FRAGILE CITY

TÜLAY ATAK, DAVID BERGÉ, ELKE KRASNY

The fragile city may be found in more than one place and more than one time. Fragility is characterized by the various layers, mobilities, and temporalities of the urban. The context is at once material and immaterial, concerning both the infrastructure and the precarization of spaces, bodies, and minds. This book asks how the fragility of the urban can be captured, how a record of it can be made in images, while taking historical models of travel, movement, photography, and document-production and -examination in order to consider these questions today.

Fragile City brings together four specific kinds of materials: photographs from Charles-Édouard Jeanneret (the future Le Corbusier) and August Klipstein's *Voyage d'Orient* from 1911; photographs by David Bergé from 2011; a selection of quotes from Elke Krasny's curatorial research in 2011; and essays by Tülay Atak, David Bergé, and Elke Krasny, which reflect upon this body of material. By bringing these materials together, we are aiming to weave an understanding of the urban where one form may relate to another in a multiplicity of ways, across spaces and times, texts and images, physical bodies present in the here and now, and by fragile connections that resist standard means of documentation while unfolding new ones.

The book developed from the curatorial research project *Le Corbusier's voyage reORIENTed, 1911-2011* undertaken by Bergé and Krasny over the course of 2011 and 2012. The project emphasized conversation and walking as methods to grasp the matter and the sense of the contemporary urban condition in Athens, Belgrade, Istanbul, Rome, and Vienna. Likewise, Atak's work on the history of the *Voyage* suggests the ways in which the photographs of 1911 may relate to the contemporary situations identified by Bergé and Krasny.

Throughout the book, we have referred to the historical figure Le Corbusier as Charles-Édouard Jeanneret. In 1911 Jeanneret had not yet evolved into Le Corbusier, an invention that took place in Paris in the 1920s. While it is true that we may not have known or have had access to the photographs had Jeanneret not become Le Corbusier — the person and the name that consolidates a body of work into an oeuvre — we also want to distinguish the photographs and consider them as particular documents of 1911. The entire set of images in La Chaux-de-Fonds and Fondation Le Corbusier in Paris comprise more than 200 photographs. Here, 68 have been selected based on the urban information they relay and how they relate to the question of what it might mean to make an image of the urban — to trace its cracks and fissures — in 1911 as well as in 2011.

It is our hope that by bringing these photographs together with Bergé's images, Krasny's curatorial work, and Atak's essay on possibilities for theorizing them, we can address what the image of the fragile city is and what its contours are, how it is and has been captured and recorded, and, critically, who participates in this capture through the making of a photograph.

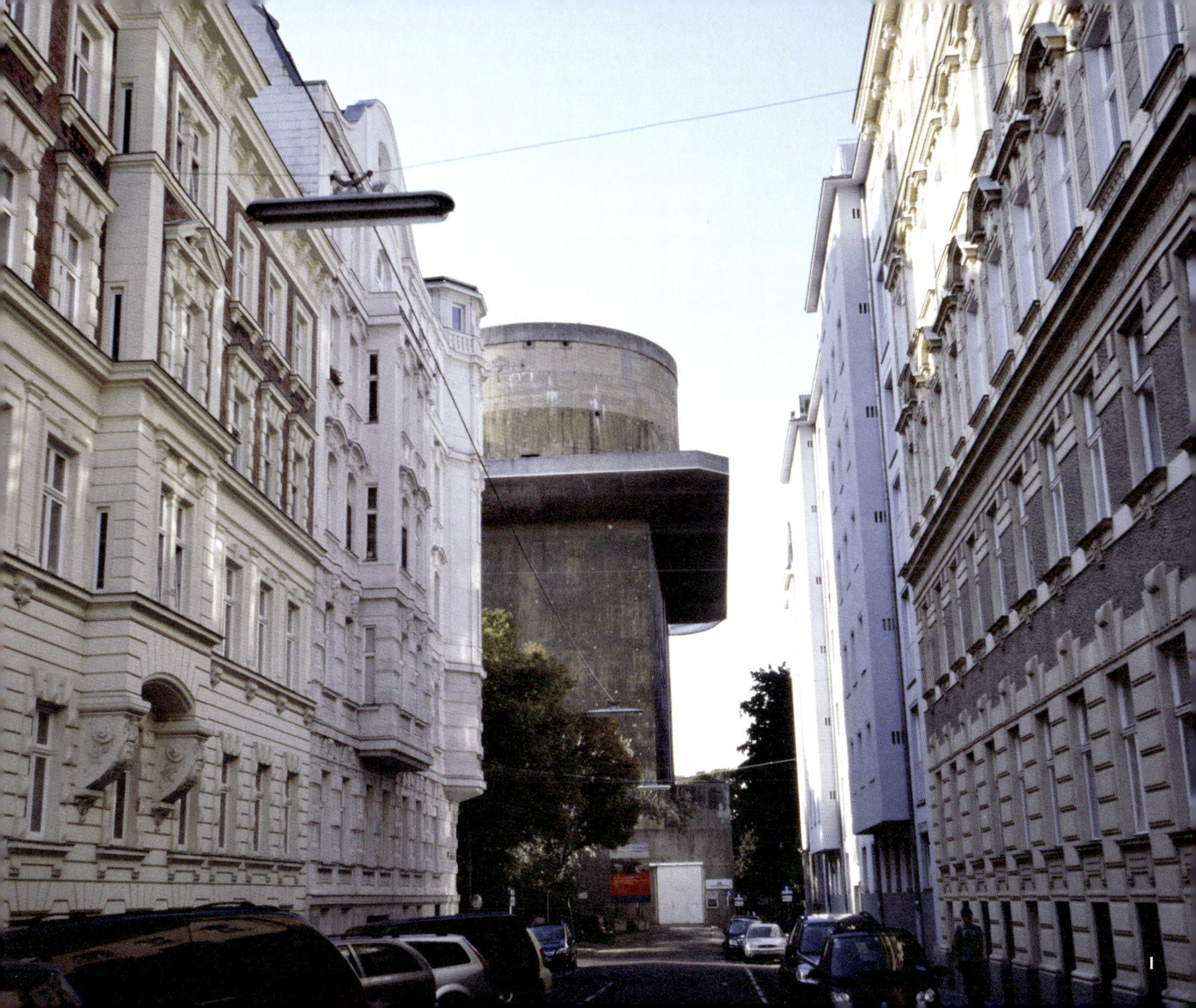

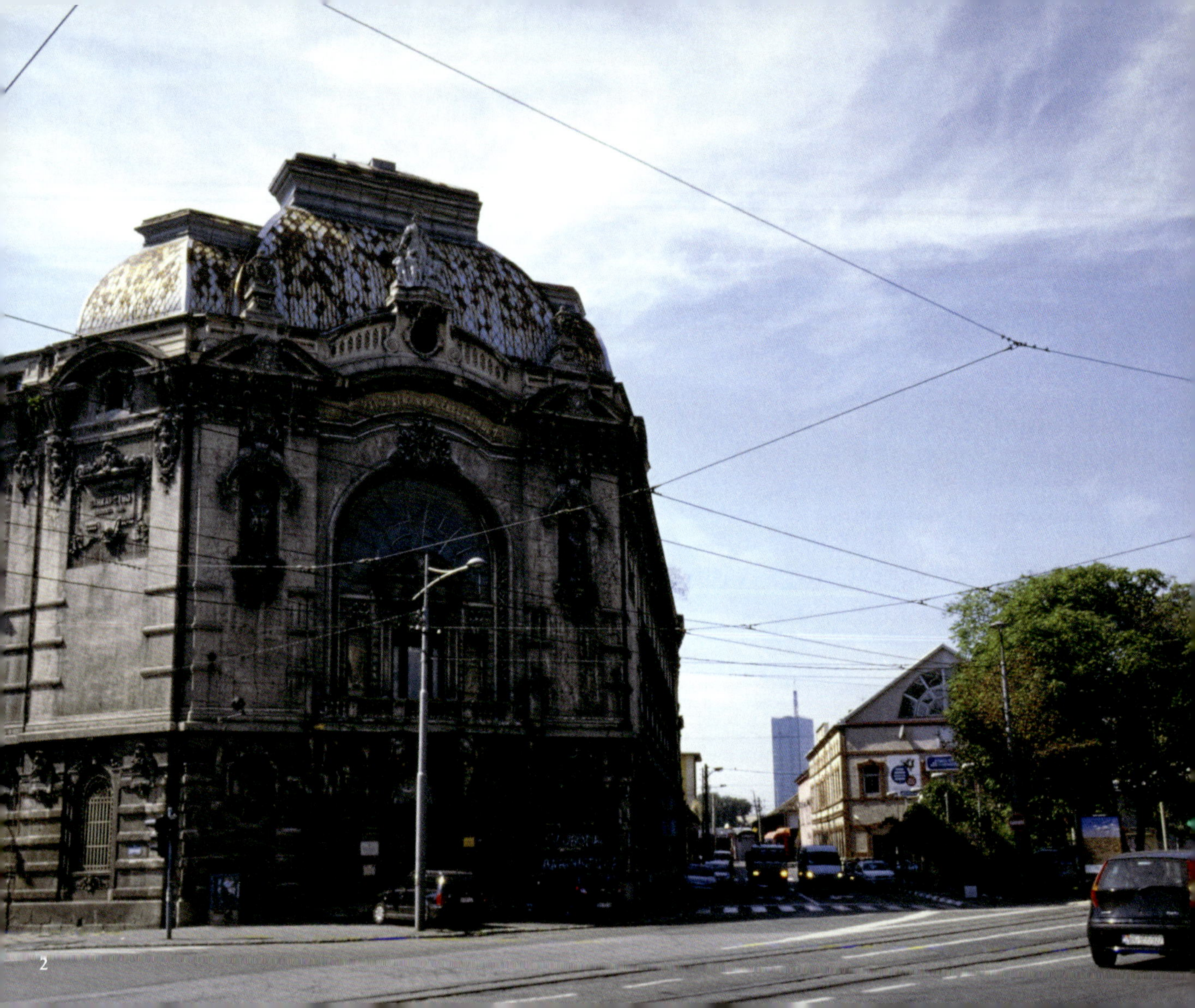

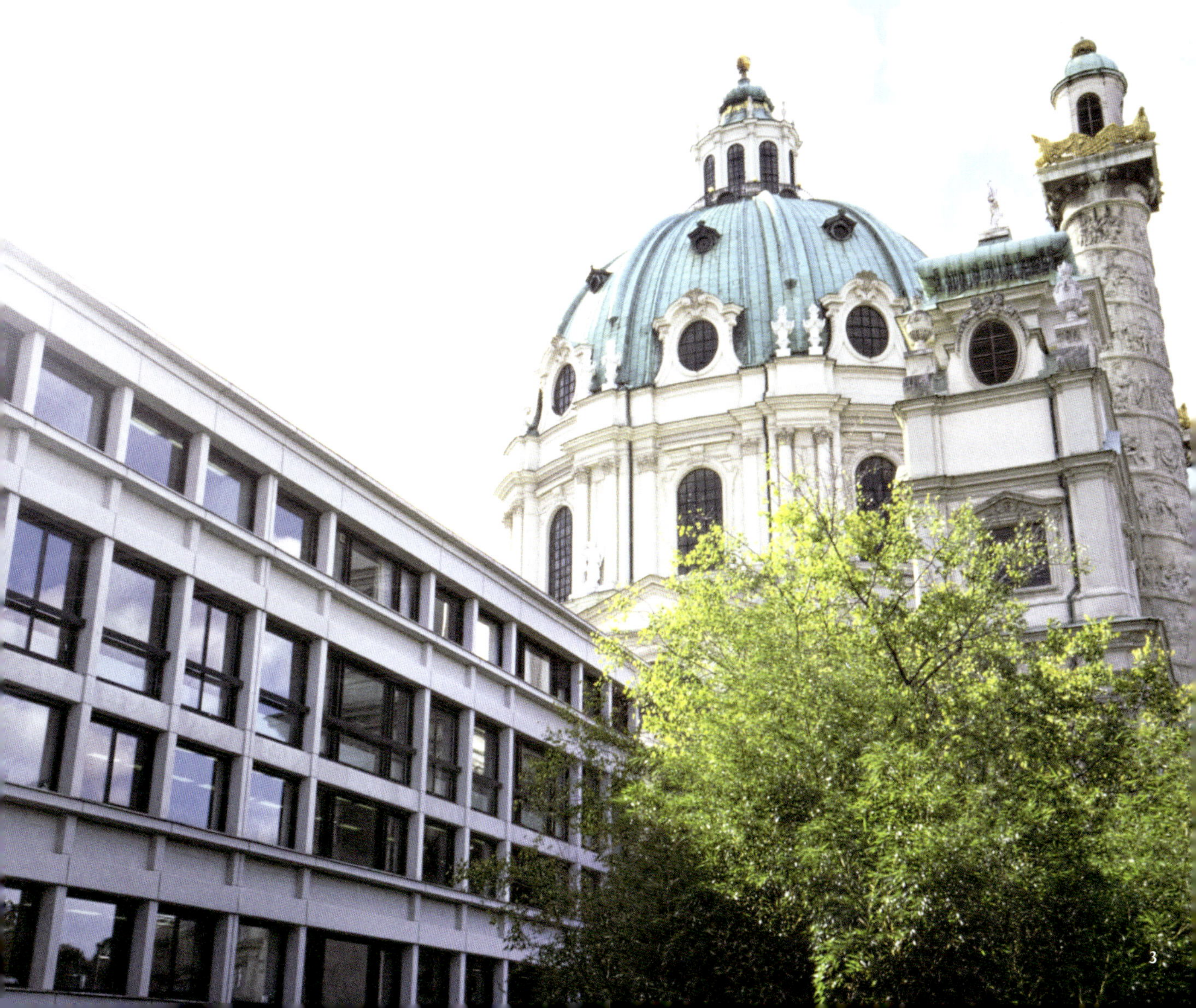

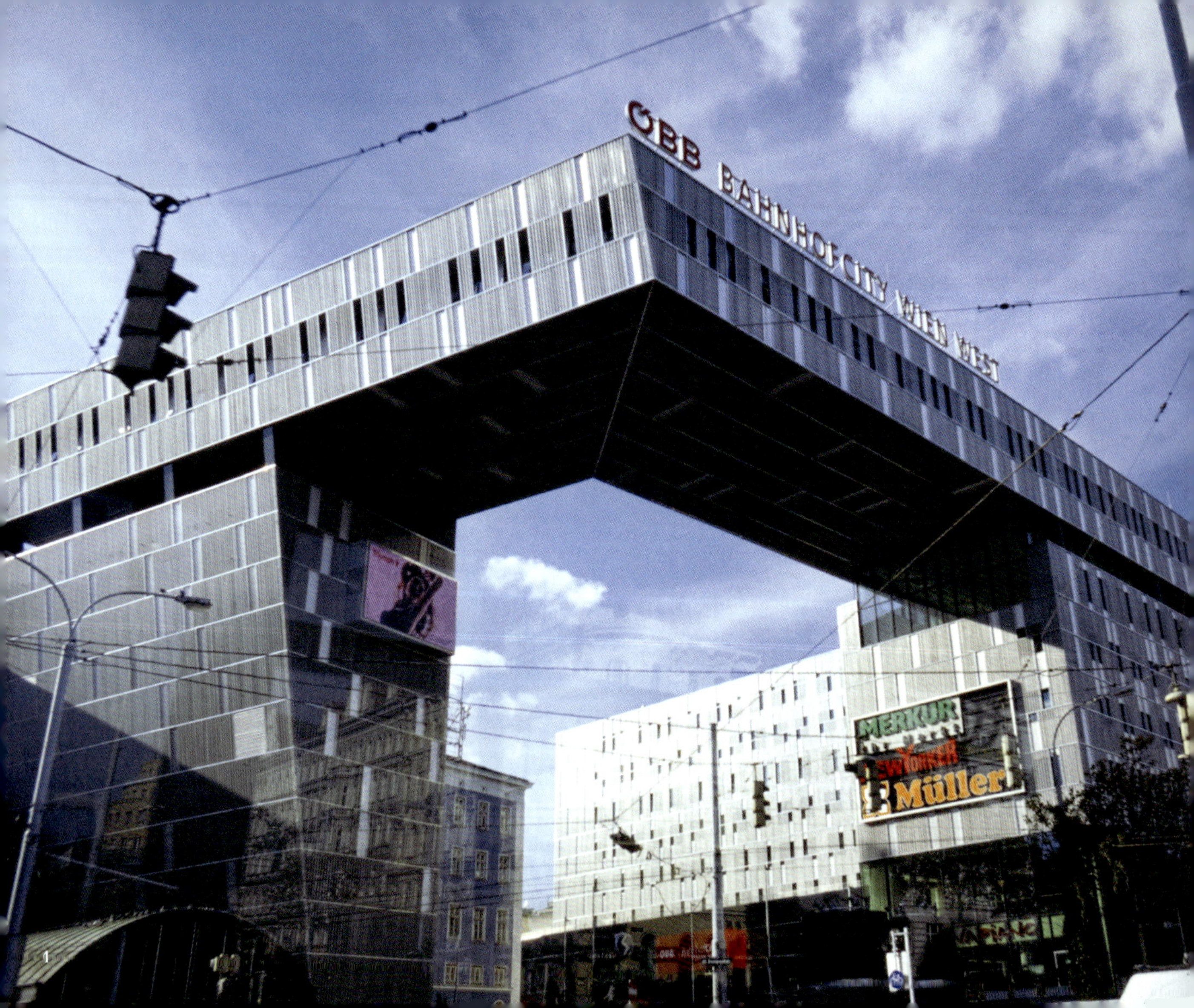

ÖBB
BAHNHOF CITY WIEN WEST
MERKUR
NEW YORKER
Müller

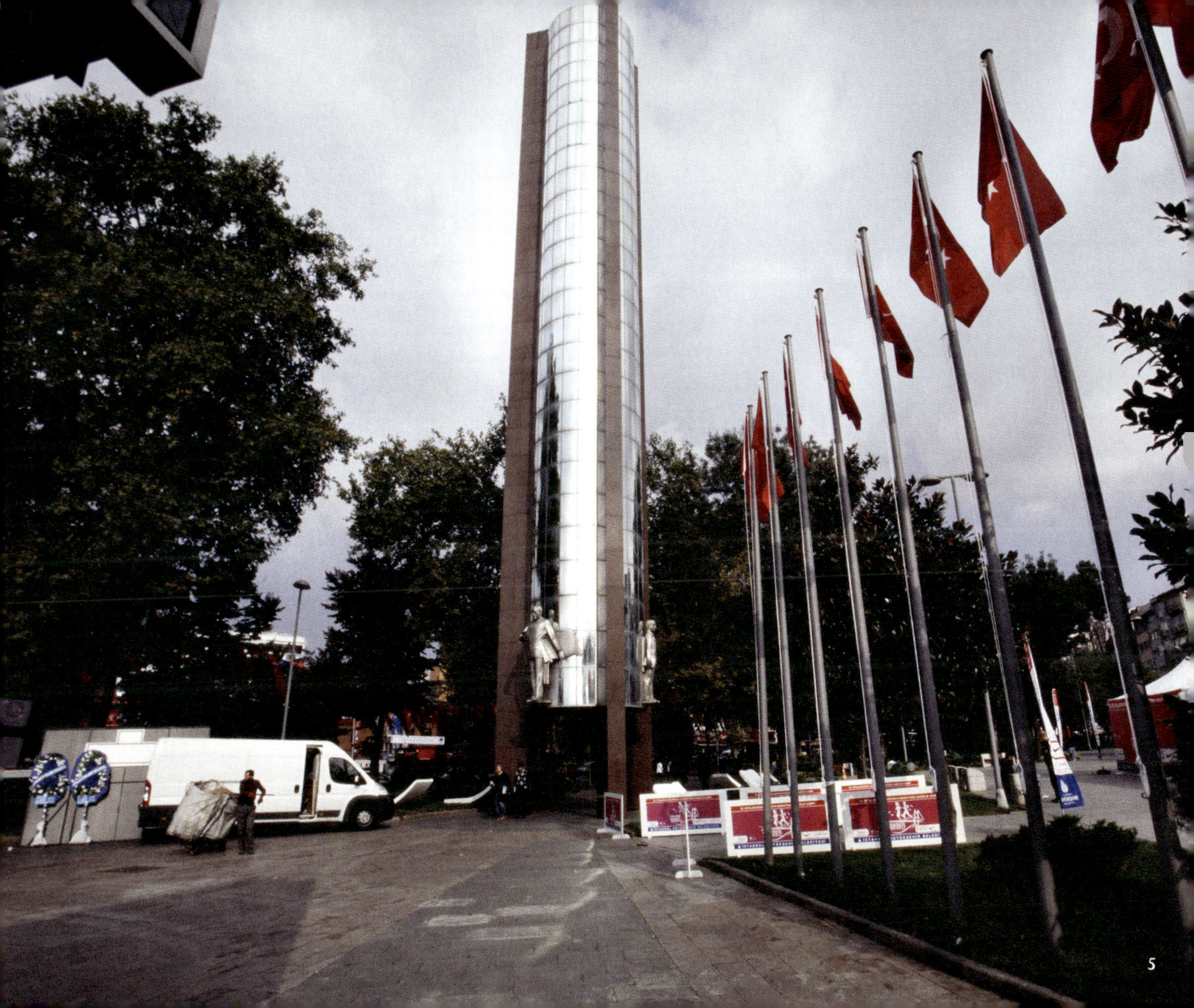

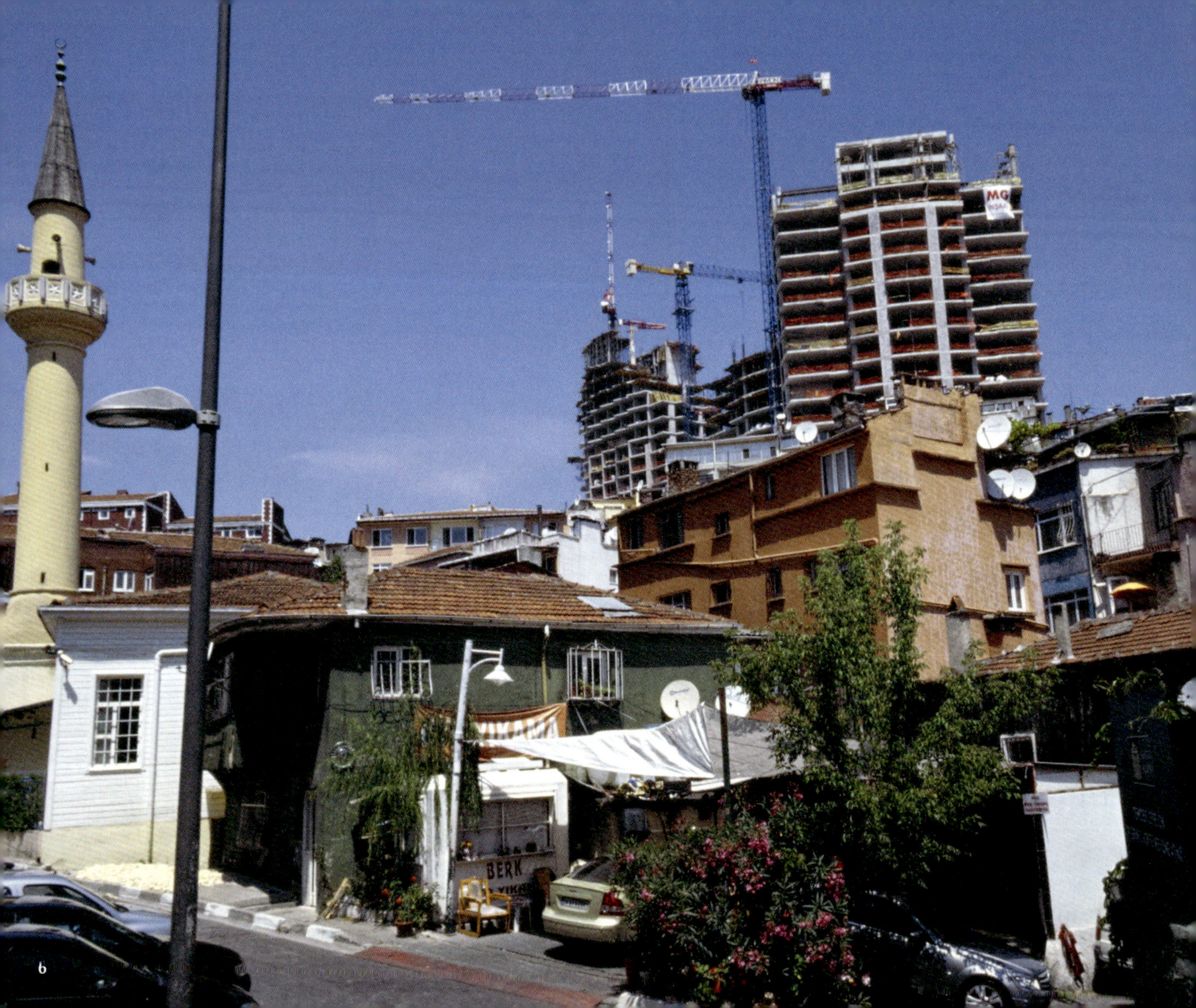

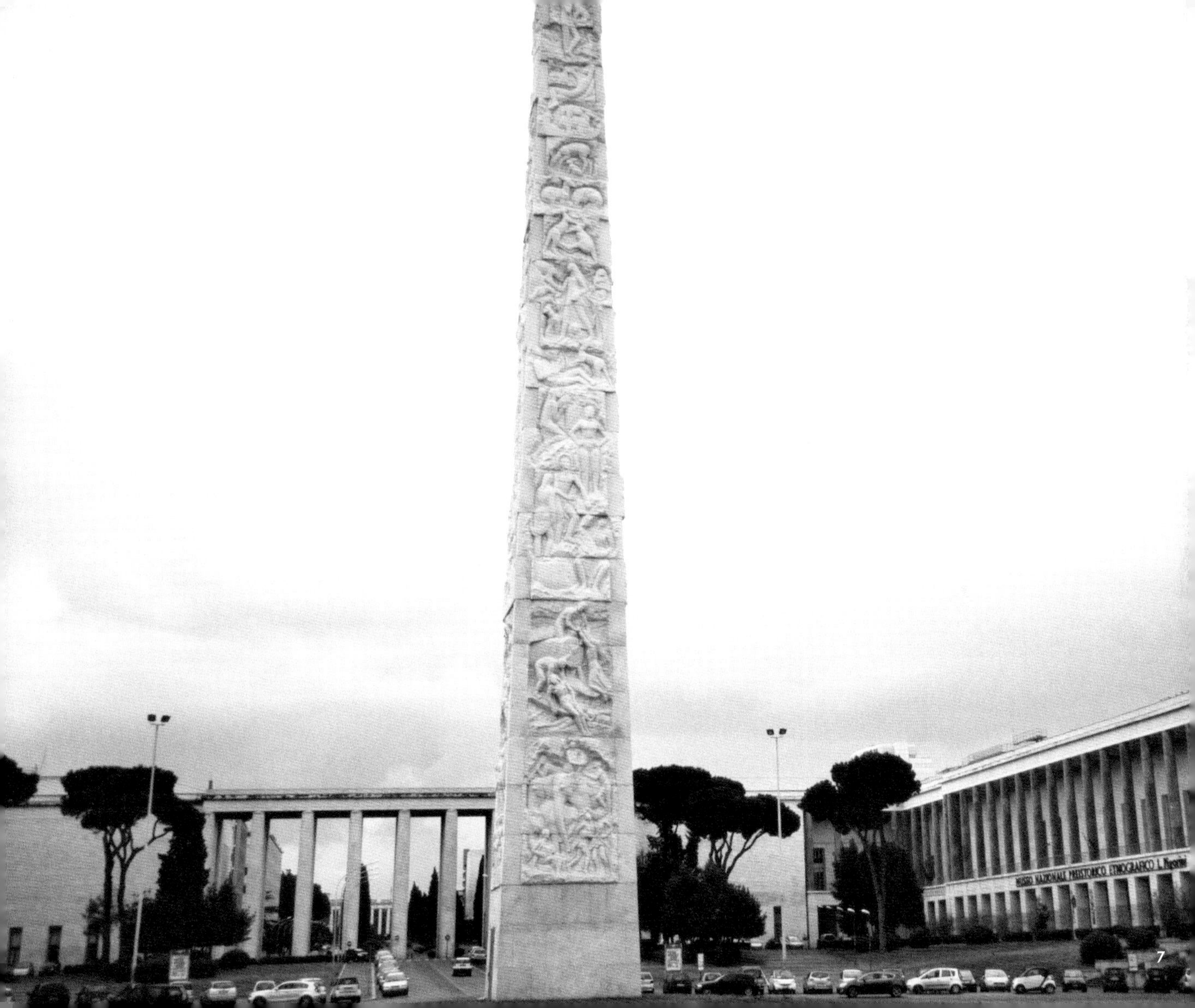
MUSEO NAZIONALE PREISTORICO ETNOGRAFICO L. Pigorini

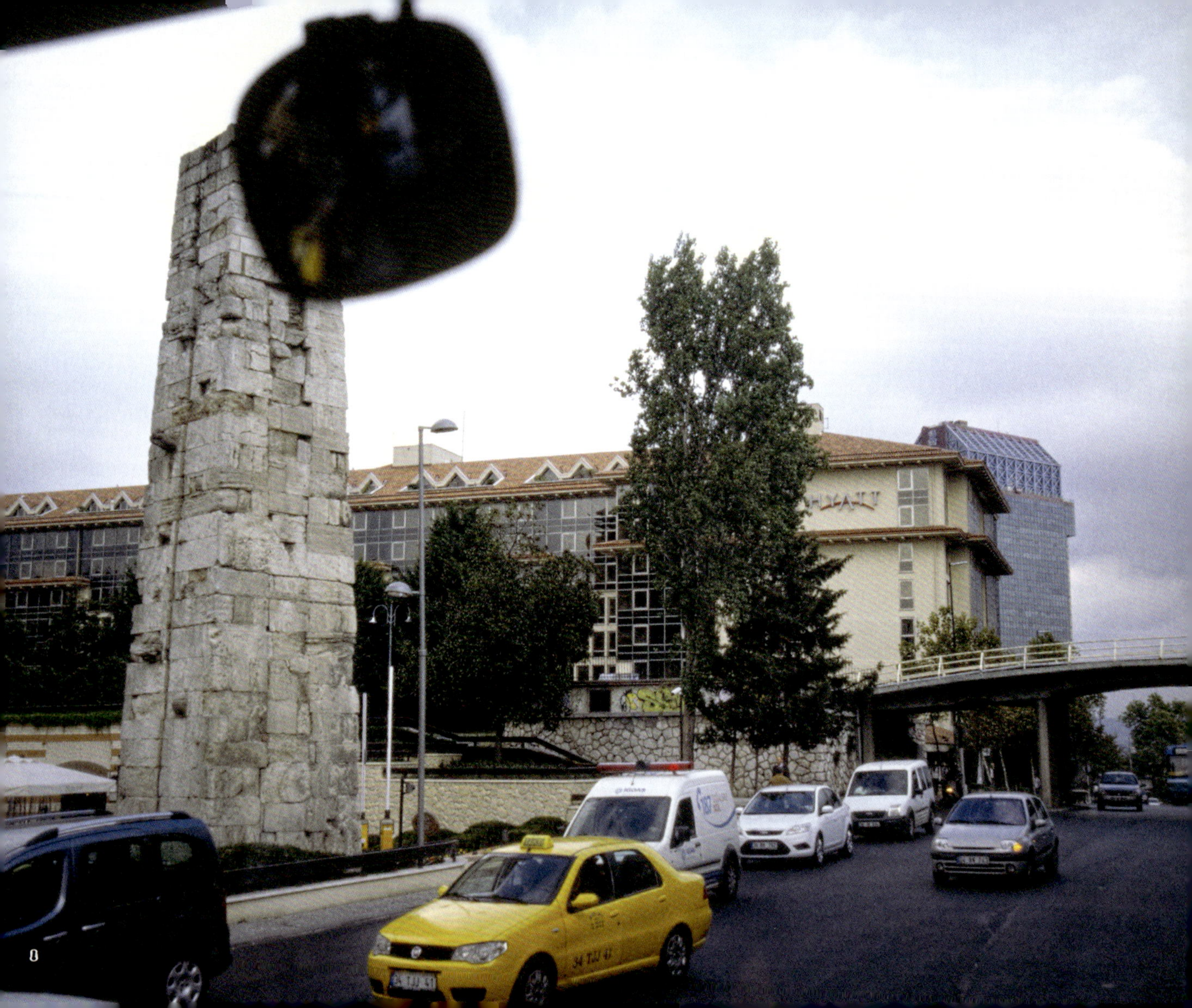

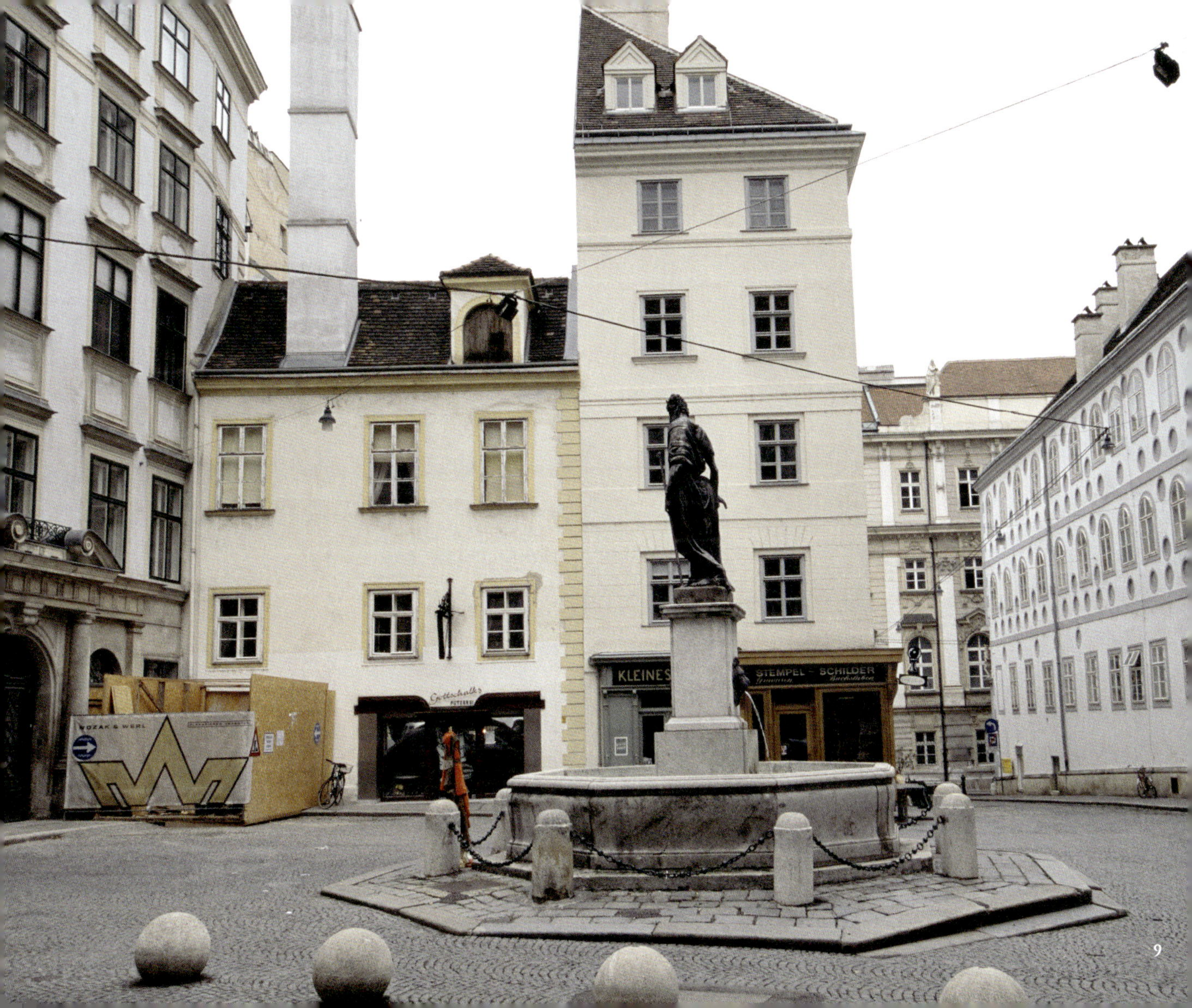

KOZAK & WERL
KLEINES
STEMPEL - SCHILDER

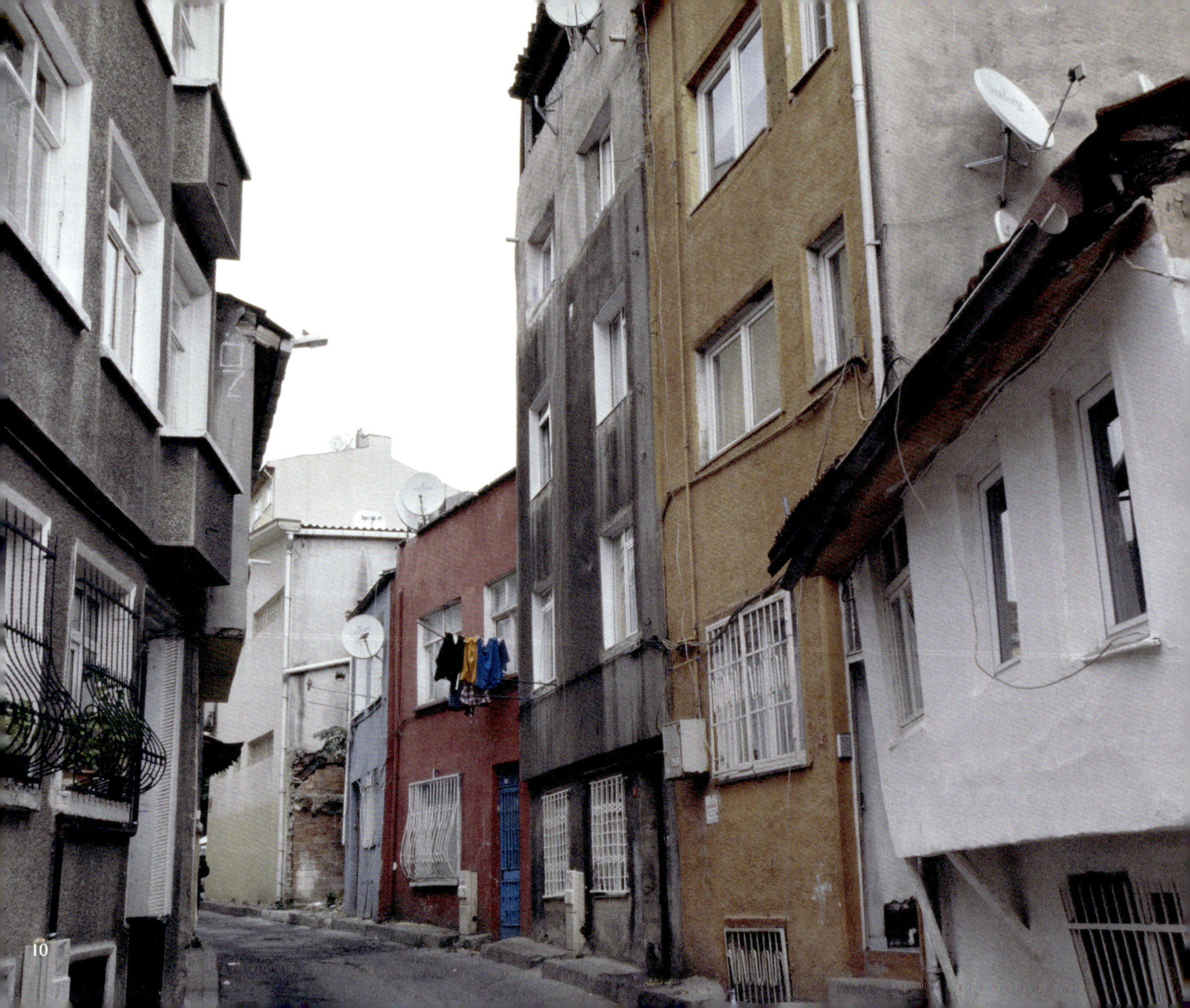

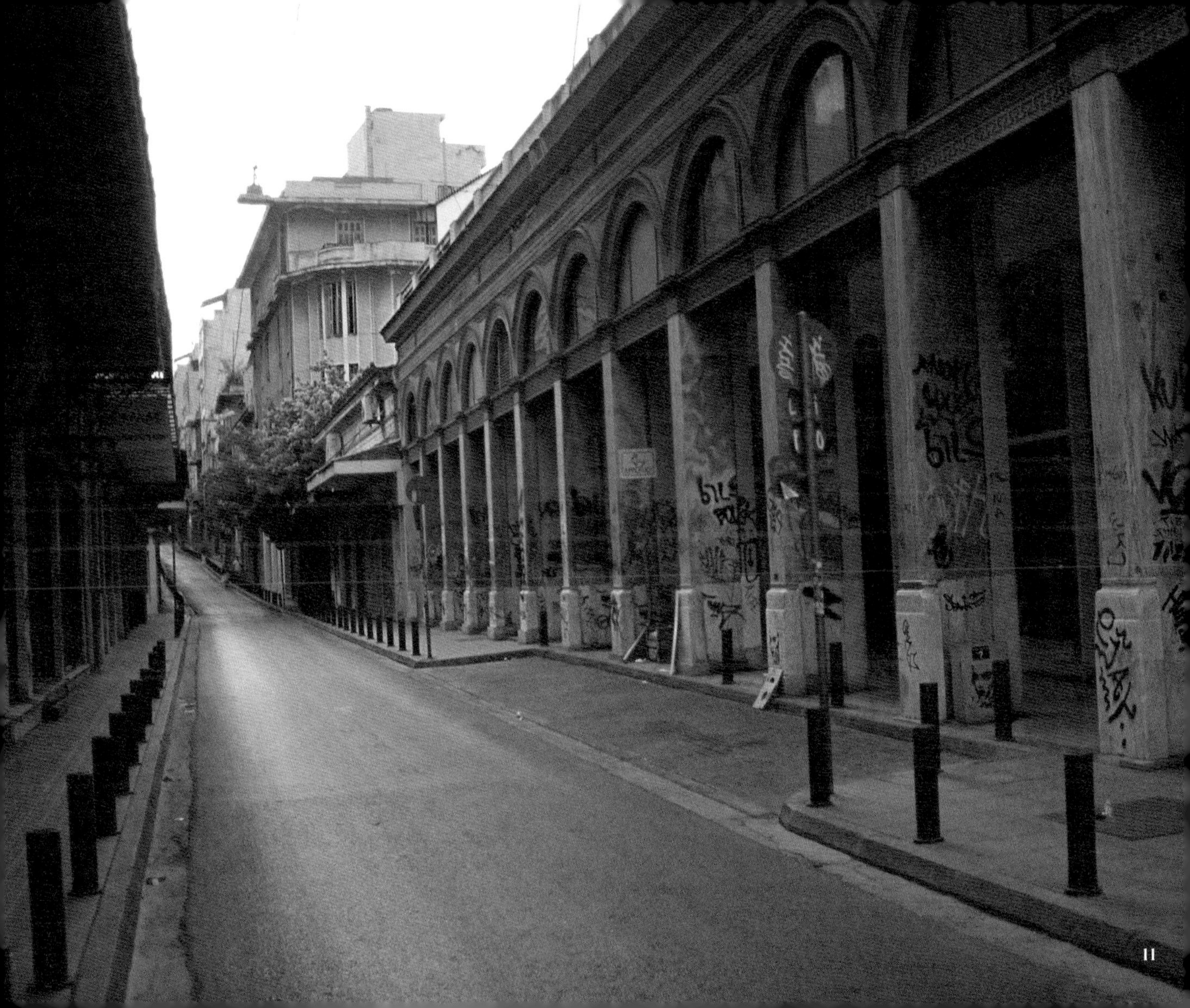

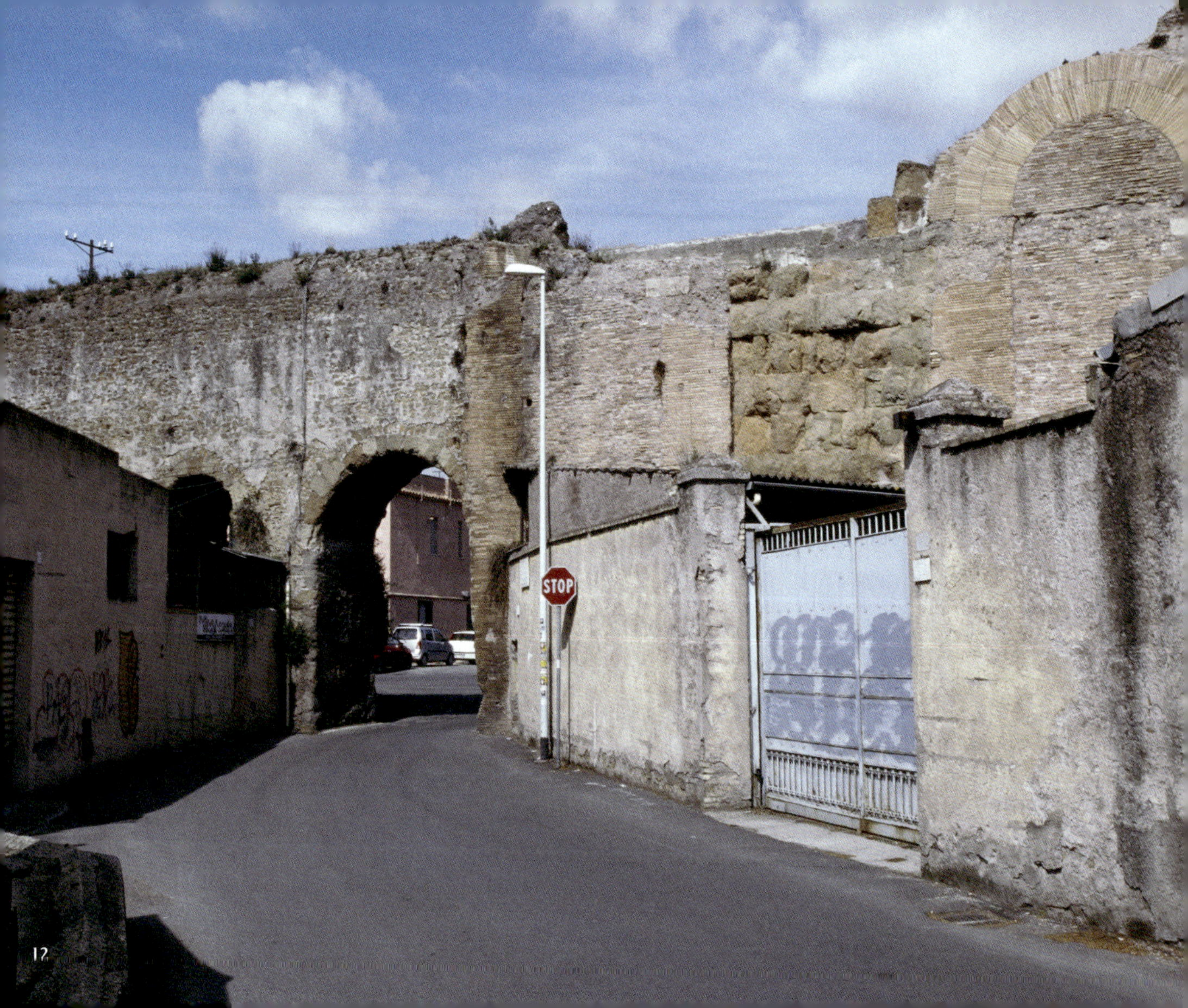

STOP

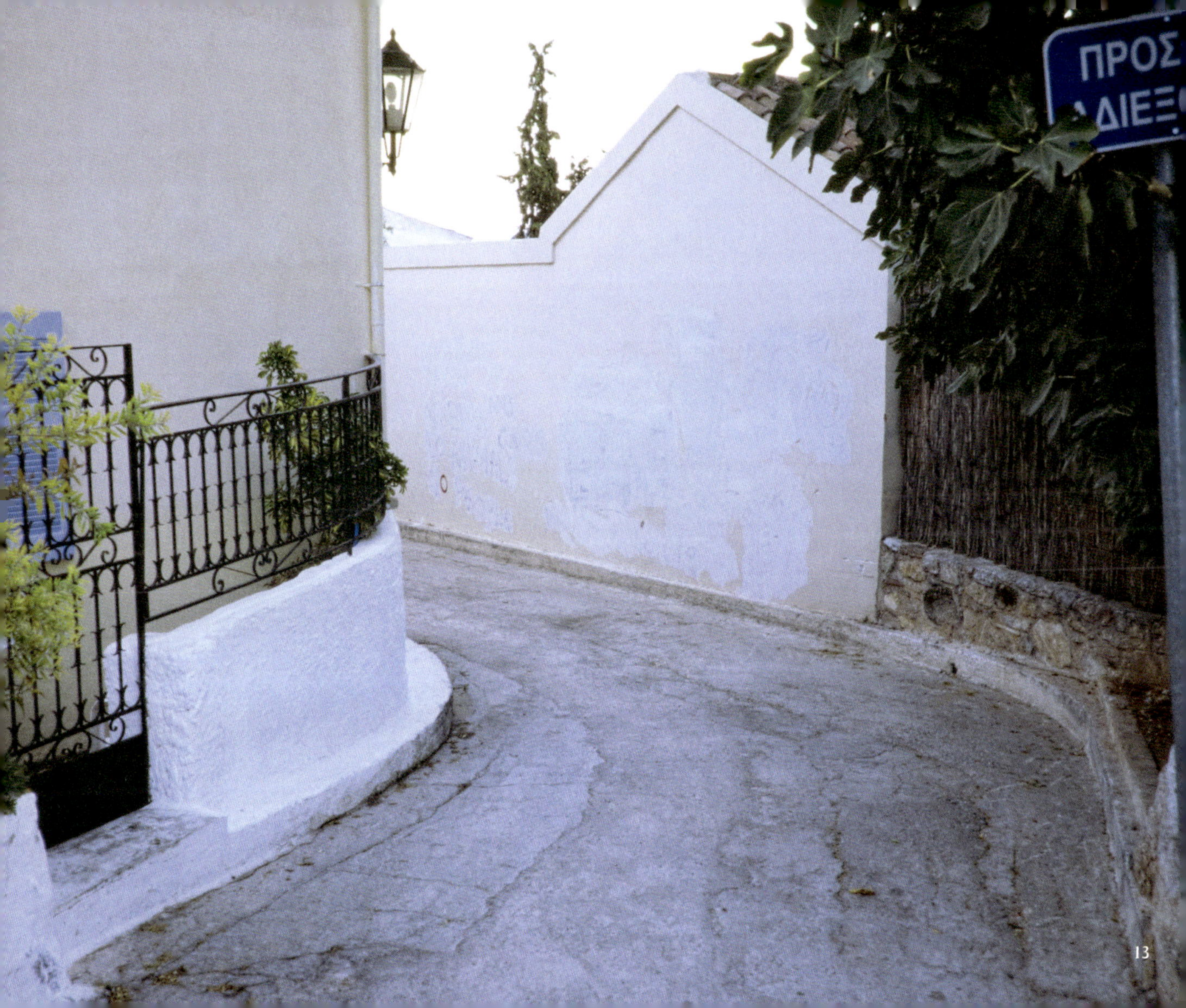

13

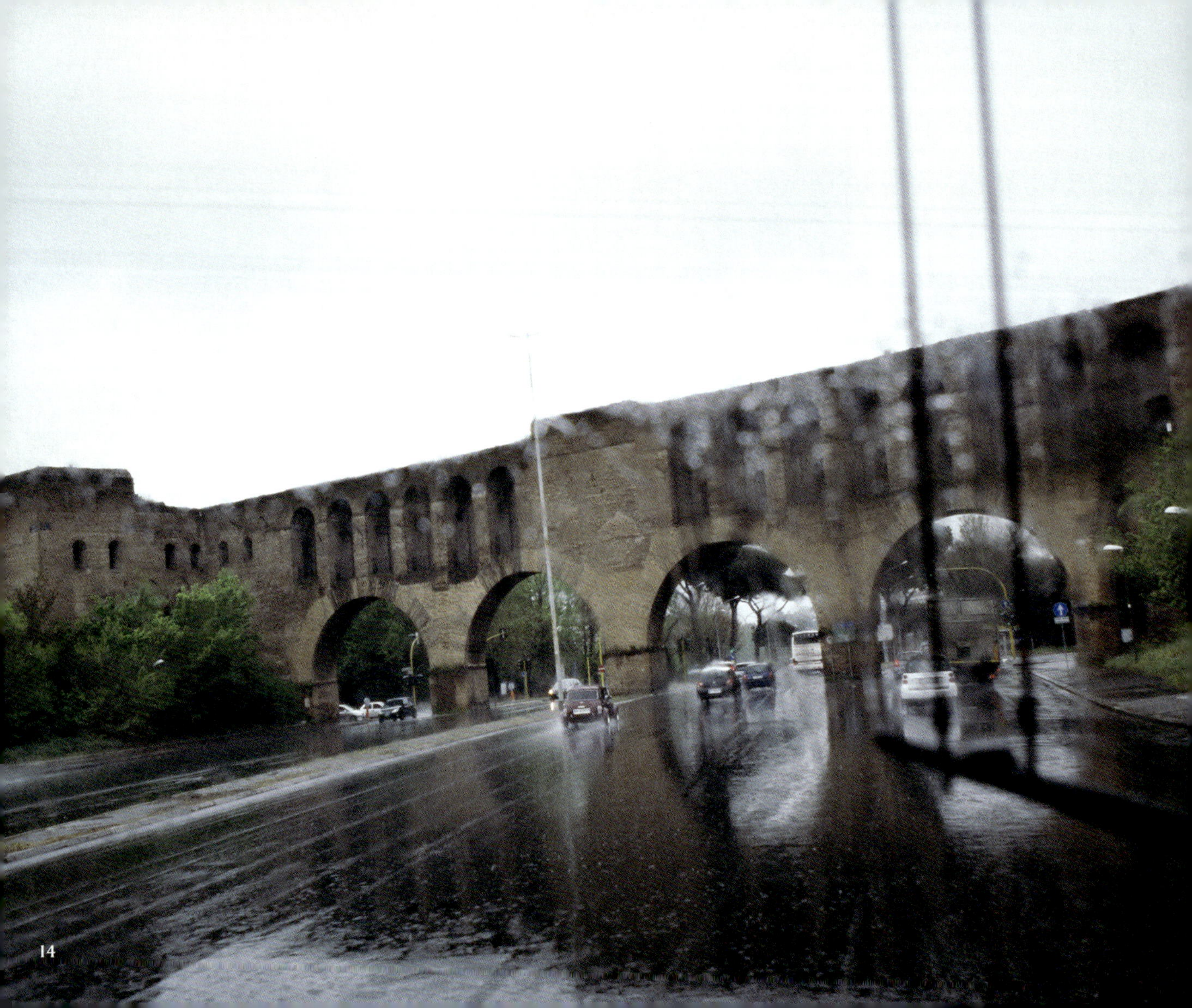

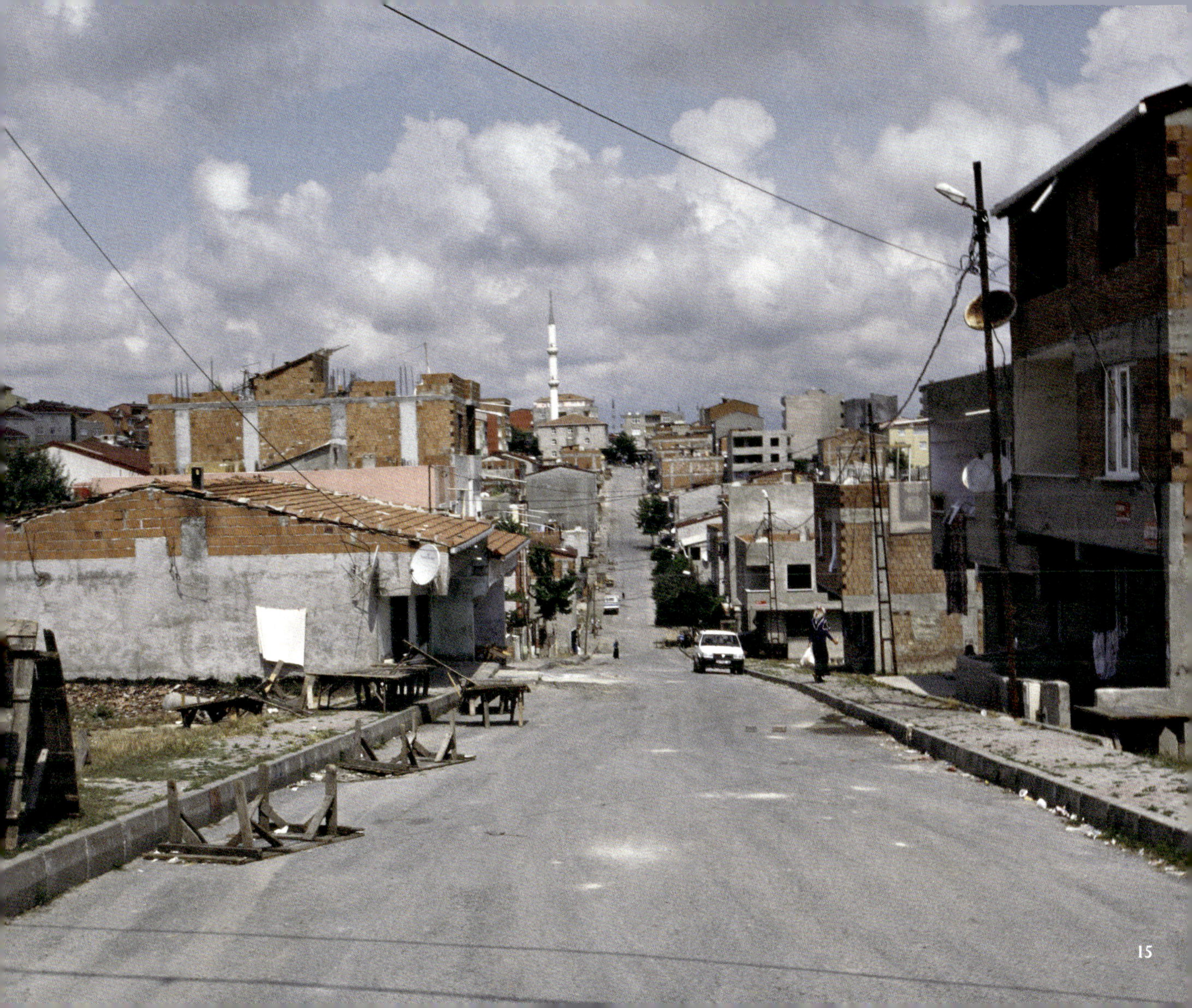

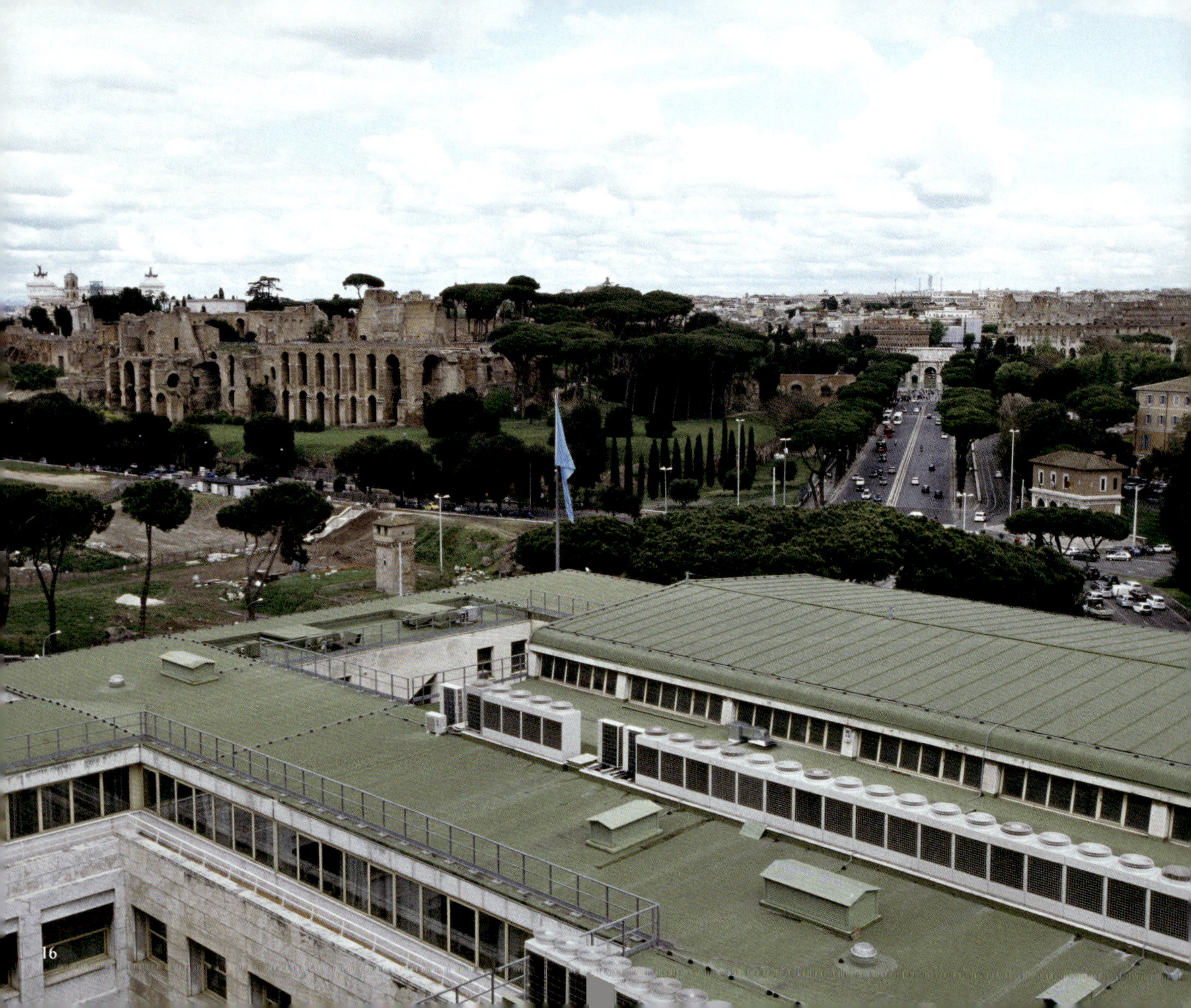

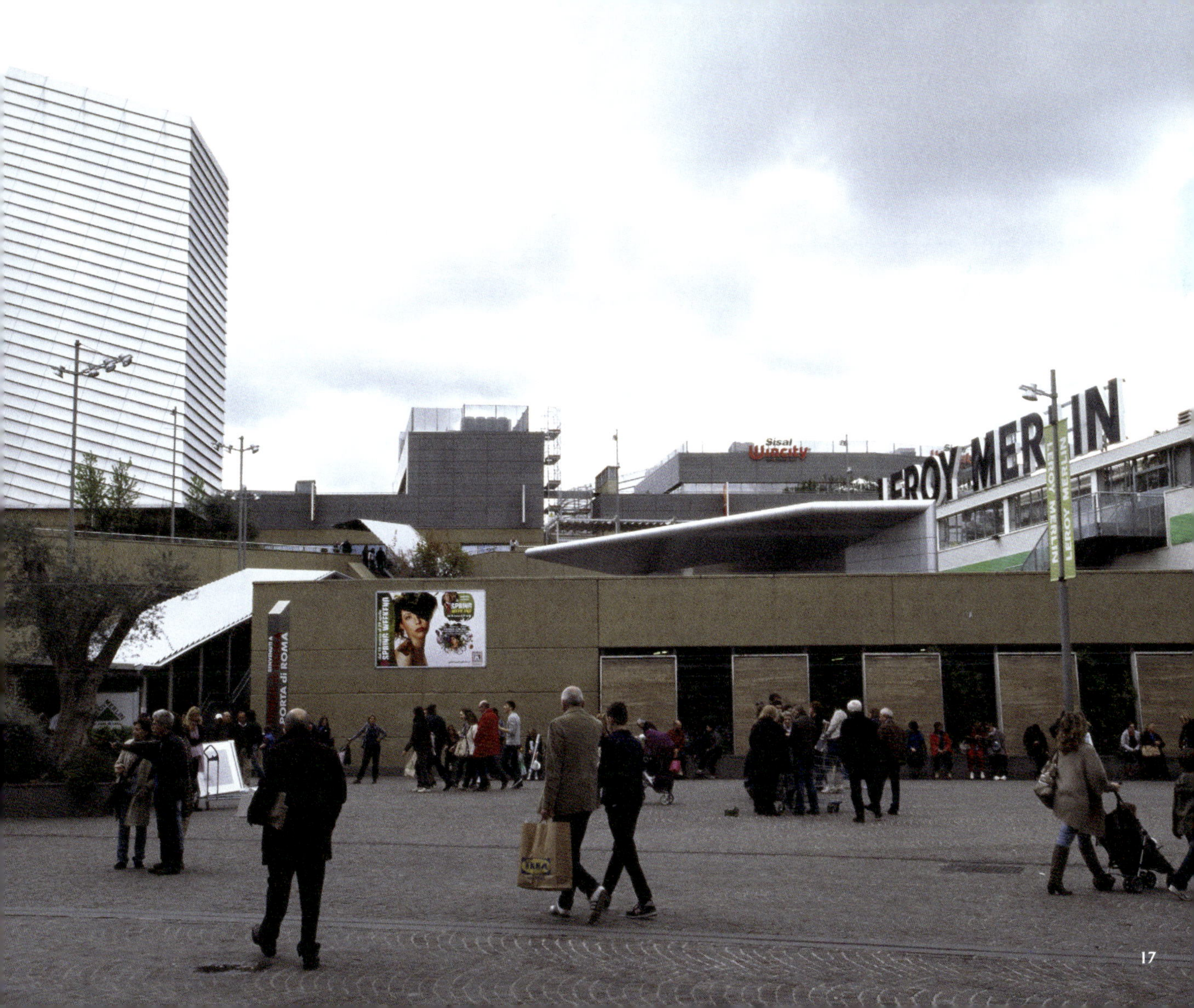

Sisal Wincity
LEROY MERLIN
LEROY MERLIN
LEROY MERLIN
PORTA di ROMA

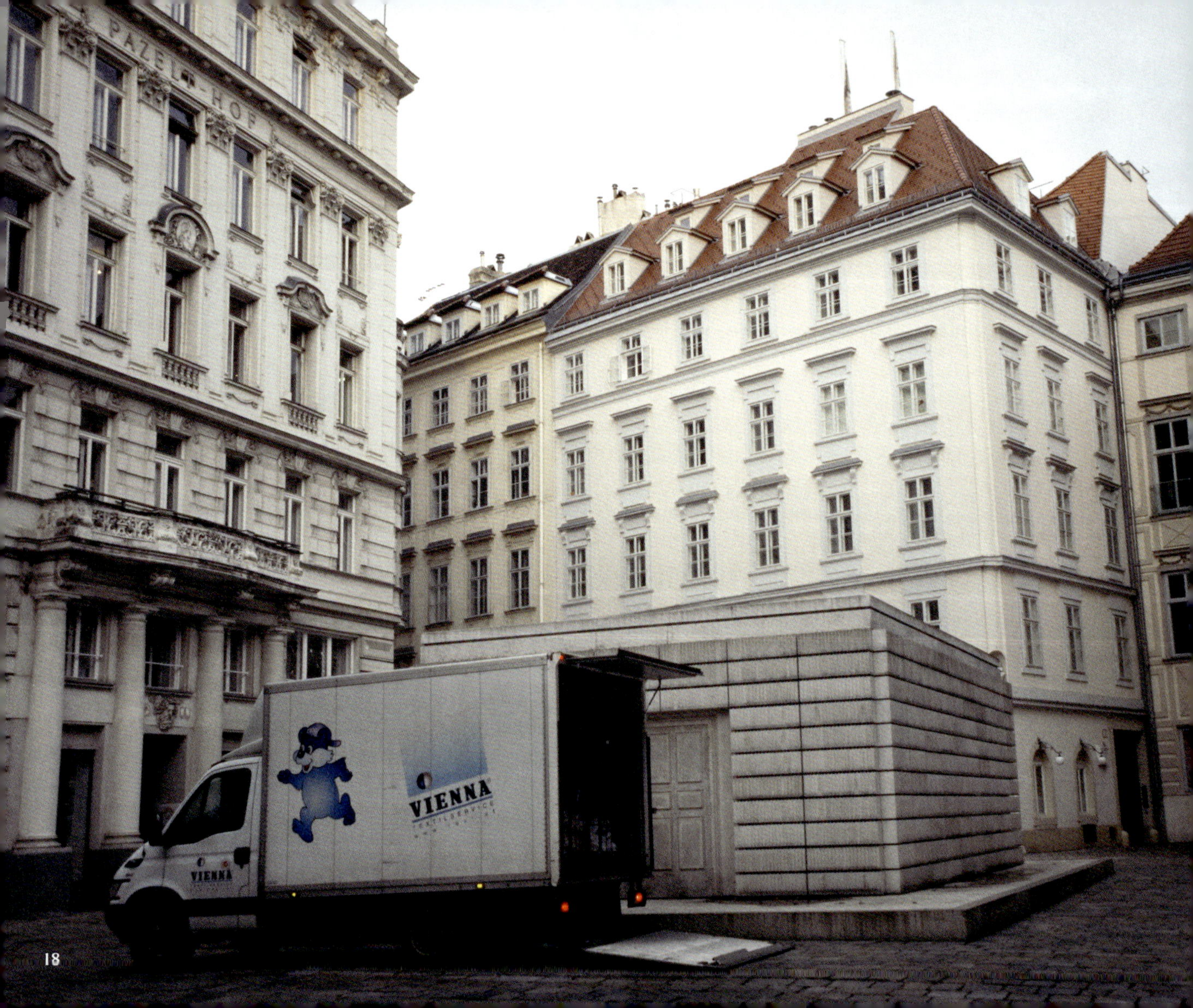

PAZELT-HOF
VIENNA

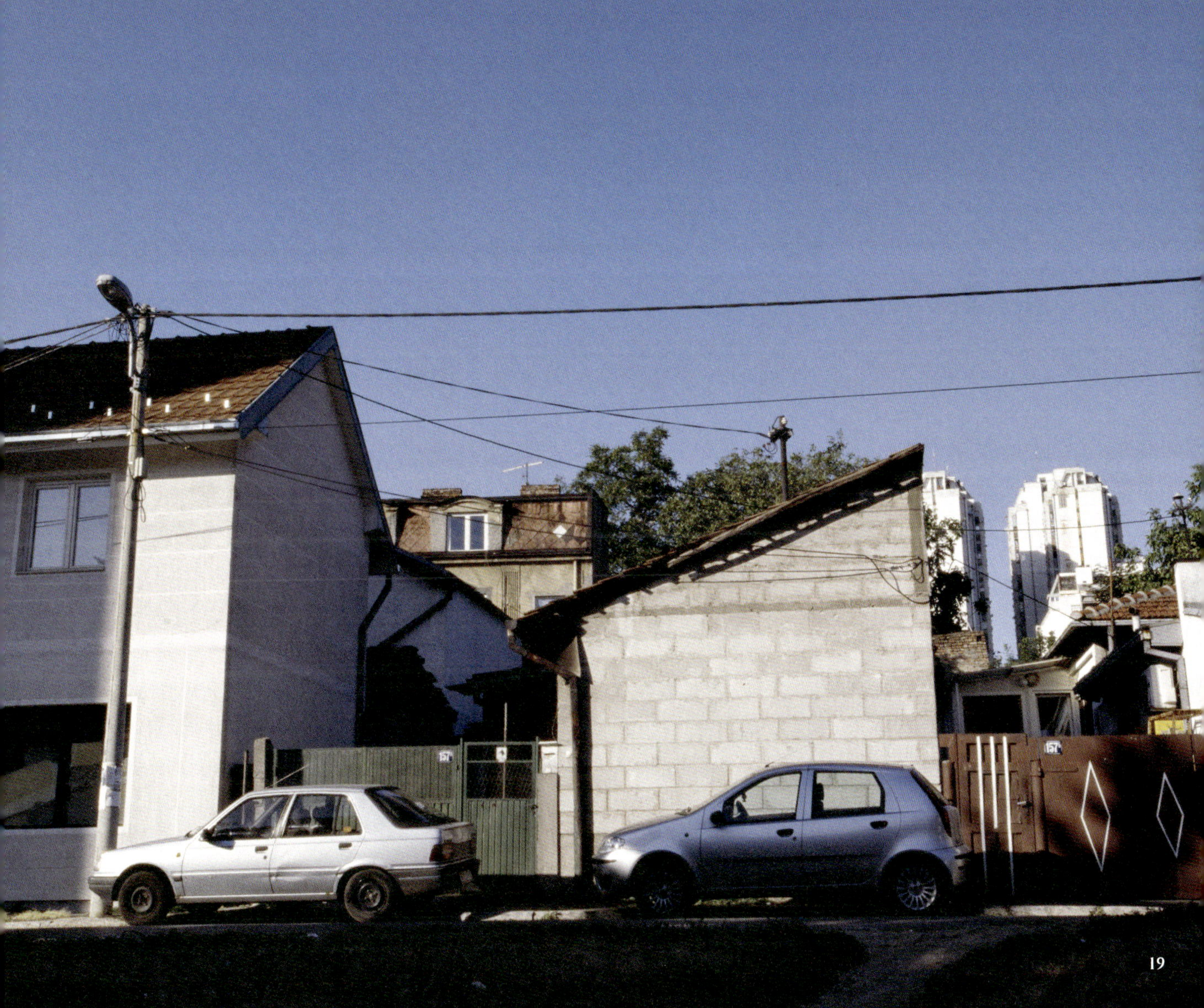

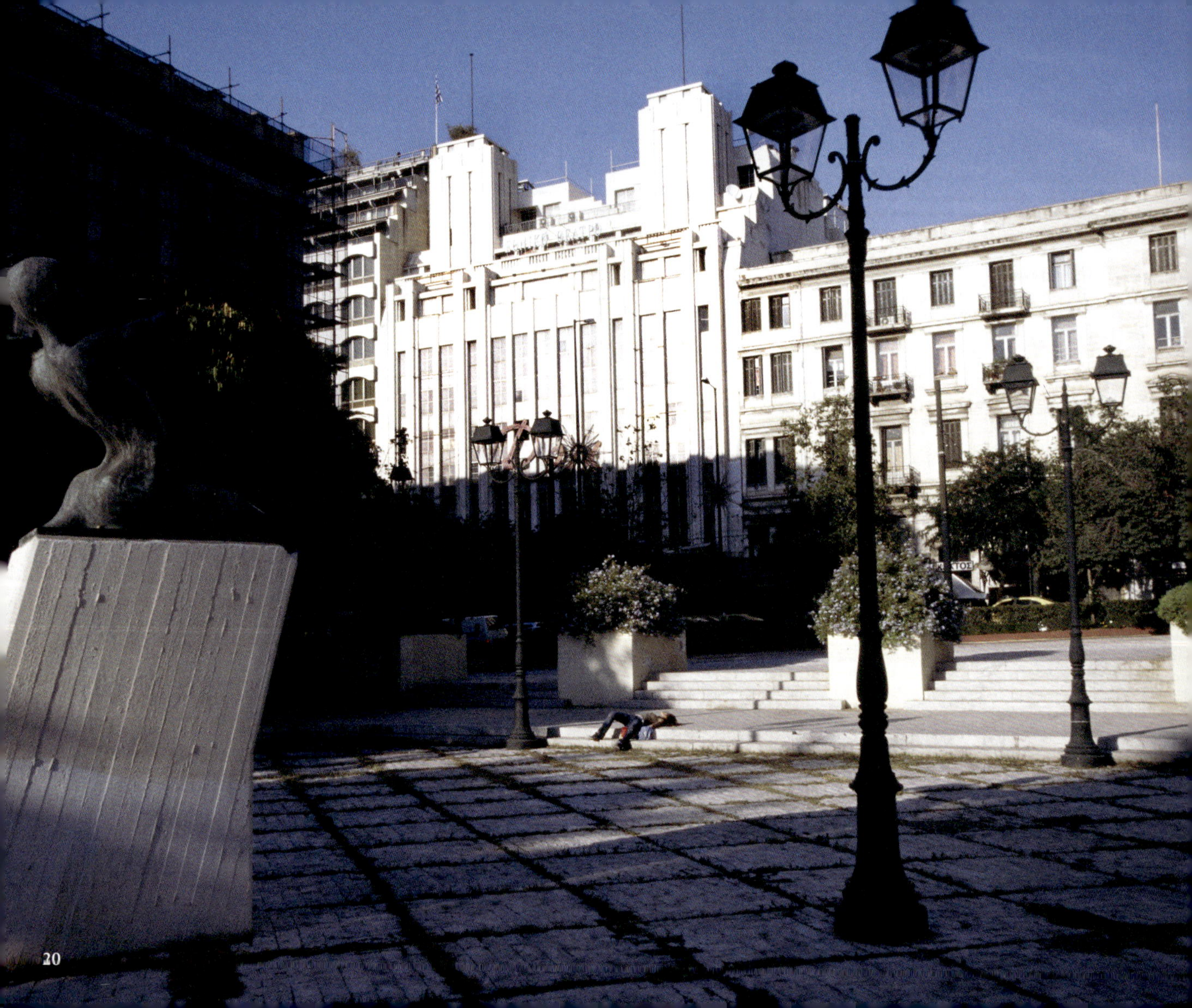

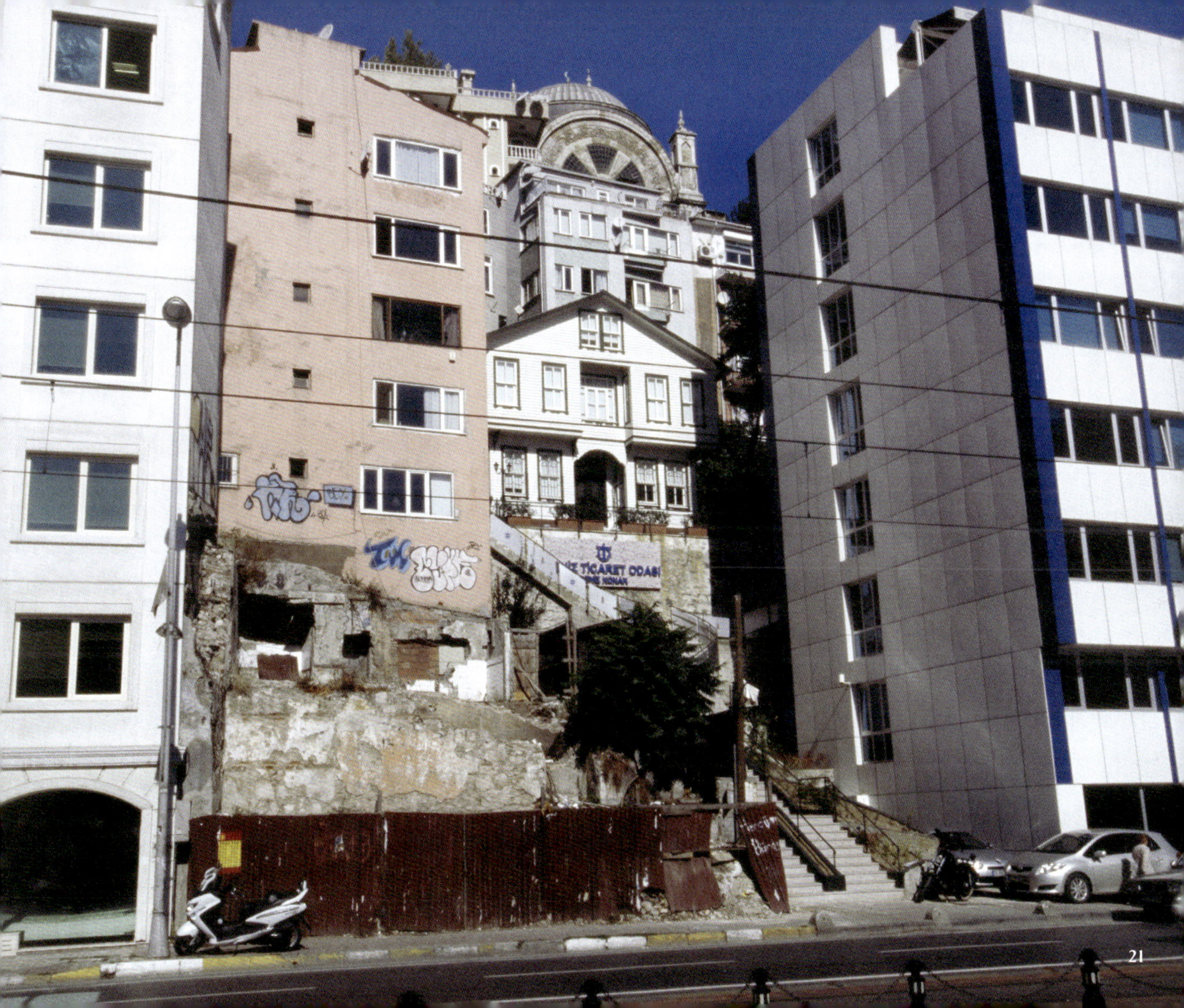

TİCARET ODASI

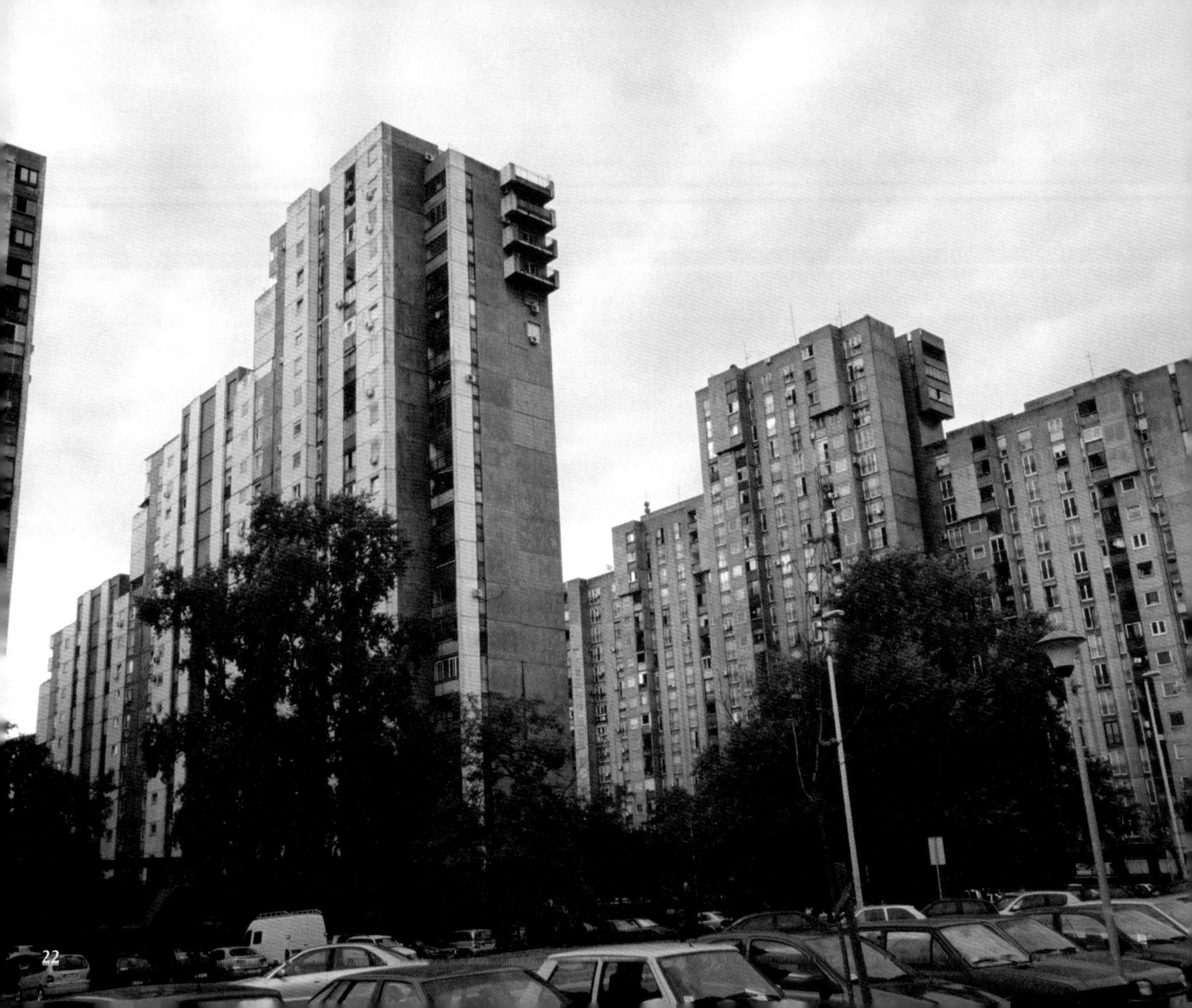

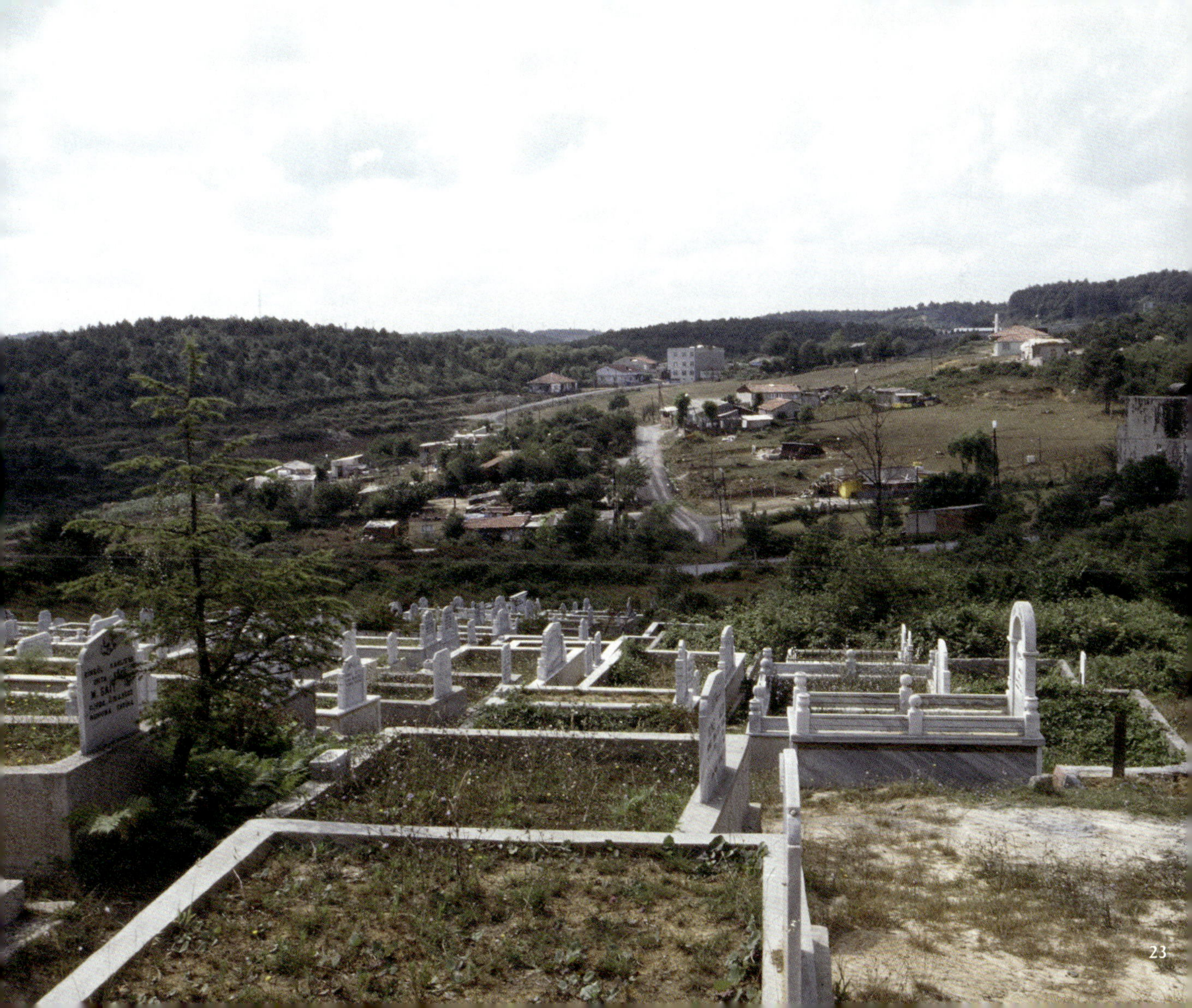

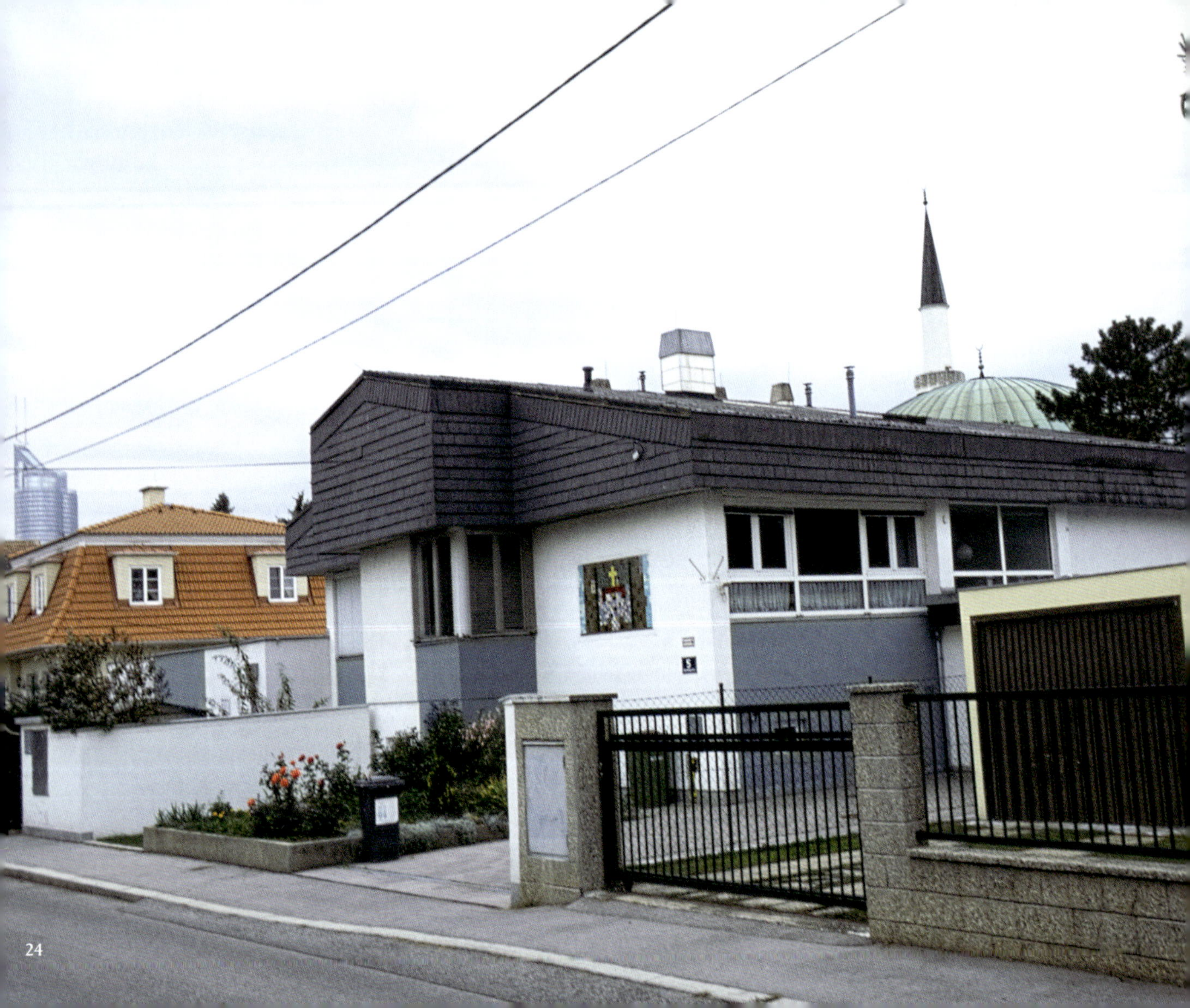

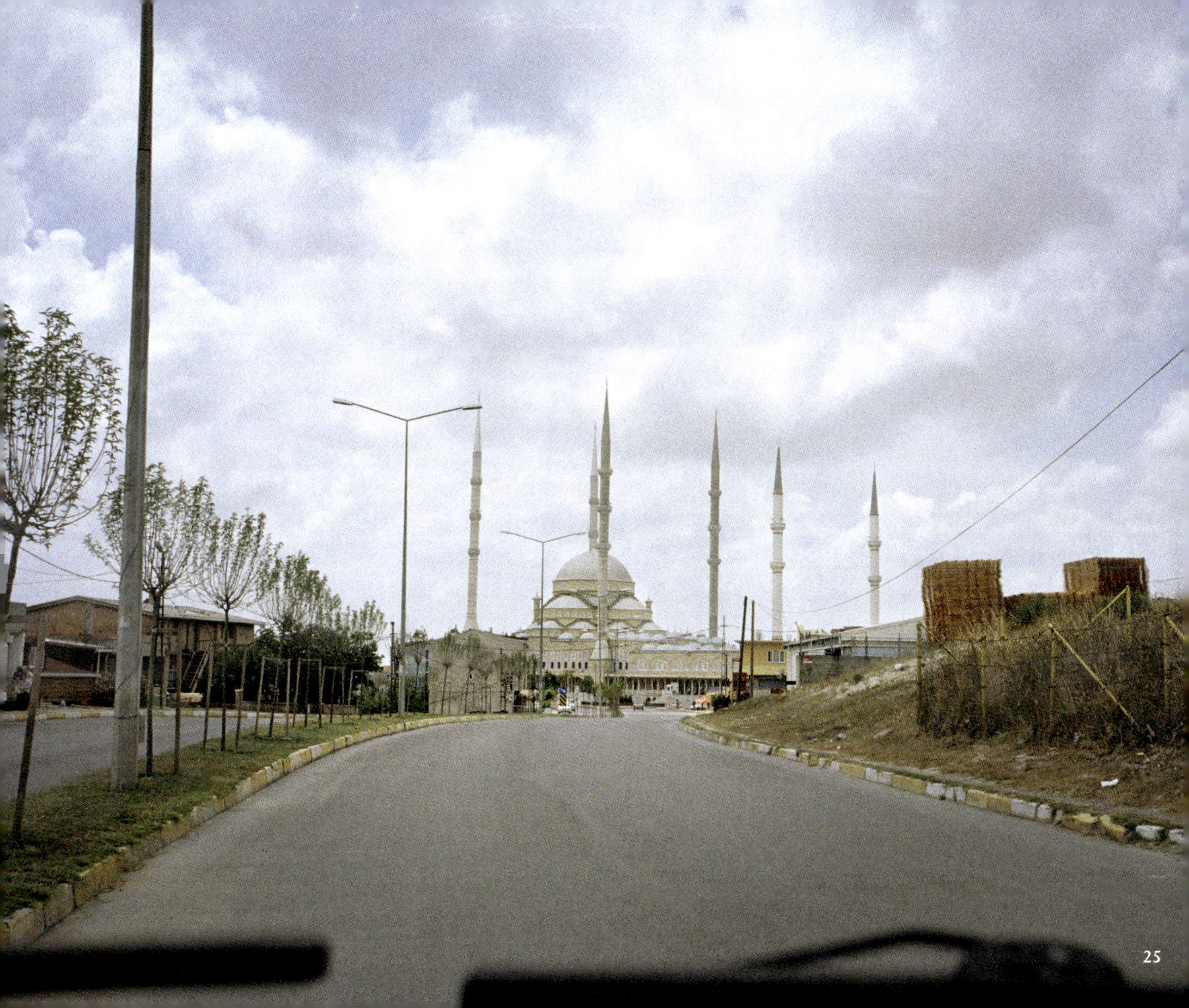

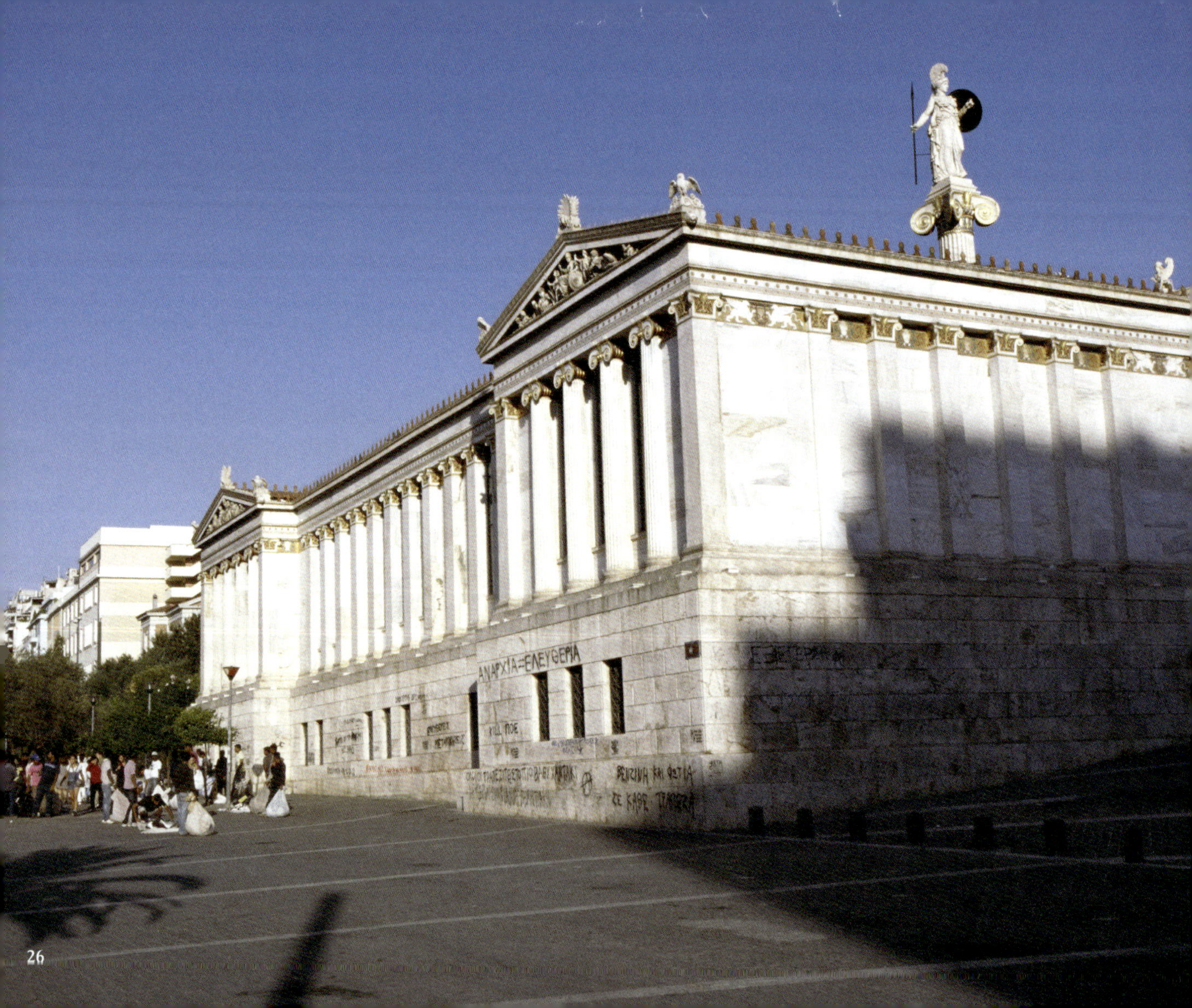
ΑΝΑΡΧΙΑ=ΕΛΕΥΘΕΡΙΑ

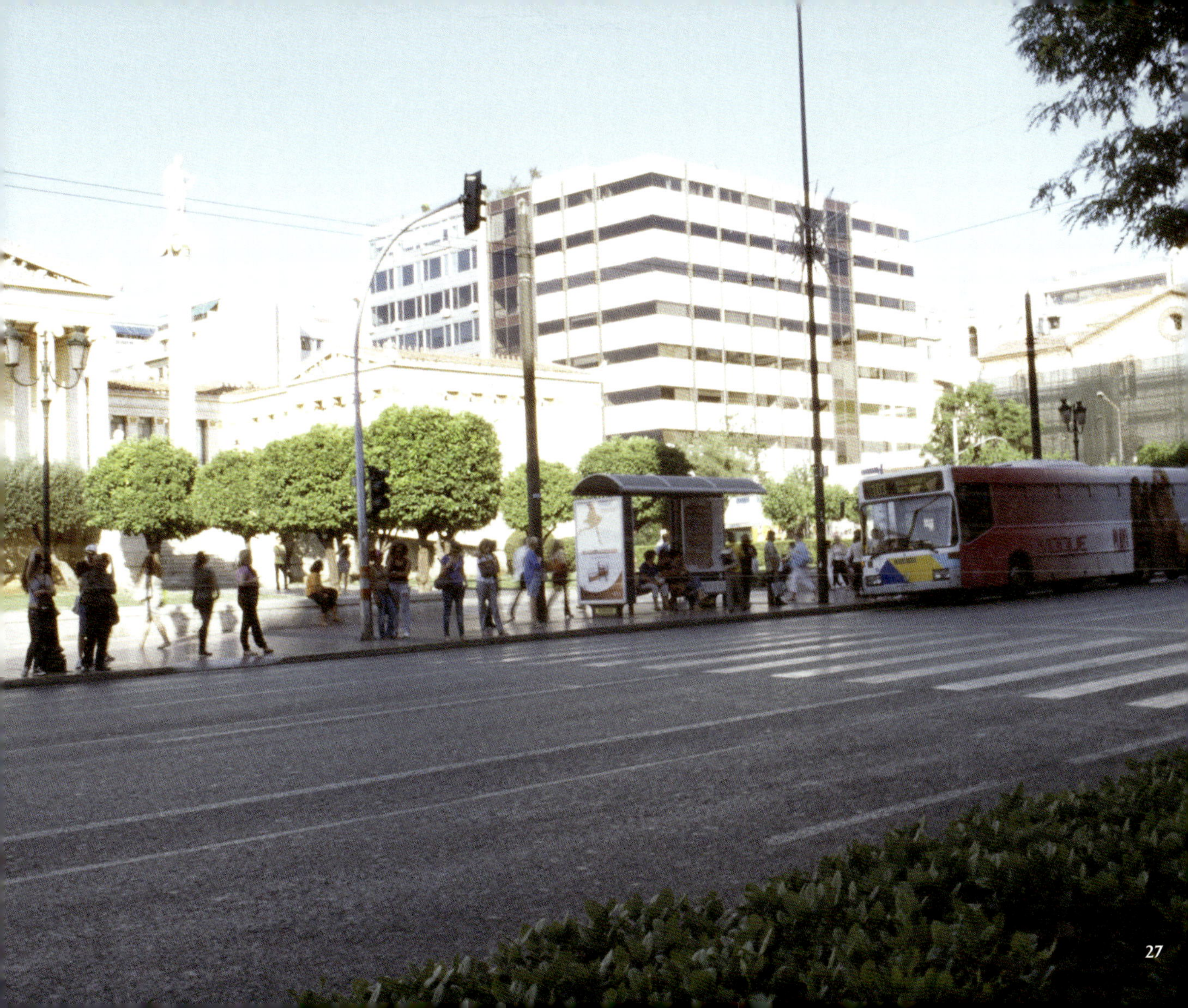

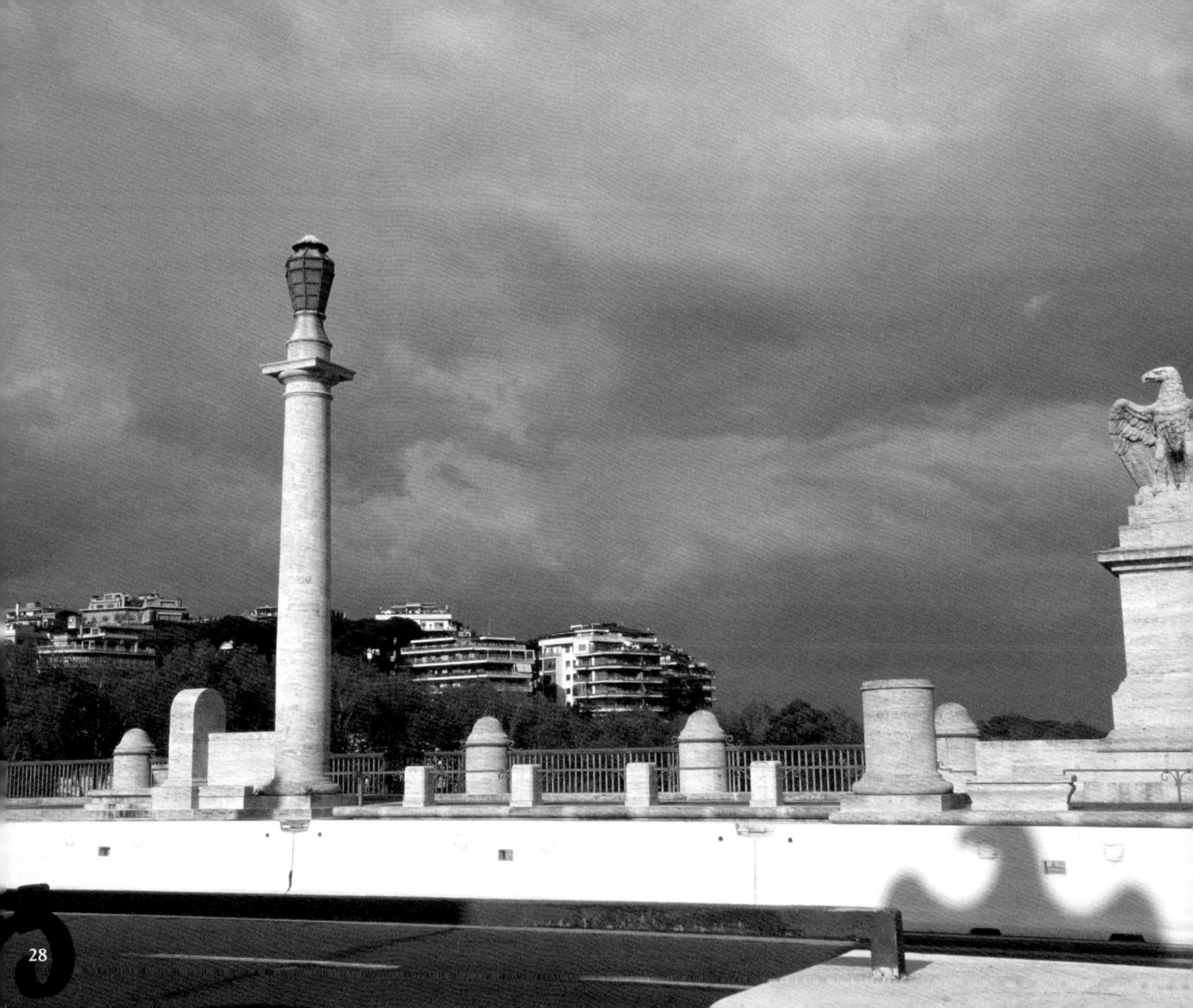

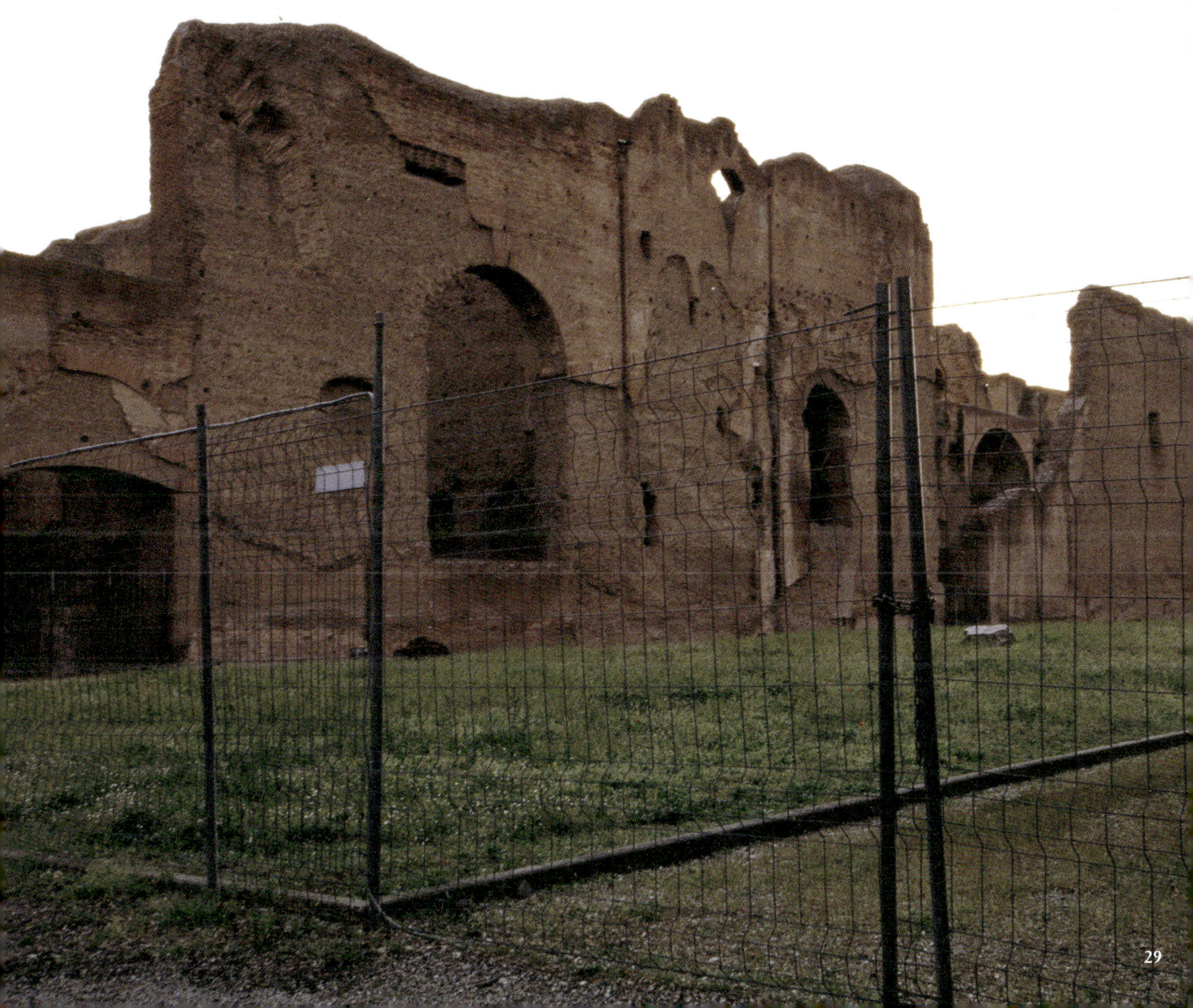

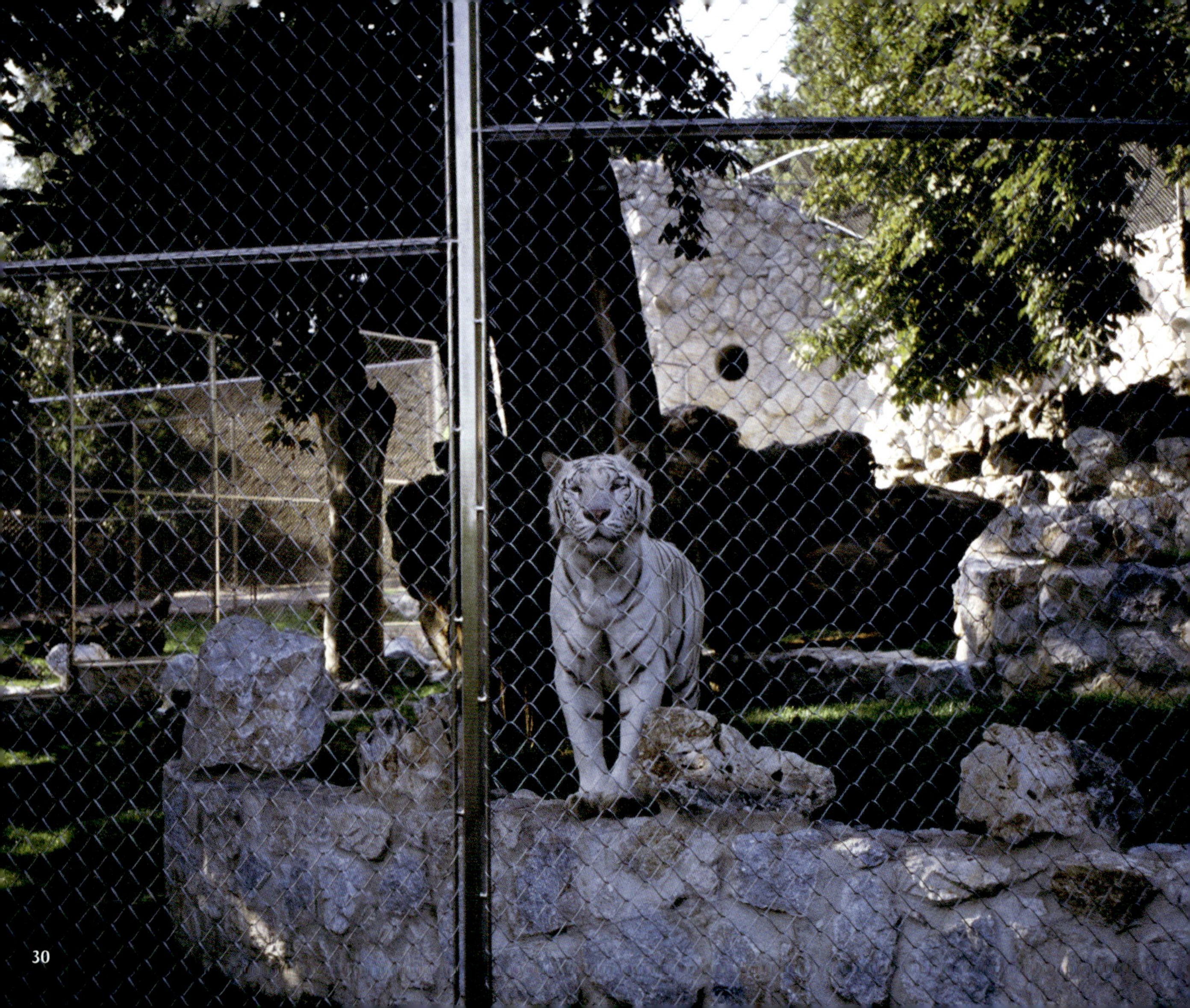

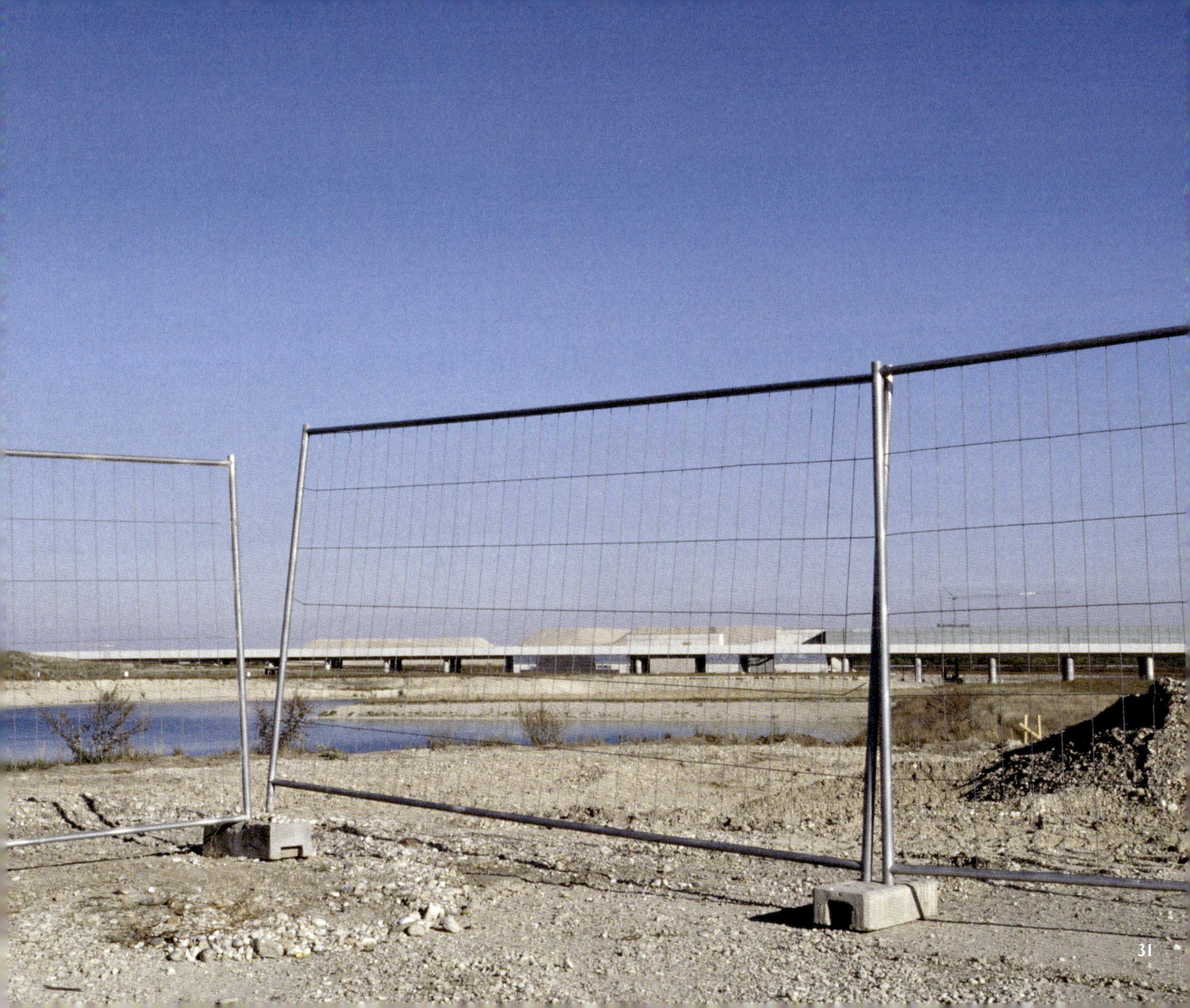

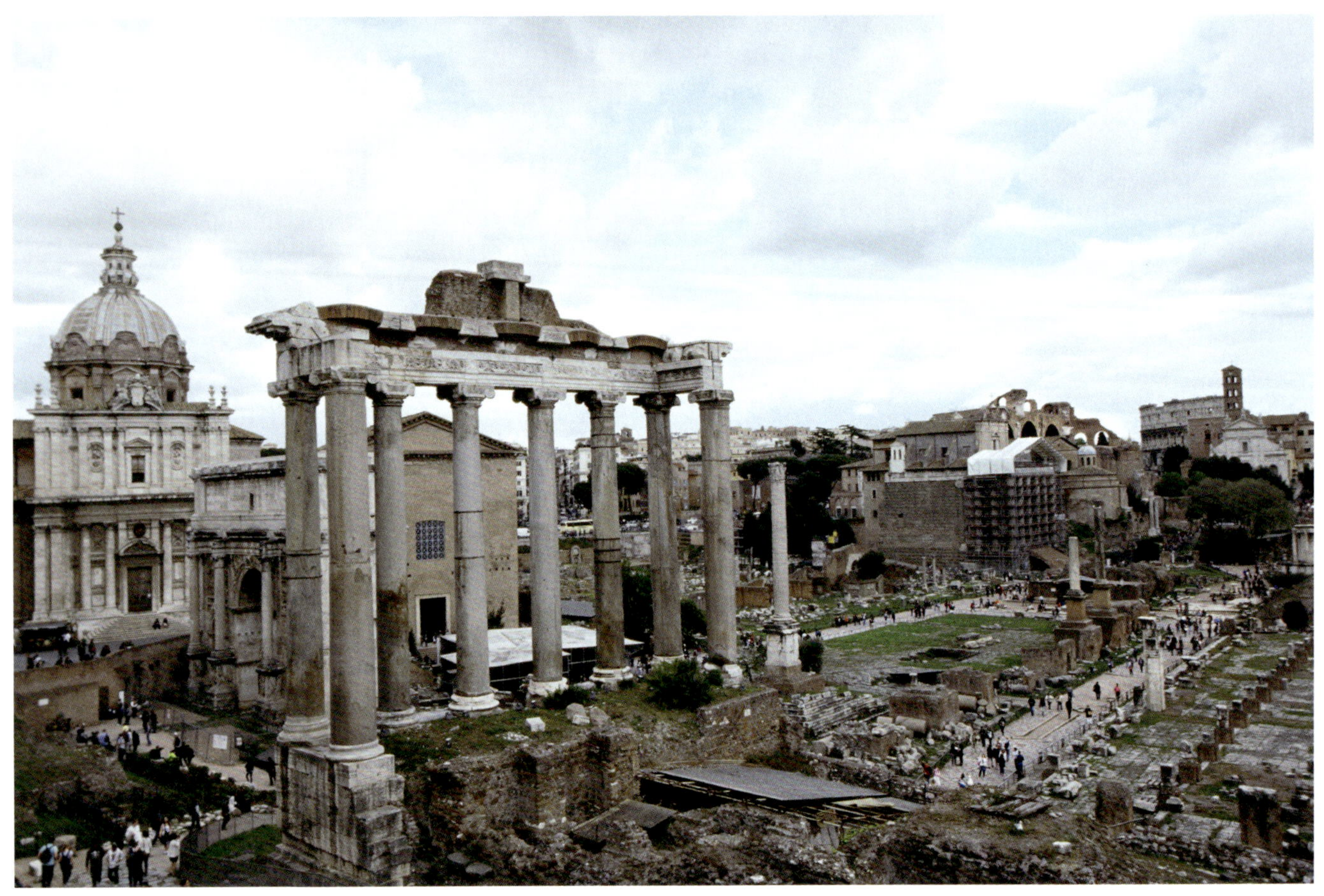

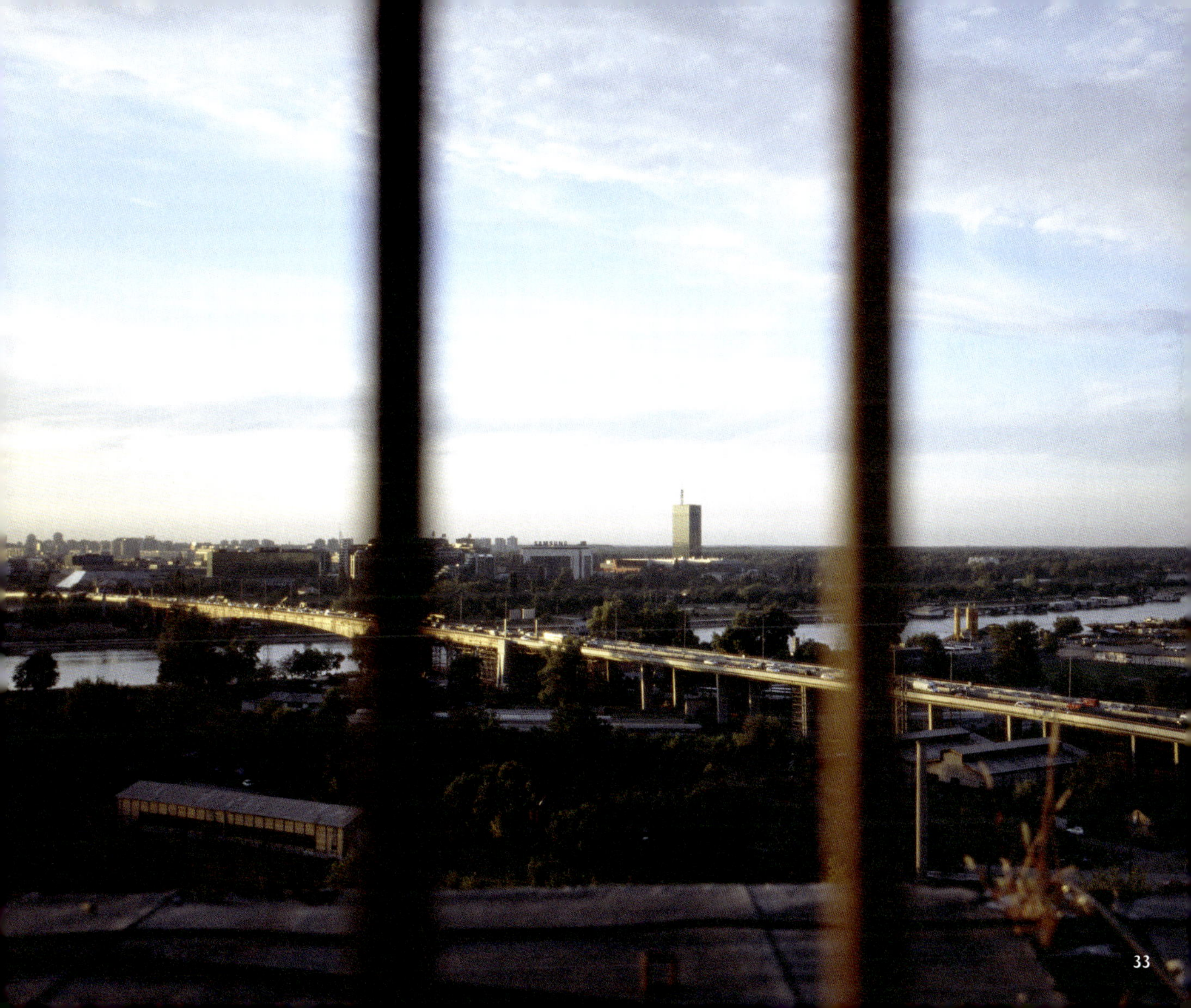

SAMSUNG

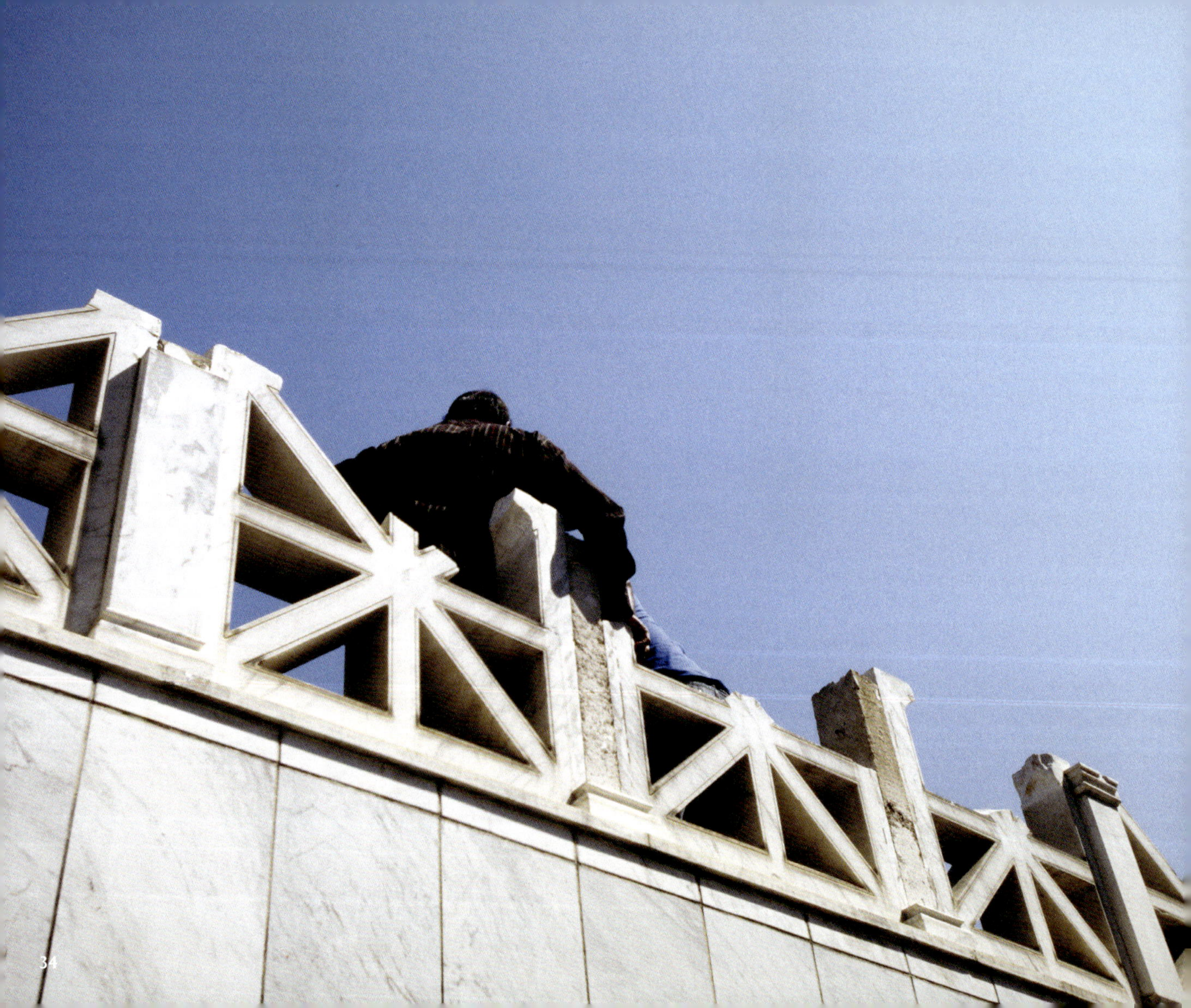

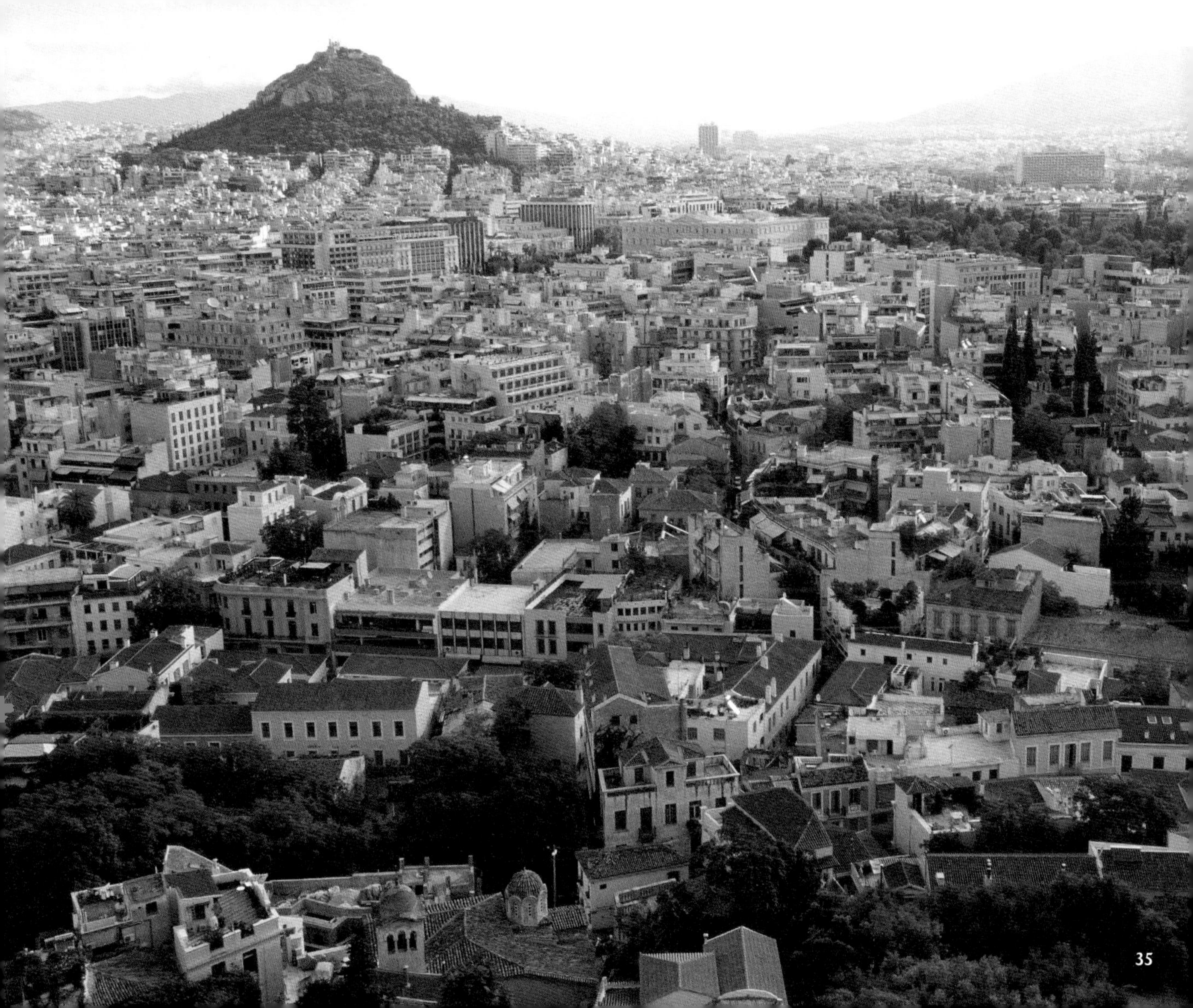

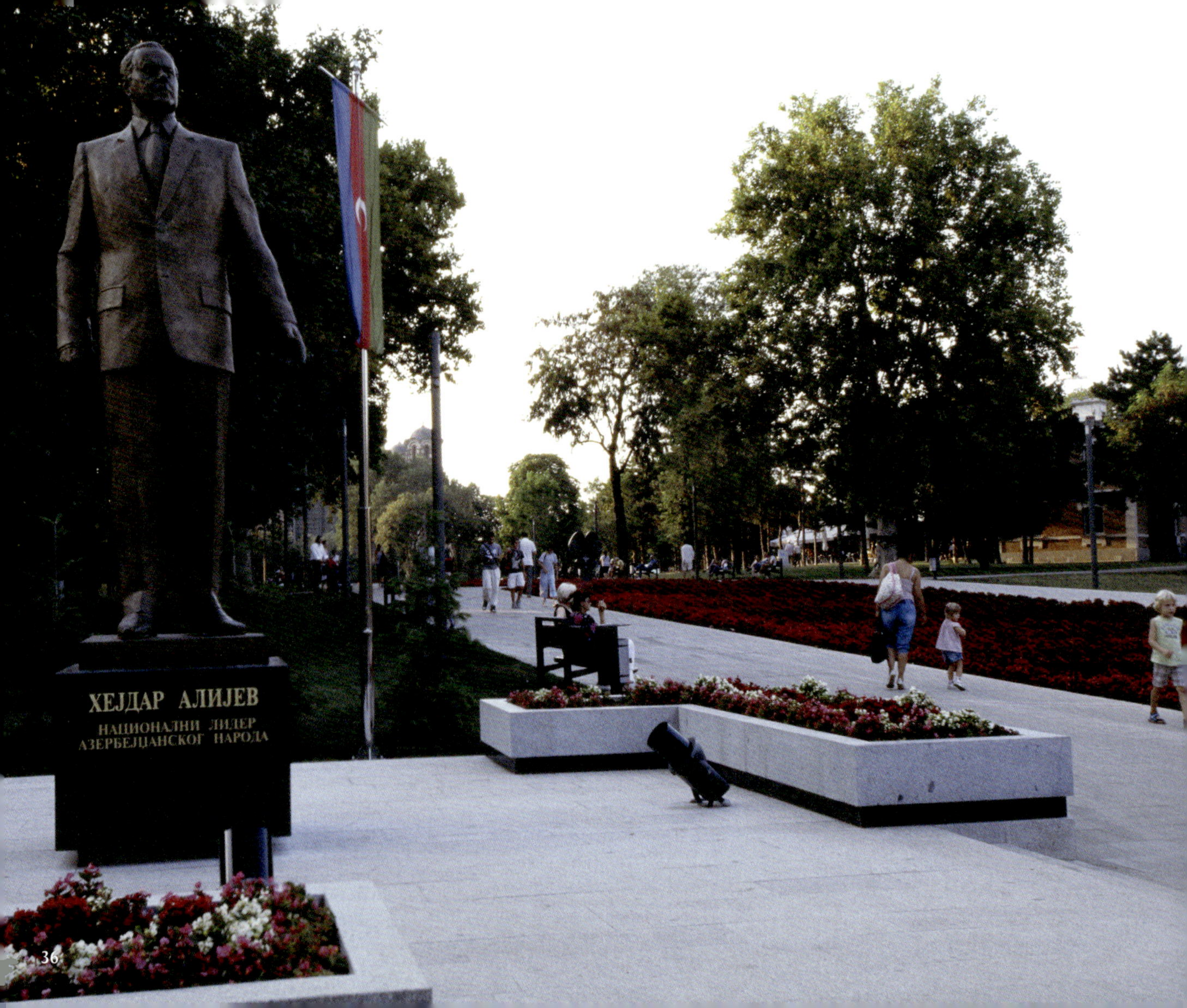

ХЕЈДАР АЛИЈЕВ
НАЦИОНАЛНИ ЛИДЕР
АЗЕРБЕЈЏАНСКОГ НАРОДА

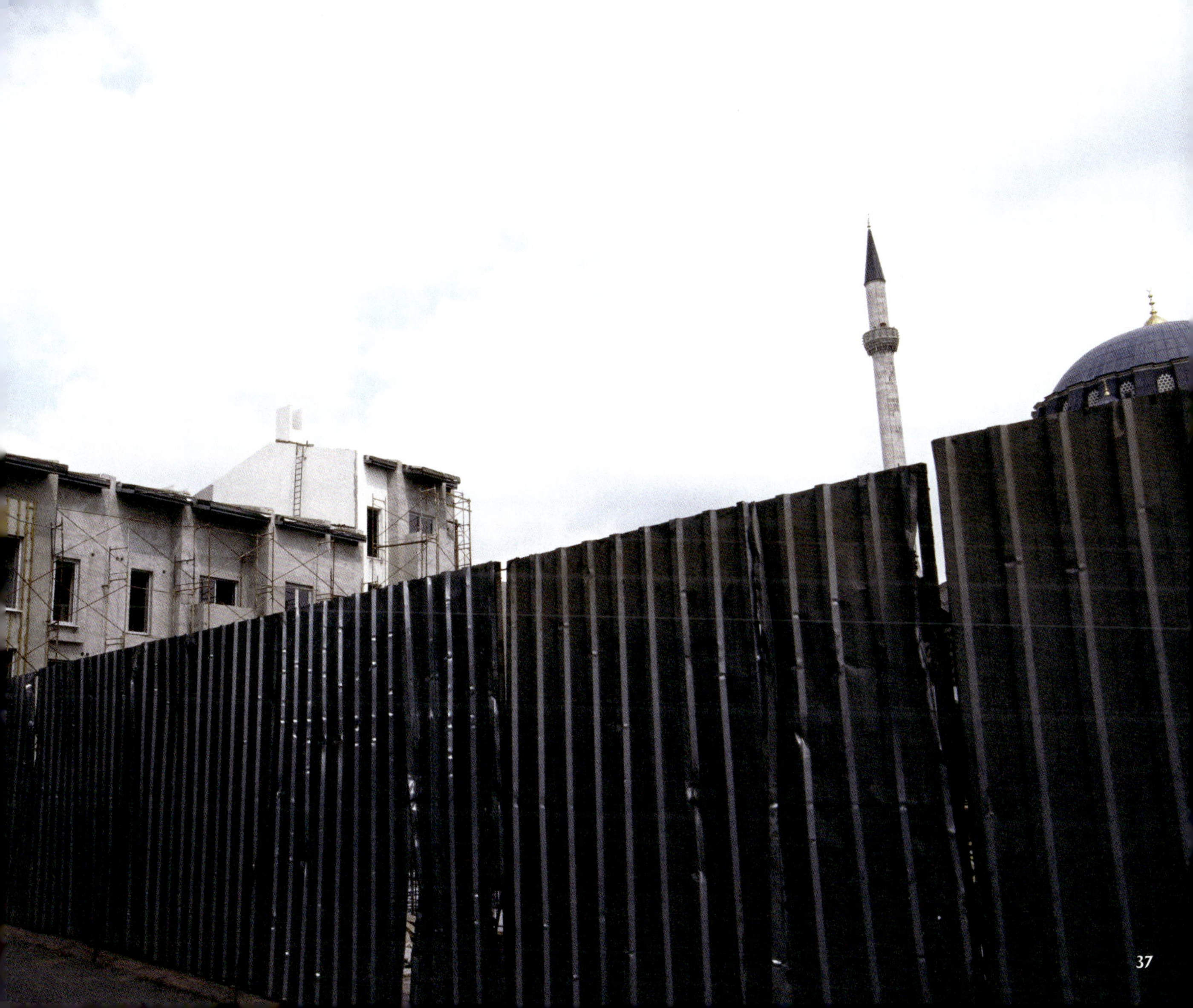

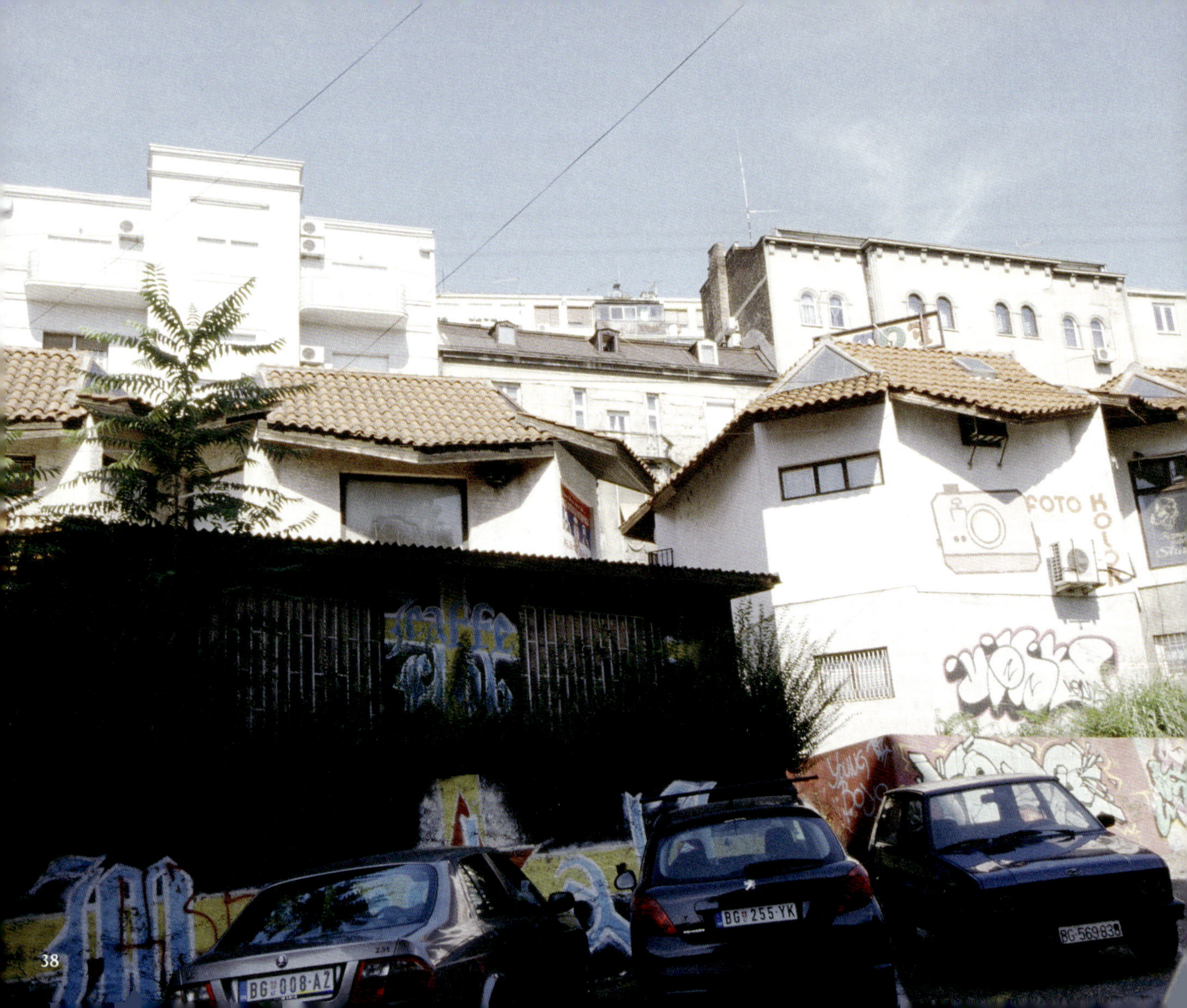

CAFFE
FOTO KODAK

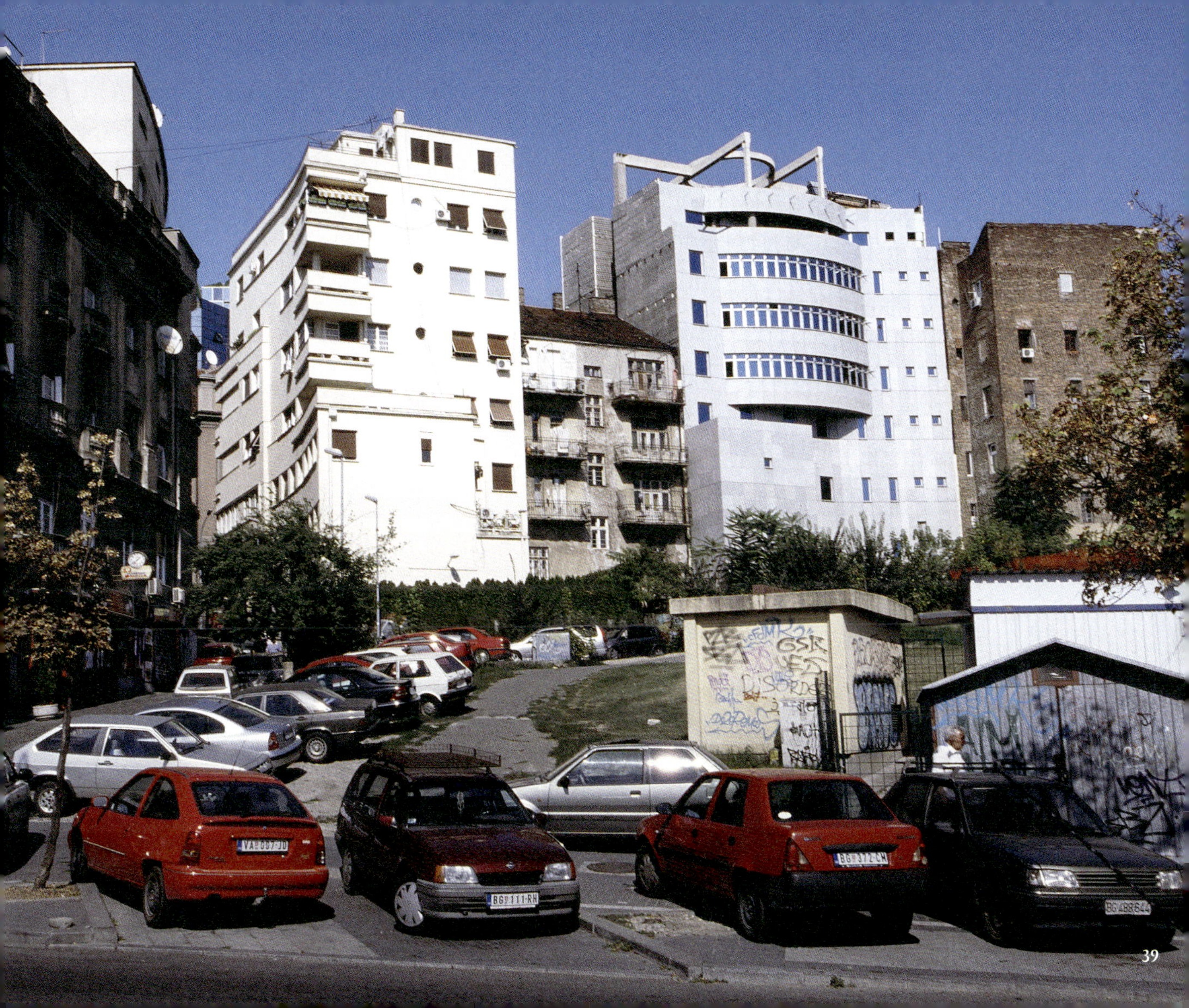

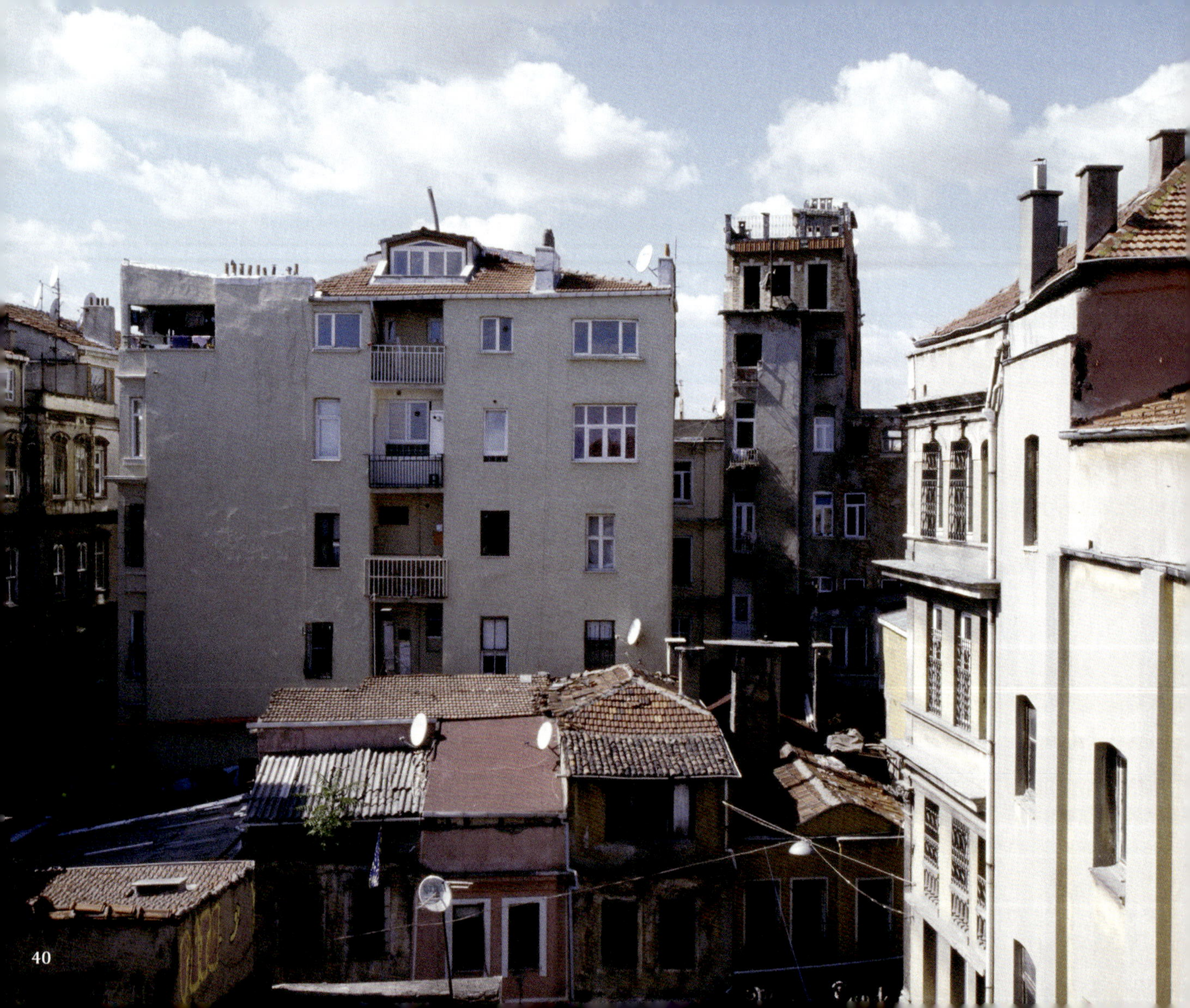

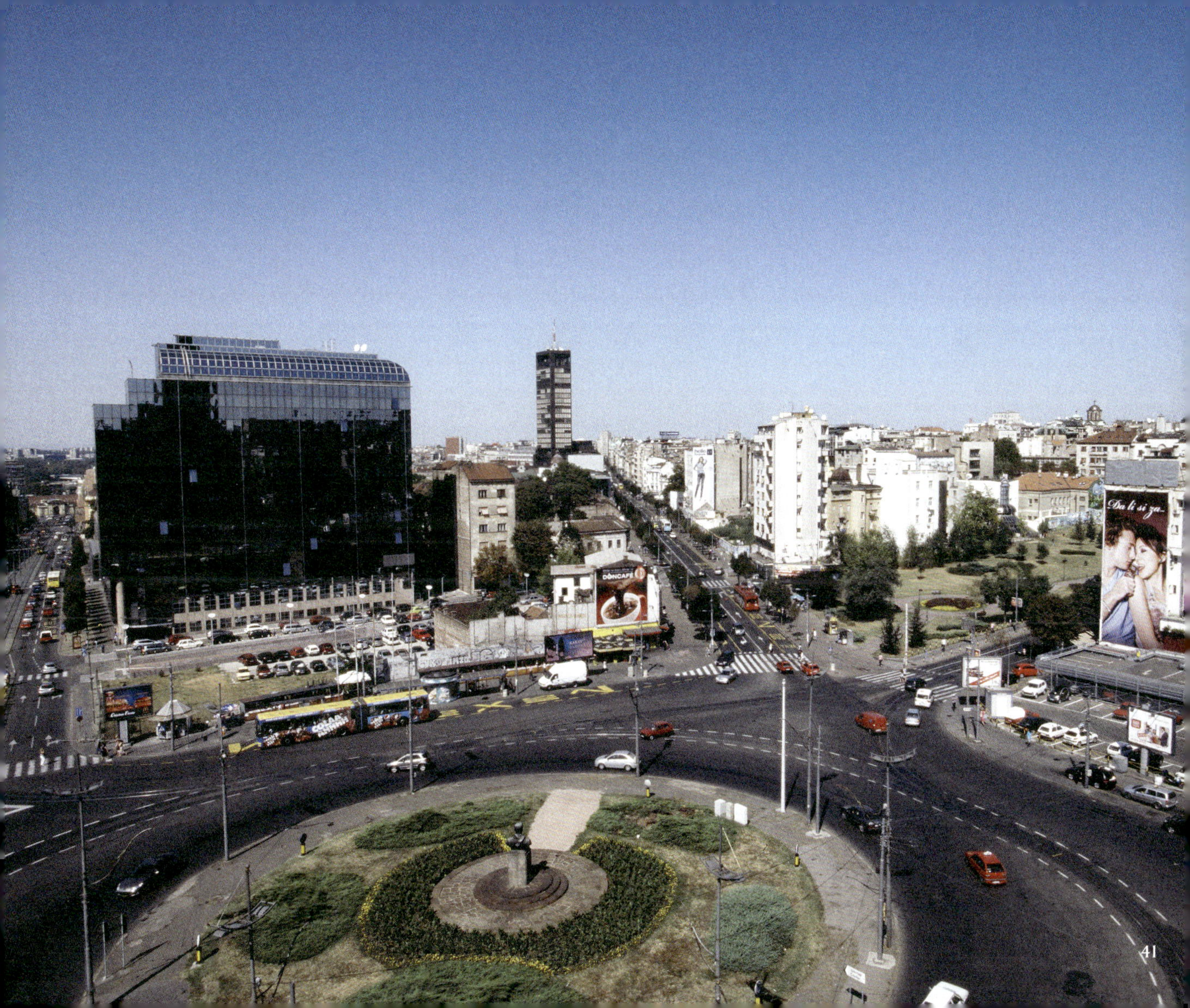

DONCAFE
Da li si za...

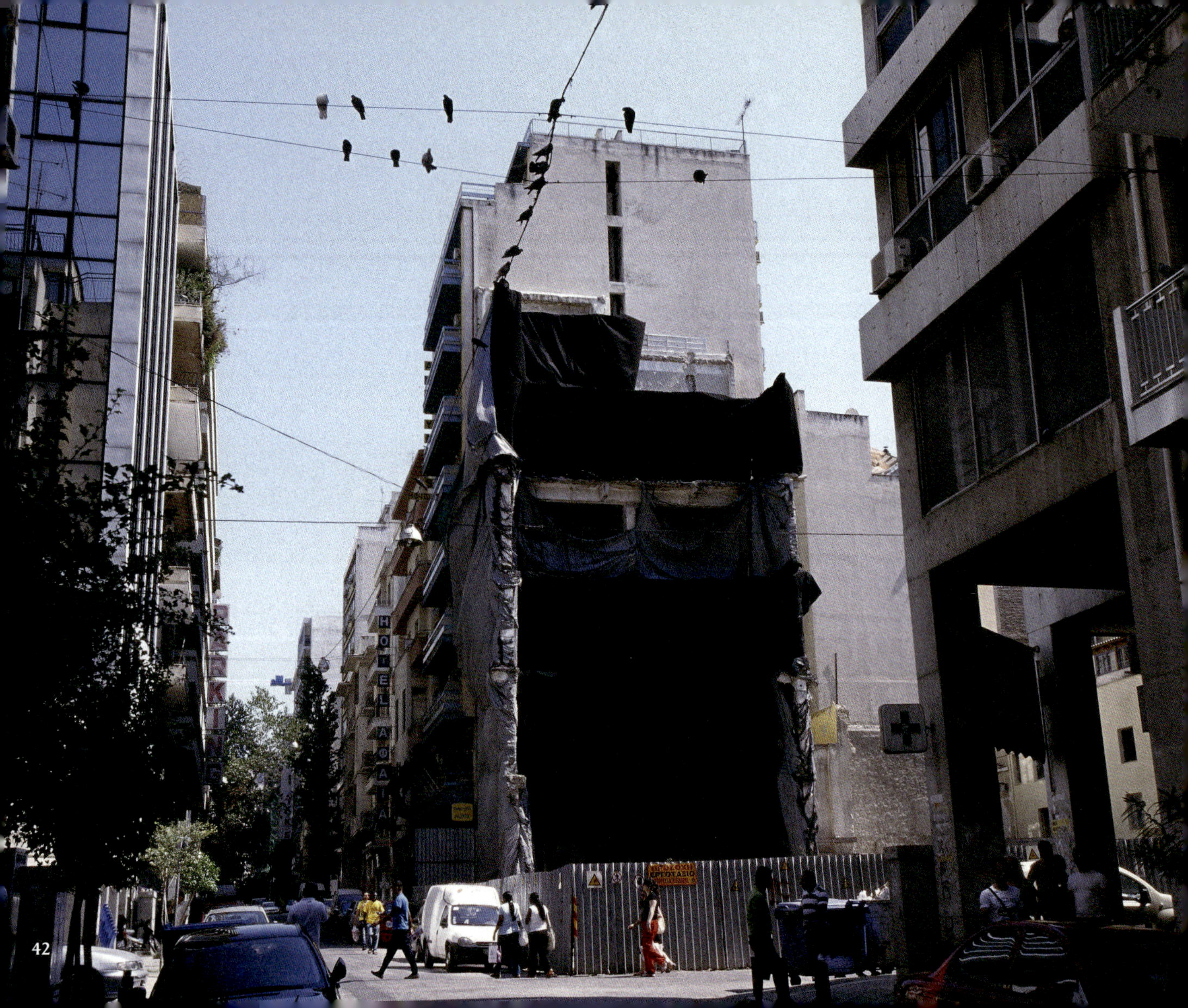

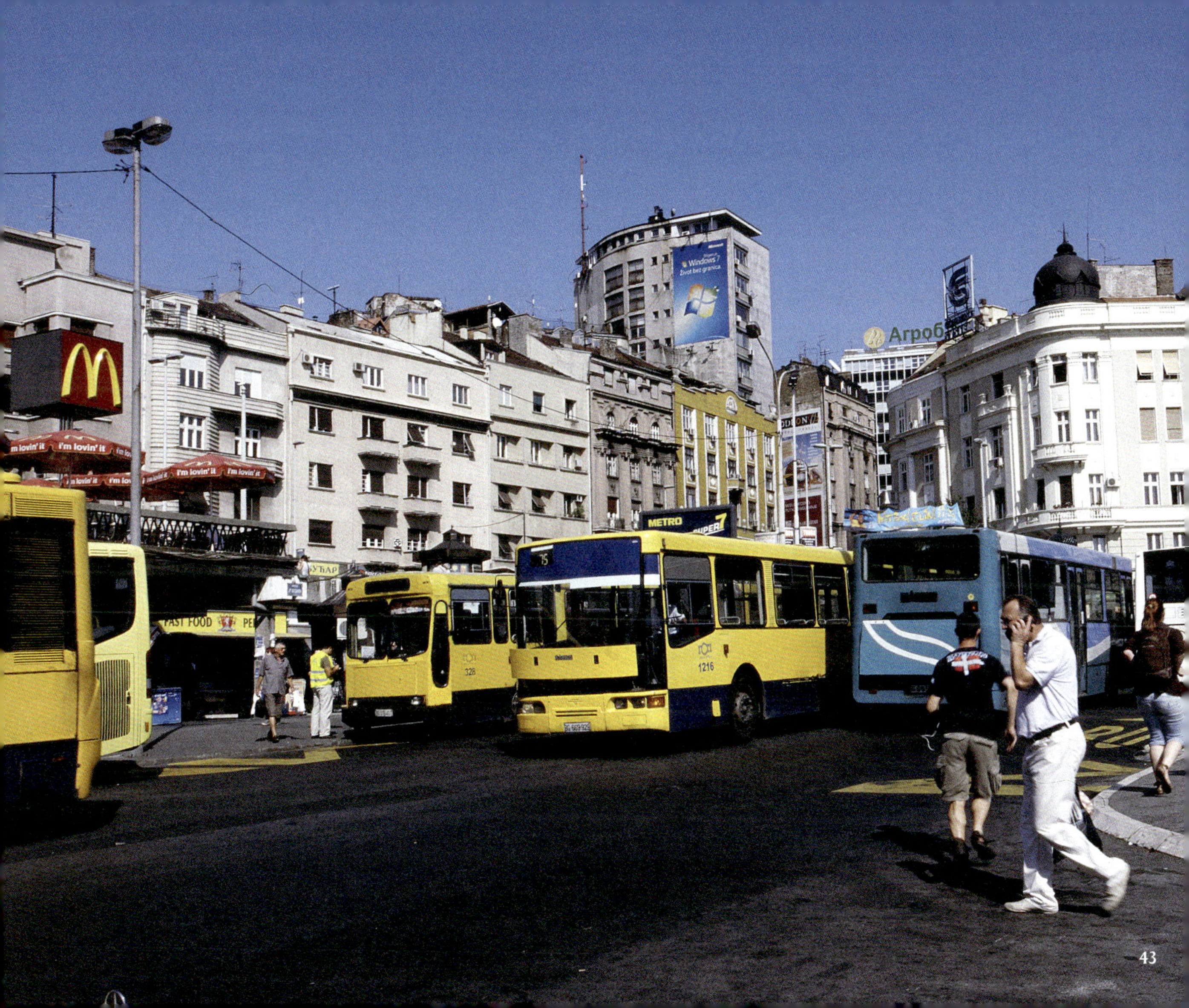

i'm lovin' it
FAST FOOD
METRO
SUPER 7
Windows 7
Агроб

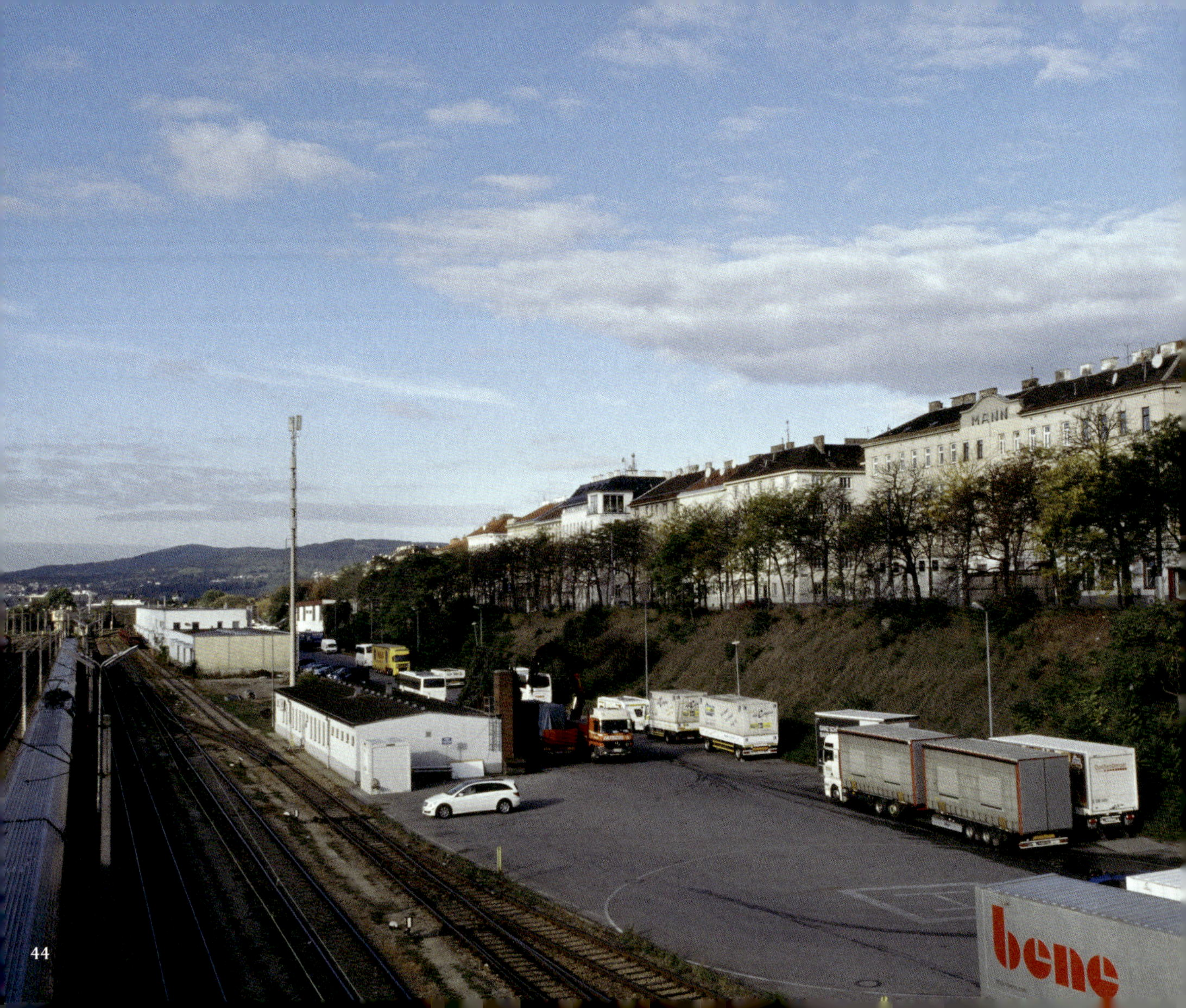

MANN
bene

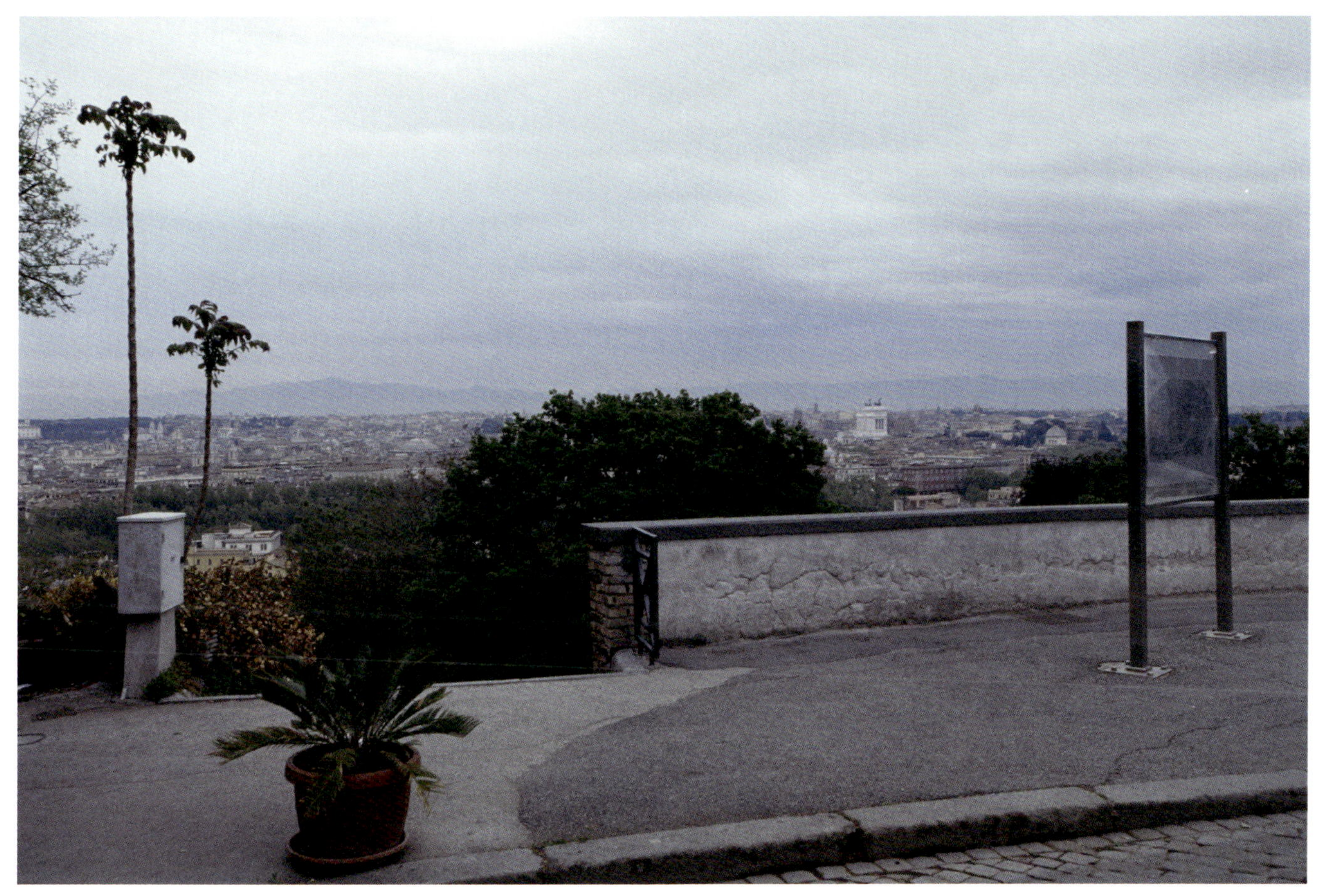

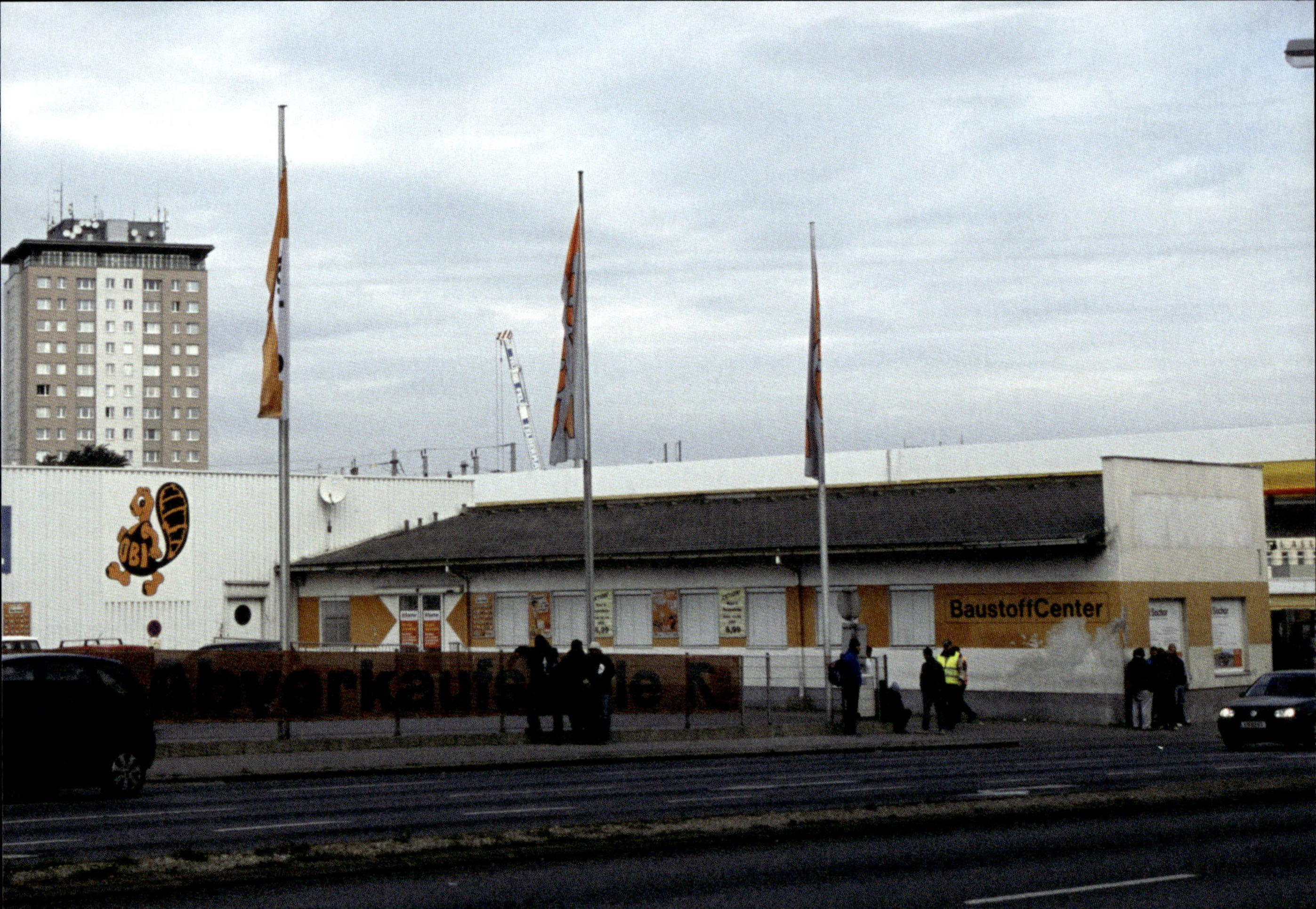

OBI
BaustoffCenter

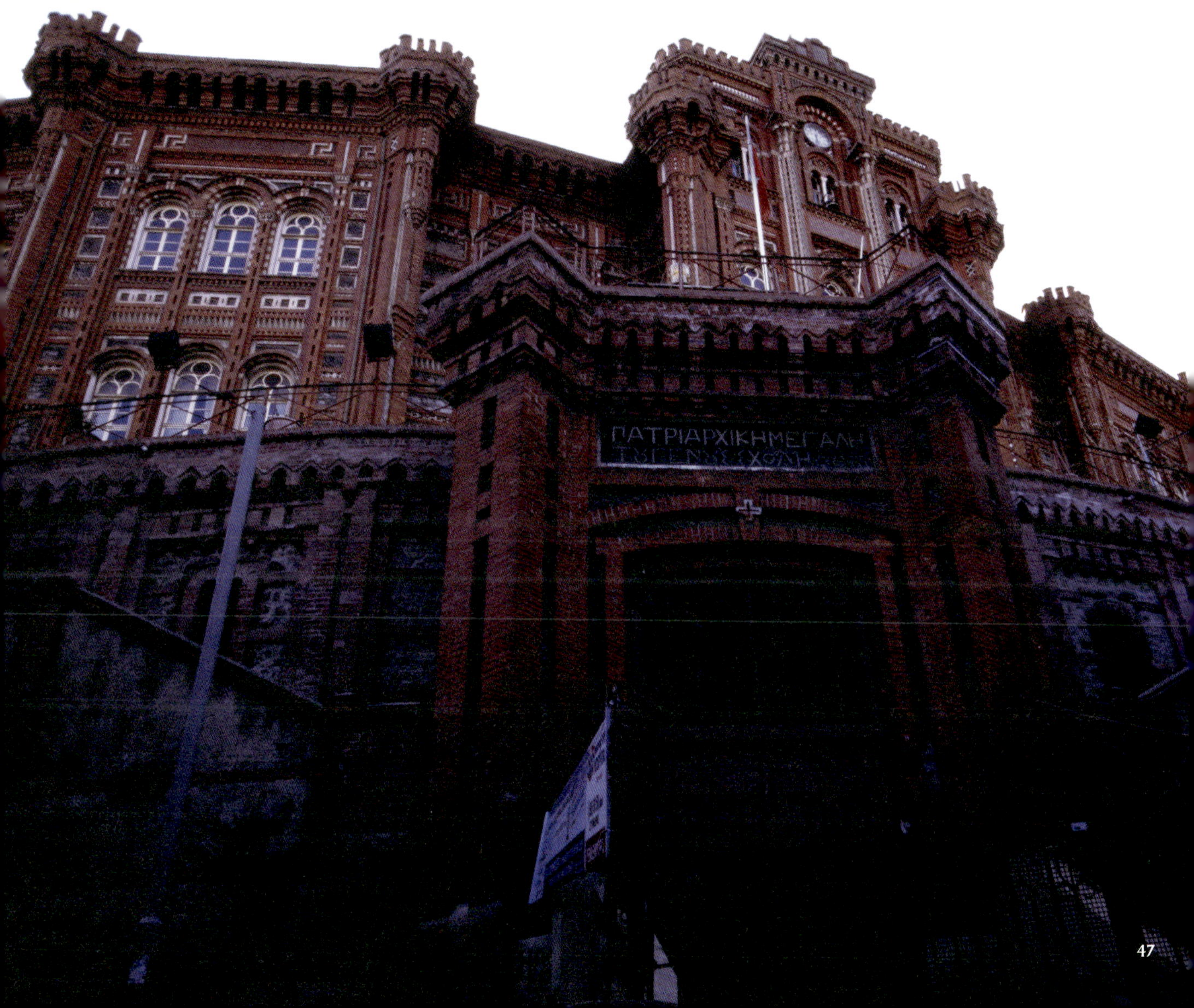
ΠΑΤΡΙΑΡΧΙΚΗ ΜΕΓΑΛΗ
ΤΟΥ ΓΕΝΟΥΣ ΣΧΟΛΗ

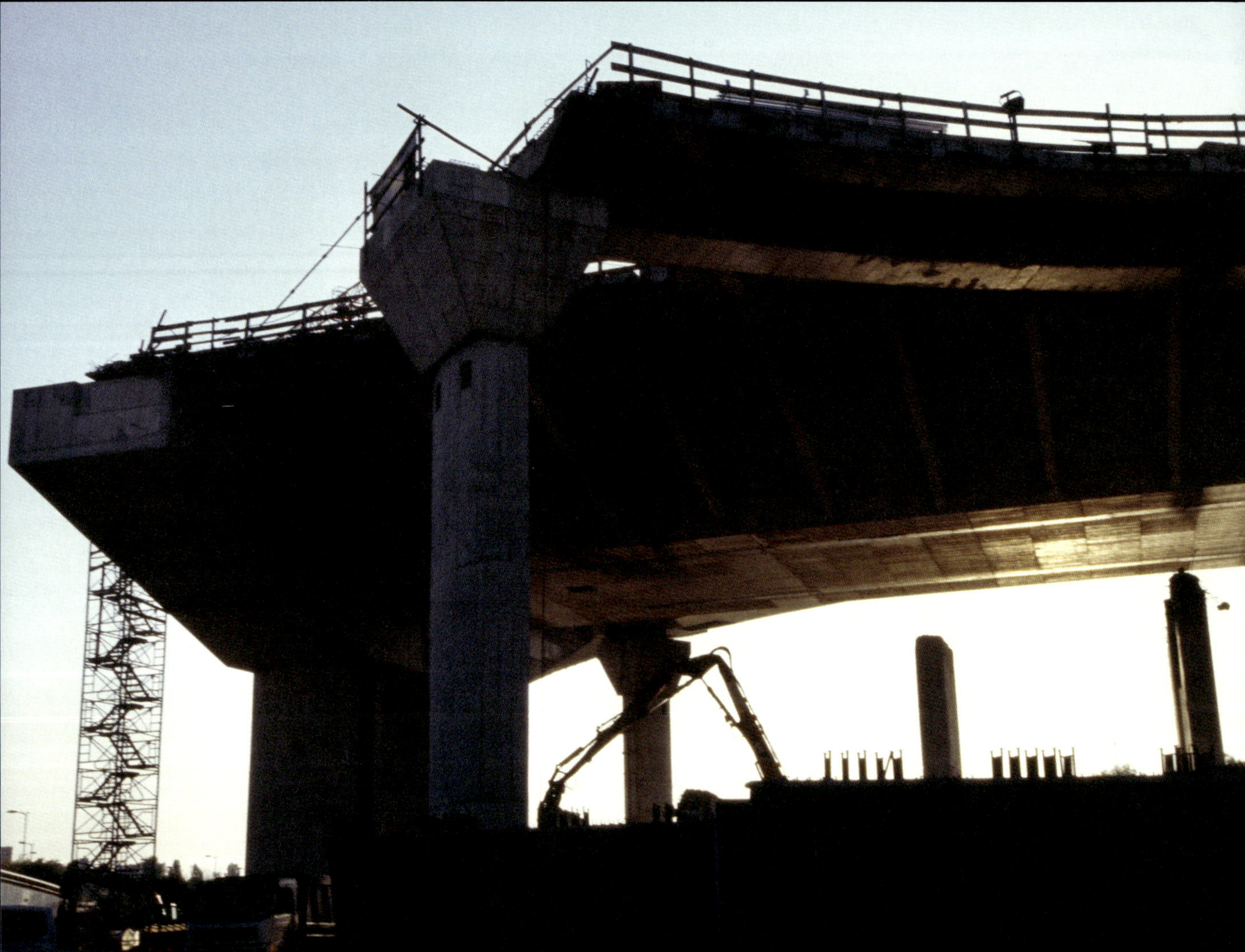

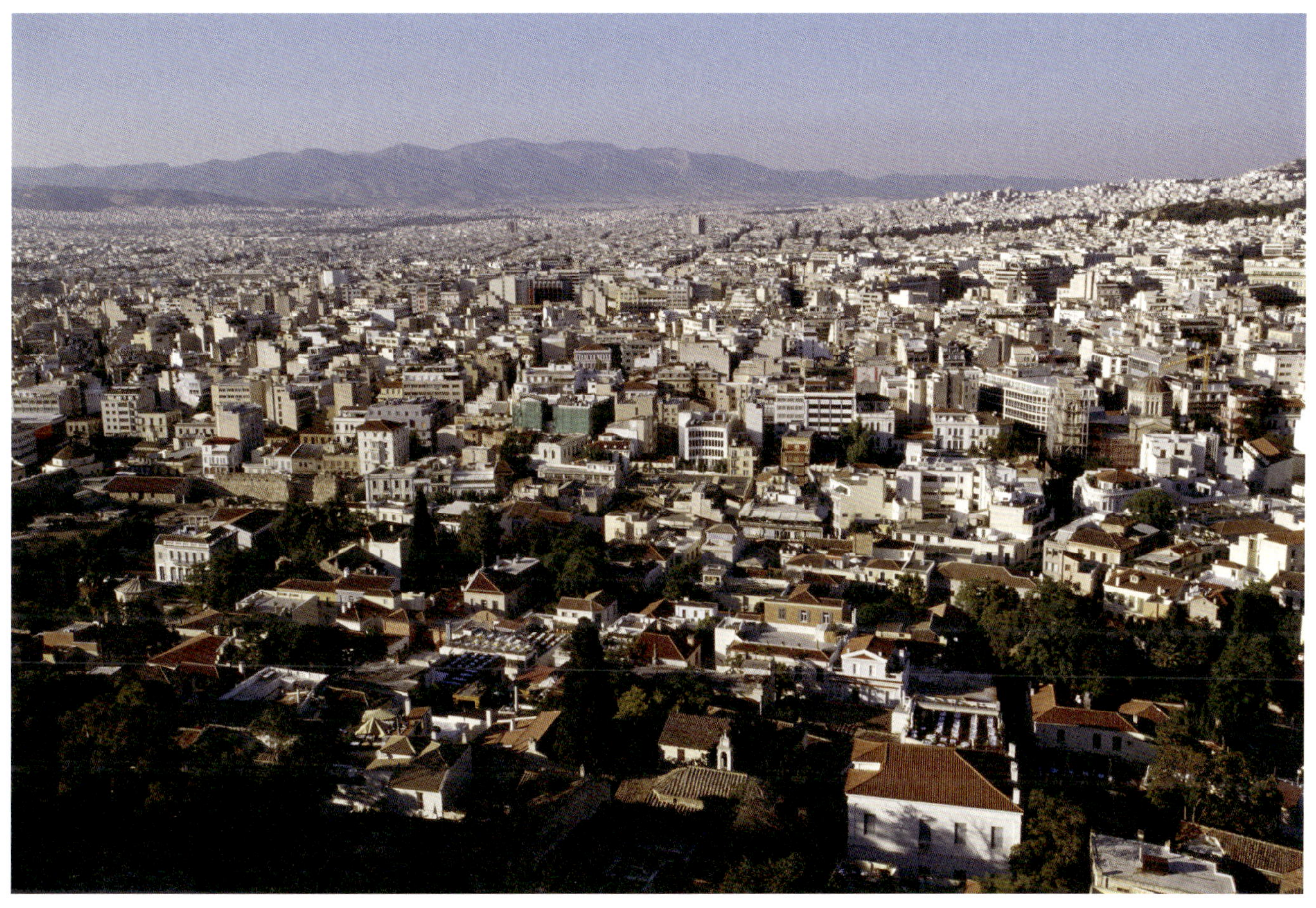

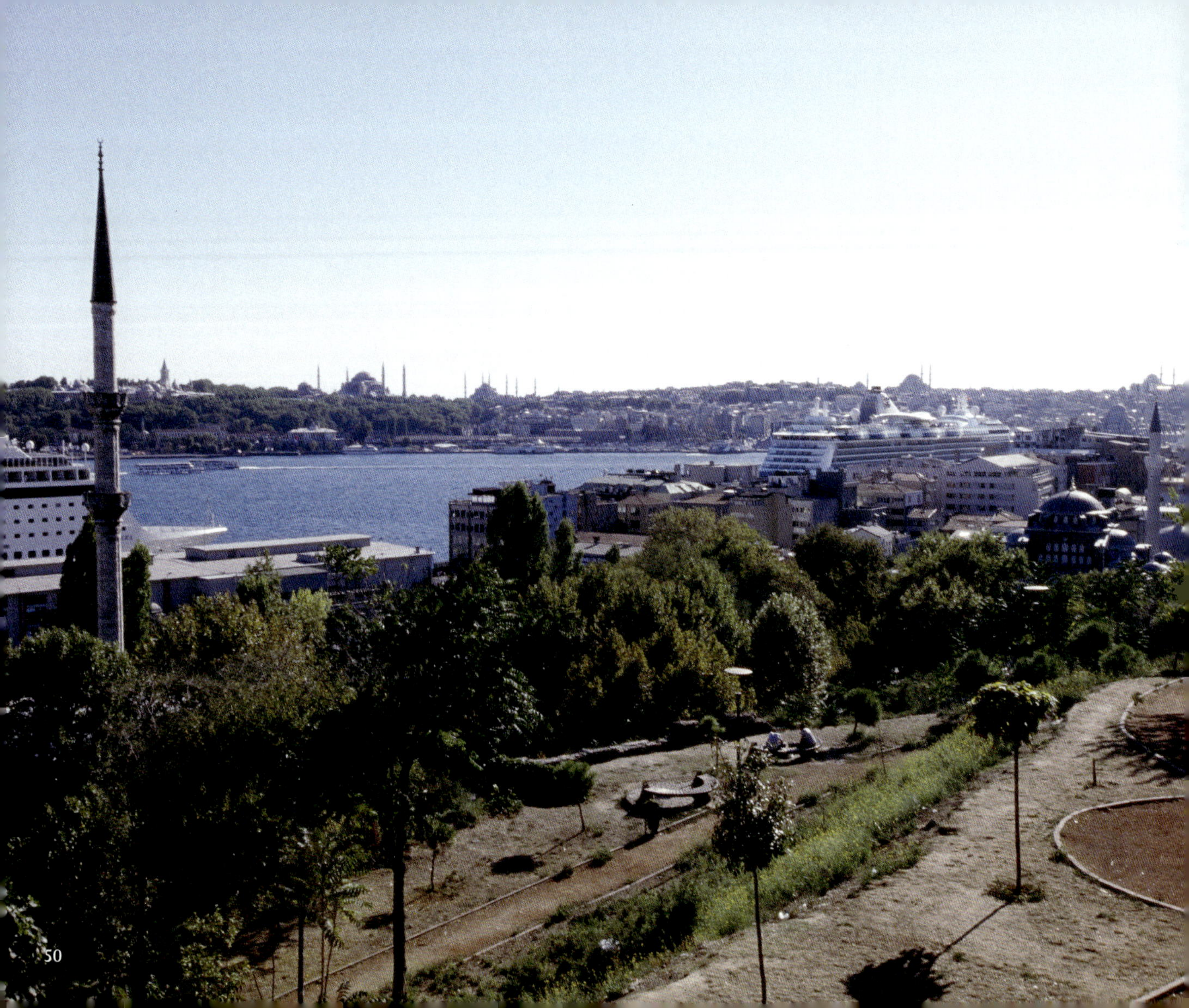

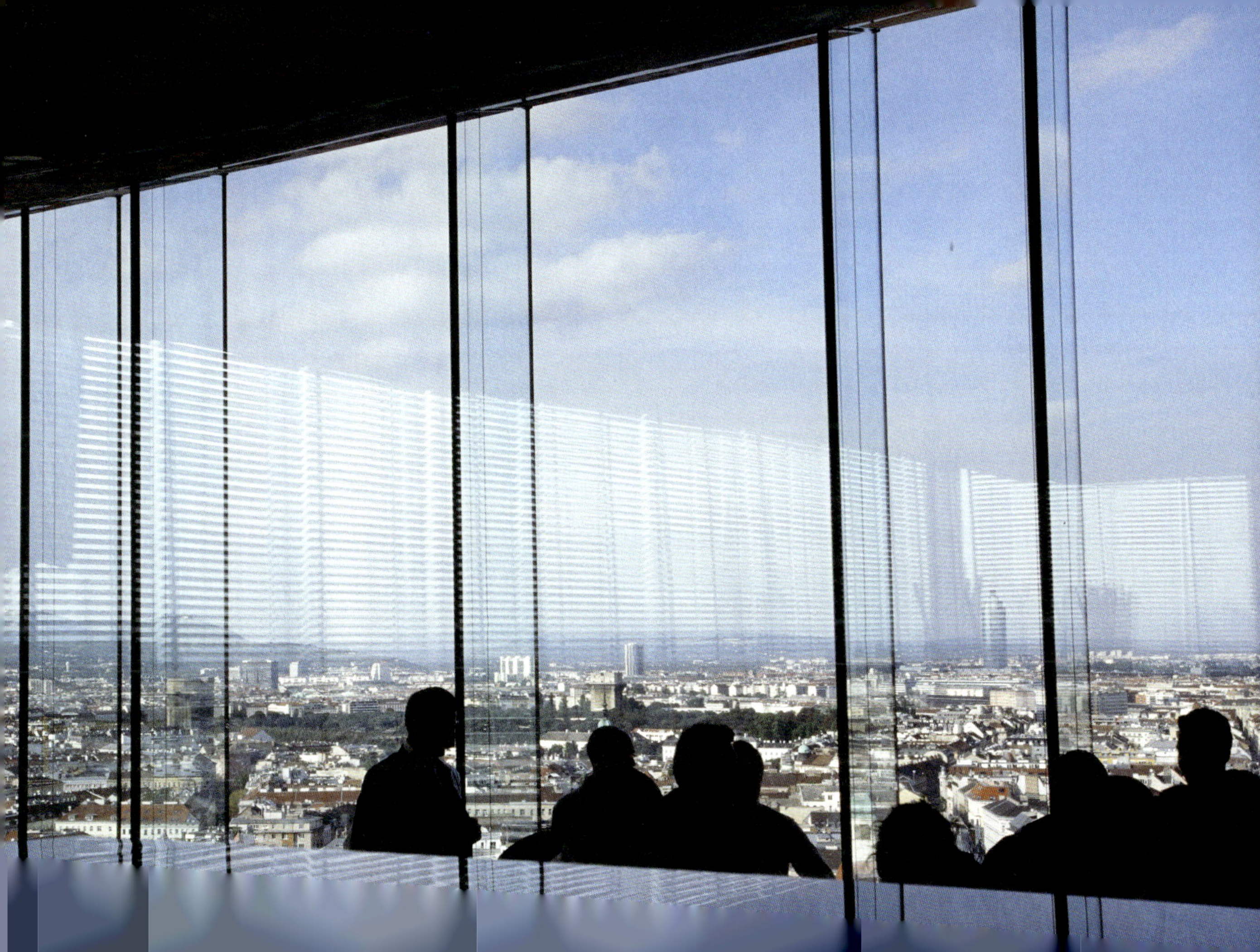

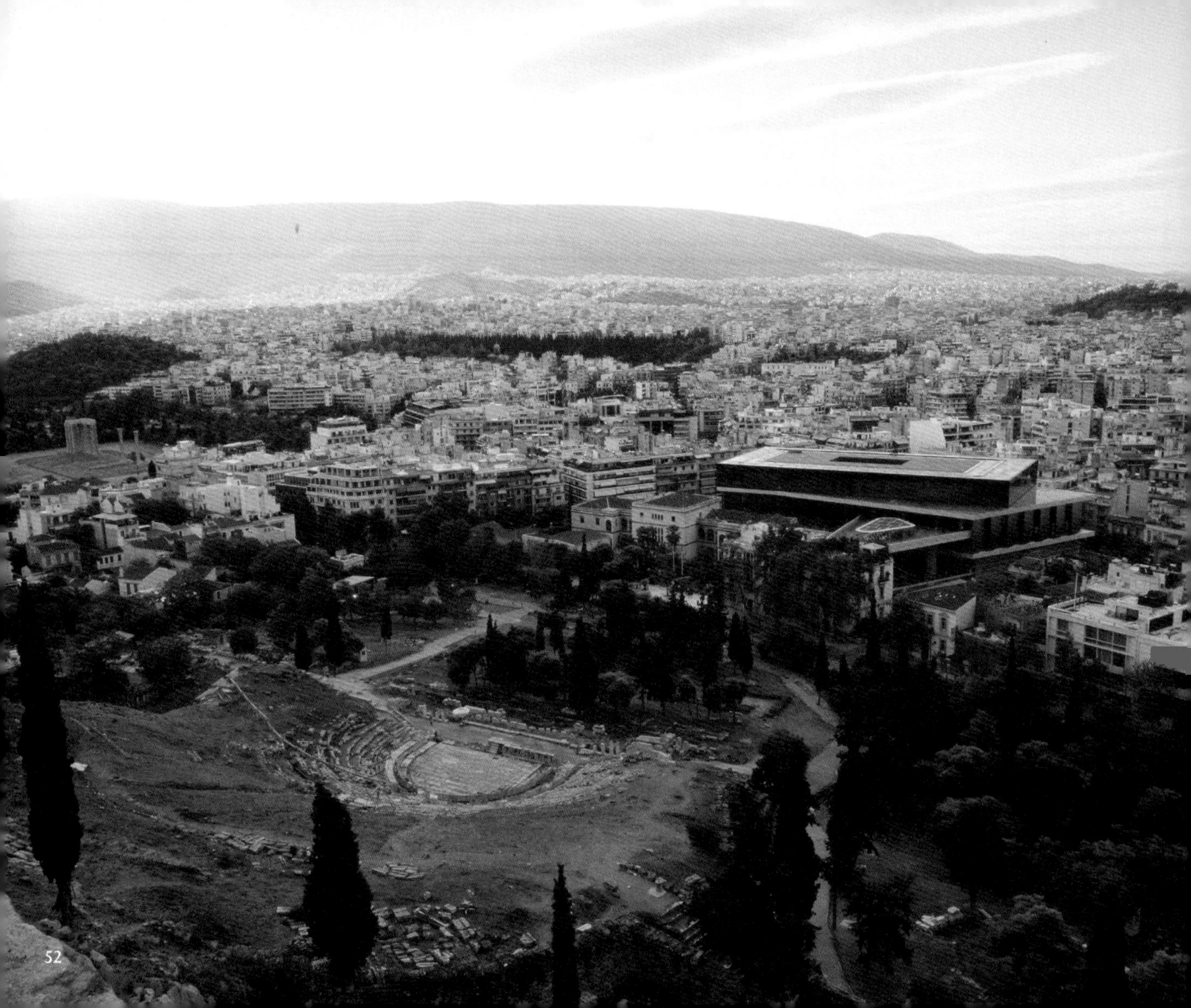

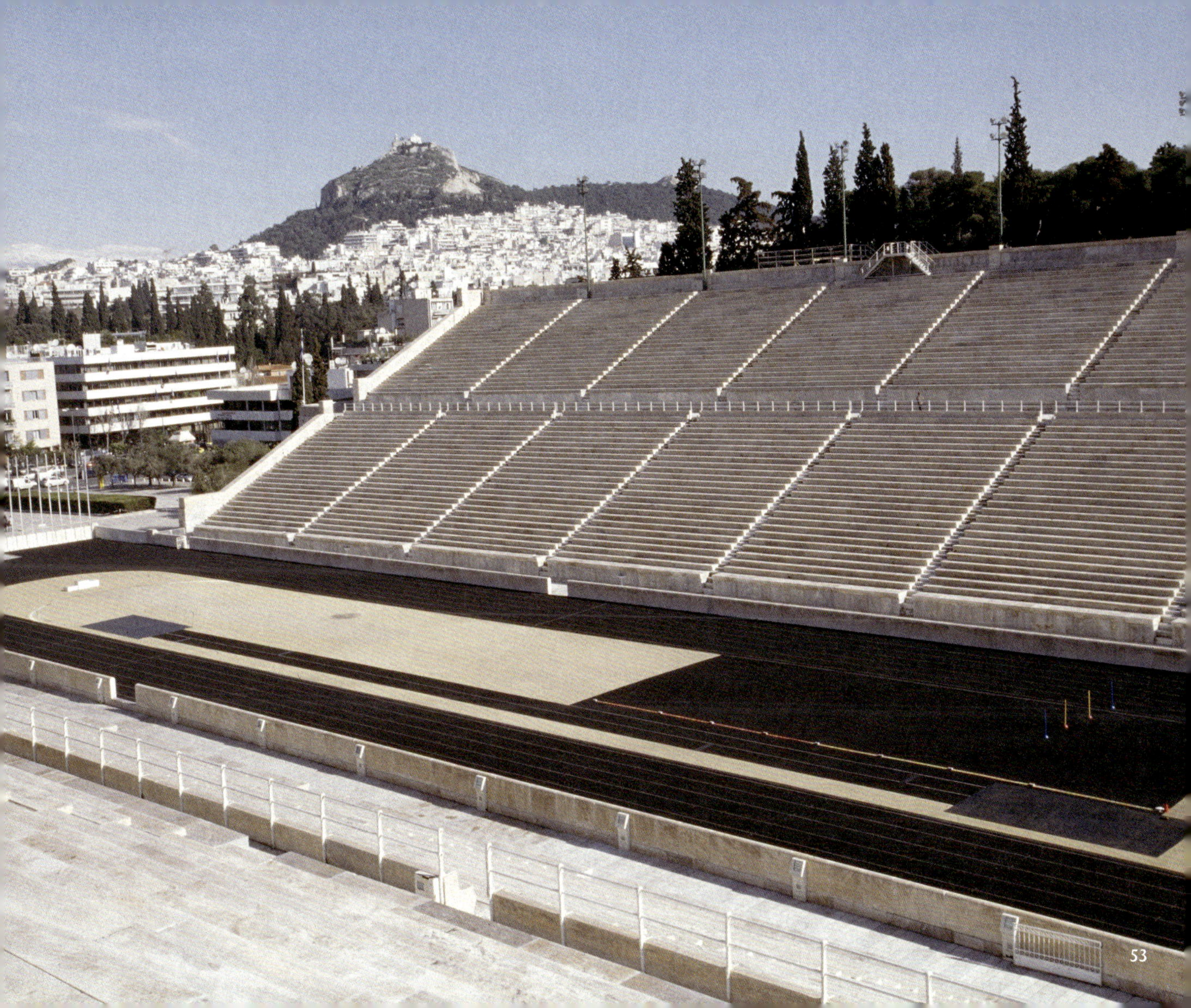

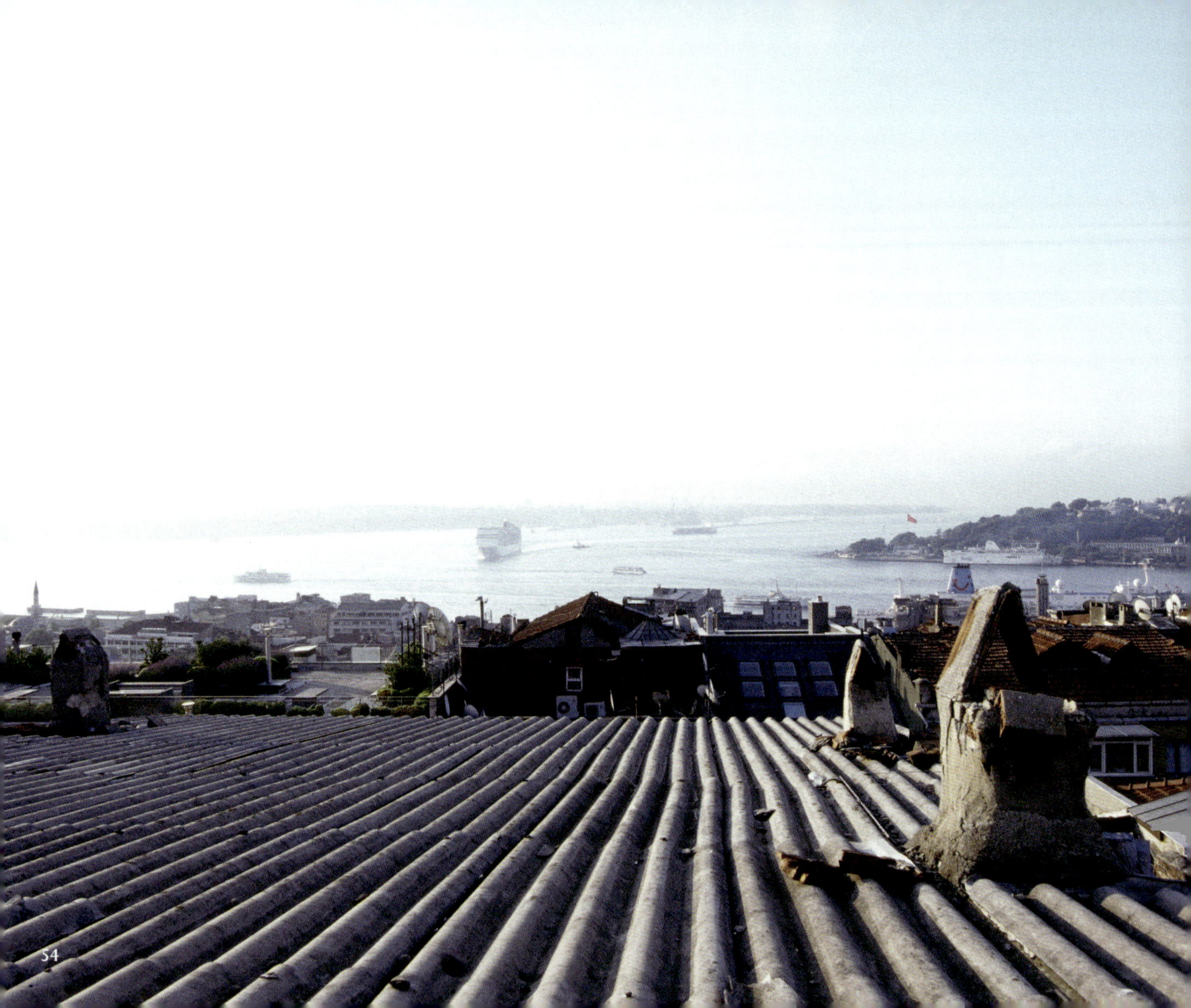

DEEP IN CONVERSATION: TRAVELLING SUBJECTS

ELKE KRASNY

BY WAY OF INTRODUCTION

The title of this essay joins together conversation, travel, and subject. In what follows I will enter into the complex cultural archive of the intersections between Western subject-formation and travel. In part, this subjectification is historically owed to formative education processes via travel. What I am referring to here is the model of the *Grand Tour* and the (ideal masculinist) travelling subjects it produced. These subjects set out to travel so they could learn from former empires and their distinct urban cultures. These subjects set out to travel and were well aware they needed to keep a record so they could show and tell/tell and show. This is of importance to understand the historical lineage a travel like Charles-Édouard Jeanneret's (the future Le Corbusier) 1911 *Voyage d'Orient* is part of.

The title speaks of travelling subjects and therefore deliberately activates the dual meaning of the word subject, i.e. subjecthood and subject matter. The subject matter I briefly sketched out above, the complex archive of Western subject-formation and travel, has to be raised when working with/as travelling subjects. Again, I am thinking of a number of issues raised by travelling subjects on several levels here: How to address travelling subjects in time/with time/over time?

The travelling subjects raised here are part of the conversation.

The research-based curatorial project, *Le Corbusier's voyage reORIENTed 1911-2011*, entered this complex cultural archive by way of making the questions travel raises the point of departure. The travel destination was not the archive holding Le Corbusier's records. The travel destinations were five cities that are part of Le Corbusier's 1911 itinerary: Vienna, Belgrade, Athens, Istanbul, Rome. The research method was conversation. How to share the complex issues raised by travelling subjects, such as Le Corbusier's journey, with others? How to make the 2011 cities part of the conversation? How to make the 1911 *Voyage* the site of inquiry by raising some of the subjects it raises into conversation: Monuments? Monumentality? East? West? Orientalization? Legacies of the 1911 *Voyage*? How to find words for these cities from a standpoint of today?

DIS/PLACING OBJECTS

Let me now approach *Le Corbusier's Voyage reORIENTed 1911-2011* curatorial research and exhibition project by way of an introductory detour that reflects the object-centricity of collection-based museums and the capitalist/colonial matrix that governed such museo-logics.[1] In collection-based museums of anthropology, history, or architecture, we might want to add, curators place a number of objects from their own museum's collections—or other collections—into new constellations. Object and placing are the key words to pay utmost attention to here. Viewed from a perspective reflecting the politics at work, one has to consider that museum objects are always displaced objects. I am not referring here to an ontological dimension, but rather to concrete social and historical conditions from which such objects in the process of being turned into museum objects have been taken/removed. The term displacement I use here seeks to capture the colonial mindset that, historically, governed much of the logic of the museum. Displacement refers to the politics of power in regards to objects being removed from their original contexts and uses and turned into museum objects. In her 1985 essay "The Rani of Sirmur: An Essay of Reading the Archives" post-colonial and feminist theorist Gayatri Chakravorty Spivak speaks of "epistemic violence,"[2] which she connects to "monopoly imperialism,"[3] which in turn must be connected to museo-logics. Not only are the objects dis/placed from their context of origin, such displacement both re/produces as much as it silences displacements. What I mean by this is that the museum often follows hegemonic orders and therefore tended not to collect what it categorizes as marginal, i.e. the material, aesthetic, and intellectual conditions and productions of all those that were othered by class, gender, race, religion. This was a very brief description of what can be understood as the re/production of ruling conditions via the objects collected, or captured, and ordered, or categorized, in museums. The second part, the silencing of displacements, is maybe even more epistemologically violent. The complex stories of what an object can tell about its place of origin before having been dis/placed in the museum have been effectively erased and silenced in

1. The term museo-logics echoes museology and seeks to at once expose and critique the logics at work in terms of the museum's foundational intentionalities: collecting, categorizing, ordering, exhibiting, and making materially manifest a web of imperial and colonial power relations.
2. Gayatri Chakravorty Spivak, "The Rani of Sirmur: An Essay in Reading the Archives," *History and Theory* 24, no. 3 (October 1985), 250.
3. Spivak (1985), 258.

many cases. The objects have come to stand in for their aesthetic value of looked-at-ness rather than disclosing the social, political, and material contexts and their complex raced, classed, and gendered conditions. In her 2002 paper "Colonial Archives and the Arts of Governance," Ann Laura Stoler argues that "scholars need to move from archive-as-source to archive-as-subject."[4] I would like to add to this the following: there needs to be an understanding from the museum/collections-as-source to museum/collections-as-subject. What the (deep) storage of museums has deeply stored has to be addressed. Therefore scholars, just as much as curators or others concerned with museums, need to move from museum-as-source to museum-as-subject. Since the 1990s, critical museum practice and critical artistic and curatorial practice with museum objects has sought to address these legacies of epistemic violence and has equally sought to find expressions for epistemic resistance.[5] Dis/placing, deployed conceptually as an actively detouring and counteractive curatorial strategy could still be used to show objects, while also exhibiting their complex situatedness of displacement differently.

(BE A) PART OF THE CONVERSATION
As a non-museum curator whose work is mostly project-based/exhibition-based I come into contact with museum collections, library collections, or archives for that matter, as part of my curatorial research. As much as I am interested in working critically with objects and finding ways of narrating stories of dis/placement/dis/placing stories, I am equally interested in doing curatorial research projects based upon working with conversations. In 2007, I began to think about a chronological fact: in 2011 Le Corbusier's Voyage to the East would be looking back upon a hundred years. For sure, there were celebrations, conferences, seminars, and exhibitions marking this anniversary to be expected.

4. Ann Laura Stoler, "Colonial Archives and the Arts of Governance," *Archival Science* 2, 1-2 (2002): 93. Stoler (2002), 93.
5. Artist Fred Wilson's seminal work, the 1992 *Mining the Museum* project, critically addressed and reoriented the collections of the Maryland Historical Society set the standard for many projects to follow. There are numerous publications concerning the postcolonial, and more recently, the decolonial critique of museum and curatorial practice. To name but a few: Belinda Kazeem, Charlotte Manz-Turek, and Nora Sternfeld, eds., *Das Unbehagen im Museum. Postkoloniale Museologien* (Vienna: Turia + Kant, 2009). Strategies of decolonizing the museum have been paid more recent attention in the fraught relationships between what is called "source (! sic) communities" and museums. Janet Marstine, "Introduction," In *New Museum: Theory and Practice*, ed. Janet Marstine (Malden, Oxford and Carlton: Blackwell Publishing, 2006), 17. From November 27-29 a series of activities, courses and seminars "Decolonising the Museum" was curated by Beatriz Preciado and took place at Barcelona's MACBA Museum in 2014.

This made me think about ways to approach such an anniversary differently. How could one navigate the controversial, and also critically con/tested territory of the legacy of Le Corbusier's Journey to the East/*Voyage d'Orient* via a curatorial project? How could one attempt to understand the 1911 voyage from today's perspectives and today's politics of location? How could one situate local urban knowledges (in plural) in regards to the 1911 voyage? How could one find voices speaking with/about/to their cities through the lens of issues raised via the 1911 *Voyage*? How could one make this part of a conversation, in fact, part of many different conversations? How could one (…)?

TRAVELLING SUBJECTS

The *Grand Tour*, which Le Corbusier's *Voyage d'Orient* was grafted upon, was an educational model requiring moneyed young English men of the aristocracy and the upper class to leave home and travel to Italy, France, or Greece. The most classical of all *Grand Tour* destinations was the Italian Peninsula and the most prominent *Grand Tour* city was Rome. One could argue that a specific Western model of modern masculinist subject-formation was grounded in leaving one's home and expand one's horizon (sic!) via travelling. In his 1615 essay "Of Travel," Francis Bacon offered the following strategic advice: "Let diaries therefore be brought in use. The things to be seen and observed are, the courts of princes, specially when they give audience to ambassadors, the courts of justice, while they sit and hear causes; […] the churches and monasteries, with the monuments […] antiquities and ruins; libraries, colleges, disputations, and lectures where any are […] cabinets and rarities."[6] The advice was written with a diplomatic career in mind. It was the ambassadorial model of imperialism in the making that takes on travel as the prerequisite of educational formation. And, etymologically, travel is connected to the French *travailler*, which is connected to travail, to labor. So, a specific kind of educational labor via travelling was necessary to form the subjects that could then assume leading roles in society and politics. During the 17th century, the century of British imperial expansion, as well as other imperial expansions at the time, began to take shape. This represents the confluence of travel, meetings with people, visits paid to architecture and museums (rarities and cabinets of curiosities in the language of the time), and the diary. Bacon also advises that "young man travel under some tutor, or grave servant."[7]

6.   Francis Bacon, *The Essays of Francis Bacon*, edited by Maria Augusta Scott (New York: Charles Scribner's Sons: 1908), 79-80.
7.   Bacon (1908), 79.

What is of interest here is that much of this sounds strangely familiar with regards to today's tourist (books). Therefore, we can concede, that the mass tourist has been formed to some extent by the educational formation of the grand tourist bound up with a masculinist subject-formation dedicated to advancing one's career. Interestingly enough though, the 'travail' (labor)[8] of travel has been replaced by the rhetorics of the 'leisure' of travel.[9] The French-born Richard Lassels, a five time tutor for English nobility on their Italian tour, wrote a book that gave this kind of travel its definitive name: The *Grand Tour*. In 1698 his book *Voyage or a Complete Journey Through Italy* appeared in English.[10]

What draws my attention here is how the travel-logic of the *Grand Tour* has a point of convergence with museo-logic. This convergence is to be made out in displacement. Travel writing is displacement writing. The dis/placed subject offers accounts, writing at once of his/her displacement from home and of the things and events seen, observed, and witnessed ab/road that are dis/placed into these accounts via being taken out of their context. Grand tourists of the 18th and 19th centuries were also in need of artworks or images referencing the places they themselves had seen and experienced. They needed visual testimony confirming what they had witnessed. This became a factor in the art economy. Local artists were commissioned to produce such visual testimony, memorabilia to take back home. The engraved *veduta* bears testimony to this development. Dis/placement is therefore crucial to the modern subject-formation: a subject able to dis/place itself and a subject able to dis/place objects, resources, knowledge from elsewhere. The *Grand Tour* and the museum are therefore cultural dis/placement practices in which an education via/through/around/with dis/placement takes place.[11]

The 18th and 19th centuries witnessed a vast production of travel literature, both travel guides as well as travel accounts. Much of travel writing, though not exclusively so, was produced by men.

8.   In her 2013 book *Gender, Artwork and the Global Imperative: a Materialist Feminist Critique*, Angela Dimitrakaki analyzes travel as labor and specifically addresses "travel as (gendered) work."

9.   When observing today's mass tourists though and their lining up to see Rome's or Paris' "cabinets, rarities, or ruins" then the concept of labor and leisure has to be reassessed. The tourist industry is one of the industries that continues to adhere to capitalism's logic of growth. Growing numbers of tourists as well as growing investment in infrastructures supporting their presence attests to this.

10.   Richard Lassels, *An Italian voyage, or, A compleat journey through Italy in two parts: with the characters of the people, and the description of the chief towns, churches, monasteries, tombs* (1698) (EEBO Editions, 2011).

Throughout those centuries fully formed colonial travel narrative conventions and tropes emerged. In his essay accompanying the 2011 republication of *Le Corbusier's Voyage d'Orient* Stanislaus von Moos firmly places the voyage in the tradition of the *Grand Tour.* "L'Architecture et l'Héritage du *Grand Tour.*"[12]

LE CORBUSIER'S VOYAGE RE-ORIENT-ED 1911-2011

Why then would one even want to enter this most contested and controversial territory of Grand Tourism, of Voyages and the legacies of masculinist subject-formation, colonial thought, and orientalism? Why then embark on a project that will only make one feel even more the most depressing weight of Western-centric, masculinist, and colonial thought and practice evidenced as educational, and in the Foucauldian sense discursive, pre-formation/pre-figuration of today's ([mass] tourist) travel? Such an entering activates the dual meaning of subject, i.e. subjecthood and subject matter. Therefore, what are the issues at stake raised by travelling subjects, and how can we from today's perspective historicize, theorize, and work practically with the subject matters raised via such past travelling subjects? How can one travel as a critical subject and turn travel into a method of working curatorially, or intellectually?

Le Corbusier's 1911 *Voyage d'Orient* is a way of raising consciousness of the archive of travelling's complex and ideologically fraught legacies. I firmly believe that ideological critique continues to be of importance for any project that calls itself critical, even if this is no longer — or has never been — the only way of working critically, or of resisting hegemonic cultures' power and narrative. At the same time I believe that new

11. There is a vast literature on the *Grand Tour.* Up until the 1990s, before the turn to postcolonialism, but even after that, a lot of writing on the *Grand Tour* was celebratory and affirmative rather than critical and deconstructing. By now there is a very large body of scholarly and theoretical work on the *Grand Tour.* I want to name the following few examples: Barbara Korte, *English Travel Writing from Pilgrimages to Postcolonial Explorations*; translated by Catherine Matthias (New York: Palgrave Macmillan 2000); Steven H. Clark, ed., *Travel Writing and Empire: Postcolonial Theory in Transit* (Zed Books: 1999). The complex cartographies and power relations of Western female subject-formation, notions of freedom, feminism, colonialism, and empire is still territory to be studied more in-depth and more critically. See for example: Clare Midgley, *Feminism and Empire: Women Activists in Imperial Britain, 1790-1865* (London and New York: Routledge, 2007).

12. Stanislaus von Moos, "Voyages en zigzag," In *Le Corbusier's Voyage d'Orient 1910-1911* (Paris: Éditions de La Villette, 2011), 105. The essay first appeared in an English version in: Stanislaus von Moos and Arthur Rüegg, eds. *Le Corbusier before Le Corbusier: Applied Arts, Architecture, Painting and Photography 1907-1922* (New York, New Haven, London: Bard Graduate Center for Studies in the Decorative Arts, Yale University Press, 2002).

approaches in combining cultural analysis and critical curatorial work have to both revisit canonized cultural objects and have to invest themselves into researching what has been historically, and is currently, marginalized, silenced, or oppressed. *Le Corbusier's Voyage re-Orient-ed 1911-2011* belongs to the former. I do not want to posit that these approaches are in any way mutually exclusive.

Eventually, the curatorial project of *Le Corbusier's voyage reORIENTed 1911-2011* turned to travel as its method of knowledge production. It did not however, choose to pay homage to the sites or locations that Le Corbusier had actually seen. It did not choose to retrace Le Corbusier' steps. It did not choose to affirm. At the same time, it also chose not to ignore that 2011 was in fact the 100th anniversary of a voyage that had resulted in (travel) writing that was formative for a powerful project(ion) of the urban imaginary as sought by artists, architects, dancers, thinkers, philosophers, and a host of many other well-educated travellers.[13] The voyage proved to be equally formative for Le Corbusier's later built work in relation to using what he had seen during his travel. So again, travel as labor-not to speak of generations of architects after Le Corbusier.

CURATORIAL LABOR, RESEARCH CONVERSATIONS

Travel became the project's method. The project set out to visit five of the cities that were part of Le Corbusier's 1911 itinerary and to engage in local conversations with the travelling subjects from Le Corbusier's voyage. The *Grand Tour/Voyage d'Orient* model serves as a historical trope that is critically understood in such a way as to not ignore its pressing/depressing legacies of canonical masculinist, colonial, and orientalizing legacies.

Over a coffee and conversation in Vienna, David Bergé expressed his interest to join the project as artist and photographer. Together we travelled to the five cities. The curatorial method relied on conversations with architects, urbanists, artists, activists, scholars, and researchers living and working in the five chosen cities. These conversations took the 1911 voyage as

13. Travel has of course been foundational for many academic disciplines that were shaped within the logics of empire and coloniality. Anthropology, ethnology, and archeology to name but a few. See for example: Talal Asad, *Anthropology and the Colonial Encounter* (New York: Humanities Press, 1973); Edward Said, "Representing the Colonized: Anthropology's Interlocutors," *Critical Inquiry*, 15(2) 1989, 205-225; James Clifford, *Routes: Travel and Translation in the Late Twentieth Century* (Harvard: Harvard University Press 1997); Faye V. Harrison, *Decolonizing Anthropology: Moving Further Toward an Anthropology for Liberation* (Arlington: American Anthropological Association, 1997).

their entry point in order to address the *Voyage*'s legacy in each city. Open-ended conversations with local experts in Athens, Belgrade, Istanbul, Rome, and Vienna led the way to understand their city. Taking part in the conversations were Phoebe Giannisi, Zissis Kotionis, Iris Lykourioti, Alexandros Maganiotis, Georgios Mostratos, Panayotis Tournikiotis and Christina Vassiliou in Athens; Mia David, Milena Dragičević Šešić, Ana Dubljević, Zoran Erić, Milica Ivić, Jovana Lutovac, Nebojša Milikić, Dijana Milošević, Dragan Protić, Dušica Parezanović, Milena Putnik, Aleksandra Spasov, Boba Mirjana Stojadinović, Veronika Spalajković Vegas, Lenka Zelenović, Jovana Rakić and Dragan Živković in Belgrade; Nafiz Akşehirlioğlu, Tülay Atak, Didem Daniş, Pelin Derviş, Defne Erdur, Irmak Kantar, Idil Kemer, Aykut Köksal, Cynthia Madansky, Meriç Öner, Ece Pazarbaşl, Jean-François Perouse, Emir Uras and Ege Yildrim in Istanbul; Antonello Alici, Francesco Garofalo, Pippo Ciorra, Luca Lo Pinto, Marida Talamona, Monika Percić and Antonella Perin in Rome; and Daniel Aschwanden, Carla Bobadilla, Hermann Czech, Antonia Dika, Jack Hauser, Sabina Holzer, Sushila Mesquita, Sandra Noeth, Luisa Piart, Hansel Sato, Angelika Schnell, and Anna Soucek in Vienna. The issues raised included the following, but were not limited to: How would you describe your city today? What

are contemporary monuments in your city? How would you describe the imagined geographies of the Orient? Where does the East begin?

How local architecture schools and architecture education deal with the legacy of the 1911 voyage was also part of the conversations. In Athens, Belgrade, and Istanbul there is an active memory of Le Corbusier's visit to the city. Professors and lecturers at architecture schools there engage students in projects related to it and it is an activated part of both architectural history and studio teaching. There are translations of (parts of the) *Voyage d'Orient* into Greek and Turkish.[14] Rome is described as Le Corbusier's *Grand Tour* destination. No mention was made that Le Corbusier's itinerary differed considerably from that of the historical *Grand Tour*. In Vienna, Le Corbusier's visit is barely remembered, and no teaching projects at architecture schools have so far used his voyage as a starting point for architectural studio teaching or research.

Le Corbusier's 1911 voyage also served as an interlocutor in these conversations. Close listening led us into each city. The conversations told us how to visit Athens, Belgrade, Istanbul, Rome,

14.   Le Corbusier, Κείμενα για την Ελλάδα (Athens: Agra Publications, 1987); Le Corbusier, Şark Seyahati Istanbul 1911 (Istanbul: Türkiye Bankasi Kültür Yayinlari, 2009).

and Vienna today with regard to the specific issues raised. Taken together, the photographs by David Bergé and my composition of quotes from the conversations form the 1911-2011 travelling subjects. Now, the book has become part of this conversation.

PS: BY WAY OF (NOT) CONCLUDING
When travelling in 2011 with 1911 in mind, the First World War is never far away. It is already in the near future. Three years after 1911, the Austro-Hungarian Empire declared war on Serbia. What followed was a most brutal war of global dimension. When travelling in 2011 with 1911 in mind, the future appears at once promising and bleak, hopeful and disaster-ridden, inspiring and foreclosed. Maybe, in the future, the year 2011 will be remembered as the year when people took to the square: Syntagma Square in Athens, Tahrir Square in Cairo, Puerta del Sol in Madrid. Maybe, in the future, the year 2011 will be remembered as the year when people were drowning, with boat after boat carrying immigrants sinking before reaching Lampedusa. As of 2015, when this essay was written, 2011 is already part of the history of the present. Travelling subjects have taken a turn toward even more brutal and more precarious meanings. Tourist destinations are at selfie-risk, with initials carved in the Roman Colosseum or statues shattered in Cremona. Refugees in forced mass travel and forced displacement find borders closed. This is why, based as it is upon travelling subjects, Fragile Cities appeared as a concept to move forward with. When we think of packages delivered to our doorstep unbroken they are often stamped: "Fragile". "Handle with Care." There are powerful political (and theoretical) connections to be made in regards to travelling subjects, fragility, care and the future of cities.

VIENNA IS A CITY
WITHOUT QUALITIES

VIENNA IS MULTIETHNIC

VIENNA IS IMPERIAL

VIENNA IS LIKE BEING
ON STAGE ALL THE TIME

VIENNA IS ANTI-SEMITIC

VIENNA IS A CITY
OF IMMIGRANTS

VIENNA IS XENOPHOBIC
AND HOMOPHOBIC

VIENNA IS A METROPOLIS

VIENNA IS THE DOOR
TO THE EAST

VIENNA AS PART OF
THE ORIENT ALLOWS FOR
A SHIFT IN THE POSTCOLONIAL
PERSPECTIVE ON THE CITY

VIENNA IS NOT
THE DOOR TO THE WEST

VIENNA IS THE BORDER
BETWEEN EAST AND WEST

RED VIENNA'S SOCIAL
HOUSING PROJECTS ARE
THE REAL MONUMENTS.
MANY OF THEM WERE
BUILT ON SITES OF
FORMER SYNAGOGUES

MASS TOURISM KEEPS
YOU FROM APPRECIATING
THE IMPERIAL MONUMENTS

THE FLAK TOWERS ARE
VIENNA'S REAL MONUMENTS

VIENNA IS A CITY OF
HISTORICAL MONUMENTS

BELGRADE IS A CROSS
BETWEEN VIENNA AND ISTANBUL

BELGRADE IS A HYBRID CITY,
CENTRAL EUROPEAN, ORIENTAL,
SOCIALIST, VERY COSMOPOLITAN
UNTIL THE 1960S

BELGRADE IS
A VERY COMPLEX CITY

NOW THERE ARE
MEGALOMANIAC ASPIRATIONS,
NEW MONUMENTS,
NEW CHURCHES

BELGRADE IS PROVINCIAL

BELGRADE IS
ORTHODOX CHRISTIAN

BELGRADE IS WELCOMING

BELGRADE IS
PREDATOR CAPITALIST

BELGRADE IS XENOPHOBIC

BELGRADE IS ANTI-ISLAMIC

BELGRADE IS HOMOPHOBIC

IT IS NOT EASY TO LIVE HERE

ACCORDING TO LE CORBUSIER,
BELGRADE IS THE UGLIEST
CITY IN THE MOST
BEAUTIFUL PLACE

THERE IS NO NEED TO
FIND THE ORIENT IN EUROPE
IN THE 21ST CENTURY

MODERNITY HERE IN BELGRADE
WAS BASED ON LE CORBUSIER

WE LIVED IN A WESTERN WORLD
BUT UNDER AN ORIENTAL SYSTEM

ISTANBUL IS A GLOBAL CITY

WE ARE USING THE MAXIMUM
OF SPATIAL RESOURCES TODAY

IT IS VIBRANT AND ENERGETIC,
BUT THE CHANGES ARE
TOO RAPID, TOO EXTREME

WE DON'T KNOW HOW
MANY INHABITANTS ISTANBUL
ACTUALLY HAS

<table>
<tr>
<td>

IT IS LIKE A WAR.
THERE ARE MASSIVE
GENTRIFICATION PROCESSES

</td>
<td>

ISTANBUL DOES NOT
HAVE A CENTER

</td>
</tr>
<tr>
<td>

ISTANBUL IS FANTASTIC
AND DIFFICULT

</td>
<td>

ISTANBUL IS DISORIENTING

</td>
</tr>
</table>

IN 1978 EDWARD SAID PUBLISHED
HIS SEMINAL BOOK ORIENTALISM.
IT IS DIFFICULT TO ADD
SOMETHING NEW TO THIS

THE ORIENT IS IDEOLOGY

THE ORIENT IS HUGELY
CONTROVERSIAL

BECAUSE OF THE IDEA
OF THE NATION STATE,
ALL THE ARABIC COUNTRIES
ARE FED WITH ORIENTALISM

TODAY WE USE
THE ORIENTALIZATION
AS A STRATEGY
FOR THE TOURISTS

SEEING ISTANBUL WAS
THE REAL PURPOSE OF
LE CORBUSIER'S REVERSED
GRAND TOUR

THE FRENCH ORIENTALISTS
DESCRIBED ISTANBUL.
ALL THE TRAVELLERS FROM
THE WEST SAW ISTANBUL
THROUGH THIS LENS

LE CORBUSIER WAS THE ARTIST-
TRAVELLER PAR EXCELLENCE

ATHENS KEEPS CHANGING
ALL THE TIME

BUT THERE IS A LOT OF
POVERTY AND MISERY INSIDE

I LOVE THE TOPOGRAPHY.
IT RELATES TO THE SEA

THE NATURAL CHARACTERISTICS
ARE VERY IMPORTANT,
NOT JUST THE URBAN ONES

THERE ARE A LOT OF REFUGEES
IN THE CENTRE OF ATHENS

ATHENS IS AN ORIENTAL CITY

ATHENS IS A WHITE CITY

ATHENS IS AN ENERGETIC CITY

THE EAST-WEST CONCEPT
IS DATED. THE SITUATIONS
IS MUCH MORE GLOBAL TODAY

WE ARE LIVING ON
THE BORDER BETWEEN
THE EAST AND THE WEST

WE USED TO BE
THE SEPARATION BETWEEN
THE EAST AND THE WEST

WE HAVE TO FIGHT ORIENTALISM

THE WEST, THIS WOULD
BE THE NEOCLASSICAL
BUILDINGS IN MUNICH

THERE ARE TWO MAIN FACTORS
THAT TURNED HIM INTO A HERO
AND THEY ARE TO BE FOUND
IN THE GREEK VERNACULAR:
THE WHITE COLOUR AND
THE PLAY OF LIGHT AND SHADOW

THE GREEK INTELLECTUALS IN
THE TIME OF EARLY MODERNISM
DID THEIR VOYAGE TO THE WEST

LE CORBUSIER IS ONE OF US

ROME IS A MEDUSA

ROME IS COMPOSED
OF FRAGMENTS

ROME IS A PALIMPSEST

ROME IS MADE UP OF RUINS

ROME IS THE BIGGEST
MUNICIPALITY IN EUROPE,
70 KILOMETERS IN DIAMETER

ROME GROWS INFORMALLY.
IT IS A CITY OF IMMIGRATION

MASS TOURISM
DESTROYS EVERYTHING

THE DISCOURSE ON GLOBALIZED
IMMIGRATION IS HIGHLY
IDEOLOGICAL, THEY ALWAYS
SPEAK OF A STATE OF EMERGENCY

LIVING IN ROME FEELS LIKE
LIVING IN A MONUMENT

THE REALITY OF THE NEW
MONUMENTALITY IS BRUTAL.
EUROMA2, THE MALL, IS SUCH
A BRUTAL MONUMENT

THE MAXXI BY ZAHA HADID
IS A NEW MONUMENT

IT MUST HAVE BEEN
A BEAUTIFUL CITY IN THE PAST

IN ROME WE ARE NOT
CONCERNED WITH A DISCOURSE
ON EAST-WEST, WE ONLY
SPEAK ABOUT NORTH-SOUTH

ITALIANS STARTED TO GO
ON THEIR JOURNEY TO
THE NORTH IN THE 1920S

LE CORBUSIER IS PART
OF THE EXTRAORDINARY
HISTORY OF THE GRAND TOUR

ROME IS BETWEEN AFRICA
AND CENTRAL EUROPE, THERE
ARE TWO SOULS IN ONE BODY

ABSTRACTING SENSITIZED SURFACES

DAVID BERGÉ

Taking a picture is always inherently appropriative. By shooting, the photographer captures, but also freezes the here and now of urban layers. Wherever one points a camera at in urban space — be it as an auteur, framing with a heavy aesthetic or a visitor loosely pointing at things — the result always involuntary documents the spatial condition of that space in that time.

Making *silent walk pieces* has been a way for me to practice photography — photography without the physical apparatus of the camera — for quite some time now. This is also how I met Elke Krasny (2010) and Tülay Atak (2012) in Vienna.

The material or starting point for the pictures I would take in Athens, Belgrade, Istanbul, Rome and Vienna, 100 years after Klipstein and Jeanneret travelled there, came out of conversations conducted by Elke Krasny with local spatial practitioners (see Krasny's essay in this book). These conversations led Elke and I to begin navigating the urban by both walking and picture-taking. Based in conversations and embodied ideas, this photography displays sensitized surfaces, shadows and layers of the contemporary built space.

In my *walk pieces* I guide small groups for 100 minutes through the urban fabric, in silence. Without me, the photographer, narrating this trajectory, the audience is given the opportunity to step outside of quotidian time and its signifiers; they construct an experience from the world around them, make their own observations and negotiate with the perceptions, memories and thoughts encountered as we move through the city. Water spilling on your arm from a walk piece that passes near a carwash; the smell of clean laundry as you cross the bedroom of an art collector at 7:00 AM; or the momentary pause in the morning sun after 70 minutes of walking when a red and blue truck finishes offloading a container and begins slowly backing down the street.

Such moments within the walks do not by themselves describe the urban (unlike the situationists, who mostly articulated the urban through language and narration). Quite the contrary:

the walks diminish prosaic meaning, they abstract
it and turn the ordinary components of city life
into colors, shapes, lights; into reflections and
movements. In this way, the walk becomes
a platform for a self-constructed experience,
employing the urban as raw material.
By slightly alternating the situational context of
existing content over the course of 100 minutes,
I produce an experience for the audience in
the present.

My walks trace the physicality of the urban space,
and make visible its layers: layers of both formal
and informal urban development, of political
decisions impacting public shared space, scars
of time, weather, use and war, left like wounds
in the urban texture, sometimes healed, sometimes still open.

This way of abstracting the urban space through
non-permanent means, through volumes
and layerings of time coinciding, are qualities
I also found within the photographs taken by
August Klipstein and Charles-Édouard Jeanneret
throughout their *Voyage* in 1911. There is a similar
kind of abstraction of the hyper-concreteness
of public shared space into something more
elemental and personal.

Just like what remains from a walk piece, those
photographs are physical witnesses to past events.
They play with imaginaries that form and mirror
the political, social and economic maps and
agendas of their (and our) times.

Using the *Voyage d'Orient* as a model of travel
from 1911, we wondered how we can travel today
and channel that heterogeneous and provisional
material into an exhibition and now into a book.

Making visible oral information by doing urban
walks.

This is how the photographs are conceived and
presented in this book: as a configuration of
spatial and temporal realities and relationships
between images that through browsing (walking)
become interpretable in multiple ways.

Who contributes to the making of a photograph? The pictures in this book suggest what
the dialogue may have been in 1911 and 2011.

About the authors

DAVID BERGÉ's practice approaches photography in an almost immaterial way. His work is concerned with the physicality of urban space and the built environment, as well as with the notion of how it is to survive as a "body" within the urban today. His practice brings forward a variety of non-object oriented formats such as *Silent Walk Pieces* and time-based photo installations. These have been presented at various international art centers including The Body Arts Laboratory Gallery, Tokyo (2012); NETWERK Center for Contemporary Art, Aalst (2012); SALT, Istanbul (2011); Maison Particulière, Brussels (2014); Goethe Institution New Delhi (2011); TanzQuartier Wien, Vienna (2010); Extra-City kunsthal, Antwerp (2015); Artefact festival at STUK arts center, Leuven (2013); and Kaaitheater, Brussels (2009). Bergé's work has been developed through residency programs such as the Cape Cod Modern House Trust in Wellfleet, USA; Haus der Kulturen der Welt in Berlin; the BOZAR in Brussels; Srishti school of art Bangalore (2015) and CAC Vilnius (2015).

www.davidberge.be

TÜLAY ATAK is an architect and an architectural historian who teaches at the Cooper Union and Pratt Institute in New York City. She received her Bachelor's degree in architecture at METU in Ankara, Turkey and pursued her PhD at the University of California, Los Angeles with the dissertation, "Byzantine Modern: Displacements of Modernism in Istanbul," which considers the agency of Istanbul's urban and architectural culture in modern architecture. Her writing has appeared in journals and edited volumes such as *Future Anterior, Invention d'un Architecte: Le Voyage en Orient de Le Corbusier,* and *Byzantium/Modernism: The Byzantine as Method in Modernity.* She has curated exhibitions at Cornell and the Boston Society of Architects and taught at SCI-Arc, Cornell, and the Rhode Island School of Design.

ELKE KRASNY is a curator, cultural theorist, urban researcher and writer; Professor at the Academy of Fine Arts Vienna; 2014 City of Vienna Visiting Professor at the Vienna University of Technology; 2012 Visiting Scholar at the Canadian Centre for Architecture in Montréal; 2011 Visiting Curator at the Hongkong Community Museum Project. She co-edited the volume *Women's Museum. Curatorial Politics in Feminism, Education, History, and Art.* Curatorial works include: the 2011-2012 project *Mapping the Everyday. Neighborhood Claims for the Future* with the Downtown Eastside Women's Centre and the Simon Fraser University's Audain Gallery, Vancouver; the research and exhibition project *Hands-On Urbanism 1850-2012. The Right to Green* at the Architecture Centre Vienna; the 2012 Venice Architecture Biennale; and the 2015 *Suzanne Lacy's International Dinner Party in feminist curatorial thought* exhibition.

www.elkekrasny.at

Additional credits

FRAGILE CITY WAS PRODUCED BY:

Platform 0090, an artist driven sustainable international platform for multi-disciplinary contemporary art production and research. www.0090.be

PHOTOGRAPHIC EXPANDED, an artist driven structure that produces the work and research of photographer David Bergé and others. www.davidberge.be

Fragile City received additional support of NETWERK center for contemporary art, Aalst and David Bergé's part was created while in residency at Kunstenwerkplaats Pianofabriek Brussels (2014-2015).

The initial research and travel that led to this book was supported by Kunsthaus Mürz (2012), The Flemish Government (2010-2011), WP zimmer (2012), CIVA (2012) and TanzQuartier Wien (2012).

A research lab took place in Vienna from February 8-12, 2012, among Tülay Atak, David Bergé, Geert Goiris, Elke Krasny, Karen Lambaek, Sandra Noeth and Pelin Derviş, hosted by TanzQuartier Wien.

The text- and photo based installation *Le Corbusier's voyage reORIENTed 1911-2011* by Elke Krasny and David Bergé was exhibited:

– at Kunsthaus Mürz, Muerzzuschlag, AT, from Nov 24, 2012 – Jan 27, 2013 as a 3-channel synchronized digital photo projection and text installation on wall. Ursula Horvath (organiser), Nanna Neudeck and Alexandros Maganiotis (set design), Alexander Schuh (graphic design), Hannes Gellner (programming).

– at Artefact festival, Kunstencentrum STUK, Leuven, BE, Feb 13-24, 2013 as a 2-channel synchronized analogue photo- and text projection. Pieter-Paul Mortier (curator), Alexander Schuh (graphic design) and Ludo Engels (programming).

– at BINA, Belgrade International week of Architecture, Kulturni Centar Beograda, Belgrade, SRB, April 18-30, 2013 as a 1-channel digital photo projection and 80 panel text installation on wall. Mia David (organiser), Alexander Schuh (graphic design) and Georg Eckmayr (programming).

– at Public Space in Progress festival, Chania, GR, June 7-9, 2013 as a 2-channel synchronized analogue projection. Lina Manaroli (organiser), Alexandros Maganiotis (set design), Alexander Schuh (graphic design) and Ludo Engels (programming).

SPECIAL THANKS TO

FONDATION LE CORBUSIER:
Isabelle Godineau

PLATFORM 0090:
Wim Viaene
Mesut Arslan
Meryem Bayram
Valerie De Visscher

PHOTOGRAPHIC EXPANDED:
Taïs Gomez de Santana
Milica Ilić
Katrien Reist
Geert Somers
Gerd Van Looy

and Ivana Bago
Veronique Boone
Daniel Clauss
Lieven De Boeck
Madame De Lil
Ursula Horvath
Milica Ivić
Johan Lagae
Paul Lagring
Jovana Lutovac
Carlos Lopez
Alexandros Maganiotis
Carine Meulders
Sandra Noeth
Dennis Pohl
Alexander Schuh
Philippe Severyns
Martin Streit
Michel Quéré
Karlien Vanhoonacker

FRAGILE CITY

WITH PHOTOGRAPHS BY:
Charles-Édouard Jeanneret (1911)
August Klipstein (1911)
David Bergé (2011-2012)

WITH ESSAYS BY:
Tülay Atak
David Bergé
Elke Krasny

GRAPHIC DESIGN BY:
Luc Derycke, Jeroen Wille
(Studio Luc Derycke) in
conversation with David Bergé

PRINT:
Graphius, Gent

PRODUCED BY:
Platform 0090 and
PHOTOGRAPHIC EXPANDED

WITH THE SUPPORT OF:
NETWERK center for contemporary
art, deBuren and Kunstenwerkplaats
Pianofabriek

PROOFREADING BY:
Zac Rose

POSTPRODUCTION PHOTOS BY:
David Bergé and Atelier KZG

PUBLISHED BY:
MER. Paper kunsthalle
www.merpaperkunsthalle.org

ISBN 978-94-9177-557-4
D/2015/7852/237

First edition, 2015
Text copyright of the authors
All color photos by David Bergé
© MER. 2015 for this edition

ALL BLACK AND WHITE PHOTOS:
© Fondation Le Corbusier, Paris.
Titles according to the inventory
of Fonds Le Corbusier, Bibliothèque
de la Ville, La Chaux-de-Fonds,
Switzerland.

FRONT COVER:
Charles-Éduouard Jeanneret and
August Klipstein. CONSTANTINOPLE.
Nighttime fire. LC-108-1 (detail).

INSIDE BACKCOVER:
Charles-Éduouard Jeanneret and
August Klipstein. CONSTANTINOPLE.
Nighttime fire. LC-108-390.

INSIDE FRONTCOVER AND BACKCOVER:
David Bergé. ISTANBUL.
Housing development in Kayabaşı.

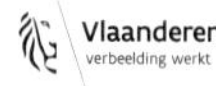 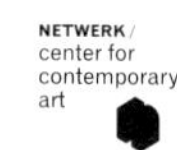

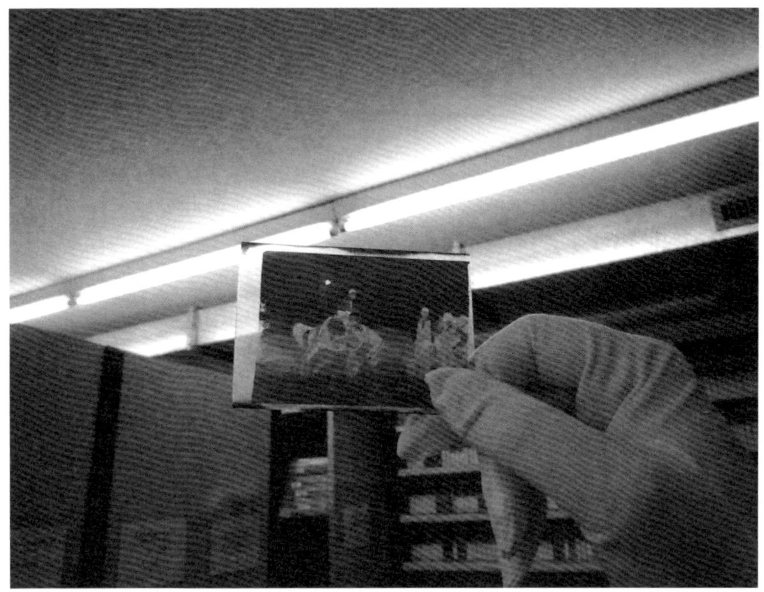

FIG. 1 Glass Plate at Fonds Le Corbusier at the Bibliothèque de la Ville, La Chaux-de-Fonds, Switzerland. Photo by David Bergé.

NOTES ON PHOTOGRAPHIC URBANISM: IMAGES FROM THE *VOYAGE D'ORIENT*, 1911

TÜLAY ATAK

Imagine all those pictures stitched together into a single image. In this ideal aerial view, neither the pervasive violence nor the sometimes cloying prettiness would be visible. Conquest and sentimentality would both be irrelevant. In other words, the image might be like the "blue marble," photograph of earth taken from the Apollo 17 spacecraft in 1972. It's our world, serene and self-contained, seen in one glance. It's not a view that excites us into plans for bombing our enemies, for it includes us as well. It is a view that reminds us of how mighty we are, how fragile, how delicately connected and how beautiful.
TEJU COLE, "The Unquiet Sky"[1]

Every present is determined through those images that are synchronic with it.
WALTER BENJAMIN, *Arcades Project*[2]

I came across Elke Krasny and David Bergé's *Le Corbusier's voyage reORIENTed 1911-2011* project while they were still doing their research in Istanbul. I was in the city for the conference on Le Corbusier's *Voyage d'Orient.* Afterwards, Bergé and I travelled to La Chaux-de-Fonds (Switzerland) in search of Le Corbusier's photographs from this trip in 1911. More than the photographs themselves (we both had seen several of them before) the *way* we saw them was what made an impact. The digital copies of the photographs projected onto a large screen in a dark room, one after the other, made it possible to think of the photographs in their entirety. This viewing enabled us to think of them as discrete images and not as part of an entire *œuvre* or as missing pieces in the *œuvre complète* of Le Corbusier. Instead, here they were, images related to the urban and territorial transformation in the "Orient" of 1911. While we would not have had access to them this way had they not

1. *New York Times*, published and retrieved online, July 22, 2015.
2. N 3, 1, as translated and quoted by Samuel Weber, "'Streets, Squares, Theaters': A City on the Move — Walter Benjamin's Paris," in *Benjamin's -abilities*, Cambridge: Harvard University Press, 2008, 229.

been connected to Le Corbusier (the fact that they were preserved, archived and presented again was because they were related to the famous name), seeing them in this context and in relation to Bergé and Krasny's work made it possible to consider them more as documents, or as interactive records of a journey and places travelled.

Much has been done on Le Corbusier's reliance on and experimentation with photography. This focus extends from those looking closely at the photographs themselves that Le Corbusier took (Gresleri, Benton), to an expanded definition of photography, which includes the photographic techniques and strategies that Le Corbusier employed throughout his work, including his publications, buildings and city plans (Tafuri, Colomina, Vidler).[3] Recent scholarship has shown that Le Corbusier may not be the sole author of the photographs, opening further our understanding of them as documents. My goal here is to consider the photographs as documents of urban transformation by situating them in relation to an ethnographic definition of travel as a spatial practice and in relation to the places where they were made. The photographs point to what I refer to as *photographic urbanism*, separate from their relationship to a viewer and what is viewed, but connected to the sense of how photographs are made and how they are uniquely able to unfold architectural and

urban space. Photographic urbanism is in this way something that is practiced more often — not as the conscious work of a singular genius — but by the observant, active urban dweller.

TRAVEL AS A SPATIAL PRACTICE,
CAMERA AS AN INSTRUMENT
In 1911, the 24-year-old Charles-Édouard Jeanneret undertook a voyage to the east of Europe, accompanied by his friend Auguste Klipstein. They embarked on a journey, travelling through major cities like Vienna, Budapest, Belgrade, Bucharest, Istanbul and Athens, crossing villages and rural

3. Giuliano Gresleri, *Il Viaggio in Oriente, gli inediti di Charles Edouard Jeanneret fotografo e scrittore*, Venice: Marsilio, 1984. where the photographs were published; Tim Benton, *LC Photo: Le Corbusier, Secret Photographer*, Zurich: Lars Mueller, 2013; *Le Corbusier and the Power of Photography*, eds. Natalie Herschdorfer and Lada Umstaetter, London: Thames & Hudson, 2012; *Le Corbusier, Aventures Photographiques*, Paris: Editions de la Villette, 2014; Manfredo Tafuri, "Machine et Memoire: The City in the Work of Le Corbusier" (although Tafuri does not explicitly write about photography, his analysis of the Beistegui house and the role that the periscope pays is significant in contextualizing Le Corbusier's work in terms of avant garde and mechanical reproduction; Beatriz Colomina, "Le Corbusier and Photography" *Assemblage* 4 (1987) and *Privacy and Publicity: Modern Architecture as Mass Media*, Cambridge: MIT Press, 1994; Anthony Vidler, "Photourbanism: Planning the City from Above and from Below," in *The New Blackwell Companion to the City*, London: Wiley-Blackwell, 2011, 656-666.

landscapes. Klipstein, a student of art history working on Byzantine Art and El Greco, wanted to see a number of important art works. Jeanneret, on his way to becoming an architect, wanted to see architecture and continued on to Rome at the end of the trip. Combining their different sensibilities, they planned the journey together, yet sought slightly different experiences.[4]

Jeanneret and Klipstein's travel can be understood as a spatial practice relating cultures and cultural artifacts to each other. By travel as spatial practice, I am referring to James Clifford's seminal account of the role of travel as a discursive and disciplinary practice within anthropology.[5] Clifford's analysis of anthropology's spatial practices is partly based on Michel de Certeau's notion of space as discursively mapped and corporeally practiced.[6] Instead of being accepted as a given, this notion of space incorporates embodied practices and relations. Considering Jeanneret's and Klipstein's travel as a spatial practice means, on one hand, that their travel was based on previous trips like the *Grand Tour*. Many of their sites, like Istanbul, Athens and Rome, were longstanding "tourist" destinations. The two planned the journey based on tips from William Ritter, the art critic and Jeanneret's mentor at the time, who had previously travelled along the Danube and down to Florence, and was fascinated by Slavic cultures.[7]

On the other hand, if previous trips provided a discursive map for the travellers, with similar itineraries and accepted points of interest, then their traversal of landscapes and urban terrains would also be disciplined and maintain an ethos. This ethos was one of observation of phenomena and environments that came from the writings of John Ruskin and Hippolyte Taine.[8] In addition, Jeanneret and Klipstein would utilize and subject themselves to the discipline of instruments, such as notebooks, sketchbooks, and cameras in order to document and record their traversal of terrains. This recording had a deeper didactic aspect: Ritter,

4. Giuliano Gresleri, "Auguste Klipstein" entry in *Le Corbusier: Une Encyclopédie*, ed. Jacques Lucan, Paris: Centre Georges Pompidou, 1987, 216.
5. "Spatial Practices: Fieldwork, Travel and the Disciplining of Anthropology" in *Routes: Travel and Translation in the Late Century*. Cambridge: Harvard University Press, 1997, 52-91.
6. Ibid. 54, and Michel de Certeau, *The Practice of Everyday Life*, Berkeley: University of California Press, 1984.
7. Giuliano Gresleri, "William Ritter" entry in *Le Corbusier: Une Encylopédie*, ed. Jacques Lucan, Paris: Centre Georges Pompidou, 1987, 349-350.
8. Ruskin's *Les Matins à Florence* (French translation of *Mornings in Florence*) and Taine's *Voyage en Italie* were in Jeanneret's library. Especially Ruskin was very didactic about what to observe, how, and even at what time of the day. He presented careful observation as an alternative to mass tourism. See Tülay Atak, "Vieille Ville, Nouveaux Fondements: l'Istanbul de Le Corbusier," in *L'Invention d'un Architect: Le Voyage d'Orient de Le Corbusier*. Paris: Editions de la Vilette, 2013, 257-267.

as Le Corbusier's mentor, wanted to ascertain the journey's pedagogical role and asked Jeanneret to write letters to him describing the topography, the cities and landscapes he passed through as an exercise to develop his eye as well as his writing skills.[9] Both Klipstein and Jeanneret kept diaries or notebooks.[10] Both turned the journey into a practice by subjecting themselves to their instruments and producing a number of textual and visual documents, spanning from diary notes and letters to sketches and photographs.

For Jeanneret, notebooks were critical instruments of travel: consistent in size and number of pages, sometimes gridded, sometimes blank, the notebooks maintained a coherent way of recording the architecture, landscape and routines of the journey.[11] When one studies the notebooks, one realizes that there are techniques for how to use them: one could write or draw; one could rotate the notebook according to the orientation of the drawing; one could use the double spread of two facing pages; one could add notes and annotations when sketches did not suffice; sometimes color could become a way of annotating. Diverse buildings, artifacts, rituals, and urban environments could cohesively come together between the covers of the notebook.

Yet, was it Jeanneret who drew in the notebooks, or was it the notebooks that were drawing

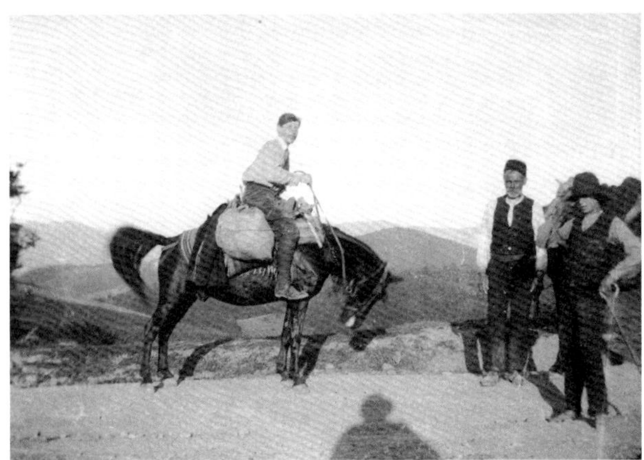

FIG. 2 BALKANS. Charles- Édouard Jeanneret on a horse. LC-108-151.

him? Considering the author/form-giver status attributed to Le Corbusier, the question seems preposterous: he drew, thus performed the action of drawing, and the notebooks were filled, passively. By following Bruno Latour's theory of action and attachment, however, the consistency

9.
Marie-Jeanne Dumont, "Bucharest to Istanbul: With William Ritter in the Balkans" in Le Corbusier: An Atlas of Modern Landscapes, ed. Jean-Louis Cohen, New York: The Museum of Modern Art, 2013, 94-100.

10.
A typescript version of Klipstein's journey diary is held at the library in La Chaux de Fonds and Tim Benton quotes some passages from it in LC Photo: Le Corbusier, Secret Photographer.

11.
Voyage d'Orient Carnets, ed. Guiliano Gresleri, London: Phaidon, 2002.

of the notebooks suggests that they were part of a series of attachments concerning what it means to travel and record.[12] Indeed, Jeanneret used the same format of notebooks in the journey he took in 1910 throughout Germany in preparation for his book *Construction des Villes*.[13] The notebooks were here part of the discipline of travel, transforming the journey into a spatial practice by imposing a consistent way of recording diverse places. In this respect, notebooks *made* the travel possible. The journey was there to collect material and Jeanneret was there to fill the notebooks that would eventually constitute the archive. When Jeanneret became Le Corbusier, he used several of his sketches (some from his notebooks) as elements of his discourse and practice. He revisited his travel notebooks in order to present this journey as the mythical beginning of his architectural inquiries.[14]

Similar questions pertain to the photographs. Who or what made the photographs and what did the photographs do? (FIGS. 1, 2) Tim Benton has challenged the assumption that Jeanneret was the sole author of the photographs by carefully analyzing the negatives, glass plates and the cameras.[15] According to Benton, the variety of negatives suggests the use of more than one camera and more than one author. For instance, in fig. 2, it is Jeanneret who is on the horse in the center of the image, therefore someone else, maybe Klipstein, shot that picture.

Aside from this specific instance where Jeanneret and his journey have become the subject of the photograph, and the camera has moved from one hand to another, the problem of authorship is one that remains intrinsic to photography and its discourse. A technology that is related to reproduction, "what makes a photograph?" is a perennial question with an uncertain answer: the photographer, the subject, the camera, the chemistry of the film, light, the relationships of elements

12. Bruno Latour, "Factures / Fractures: From the Concept of Network to the Concept of Attachment," *RES: Anthropology and Aesthetics* 36, special issue *Factura* (1999): 20-31.
13. Le Corbusier, Les Voyages D'Allemagne Carnets, ed. Guiliano Gresleri. New York: Monacelli Press, 1995 On the book *Construction des villes*, see Christoph Schnoor, "Munich to Berlin: The Urban Space of German Cities." In *Le Corbusier: An Atlas of Modern Landscapes*, ed. Jean Louis Cohen, New York: The Museum of Modern Art, 2013, 84-90.
14. The first volume of *Œuvre Complète* began with the sketches from the journey. *Œuvre Complète*, 7 vols., Zurich: Editions d'Architecture, 1965, Vol. 1, 17-21. In several of his books, Le Corbusier presented this journey as his discovery of architecture, notably in *L'Art Decoratif d'Aujourd'hui*, Paris: Flammarion, 1996, 197-218.
15. Tim Benton, *LC Photo*, 100-120.
16. While the bibliography on this questions is extensive, the work of the "Pictures Generation" is seminal. See for example the questions Rosalyn Deutsche raises in response to James Welling's work, in "Darkness: The Emergence of James Welling" in *James Welling: Abstract*, exhibition catalogue, Brussels, Toronto: Palais des Beaux-Arts and Art Gallery of York University, 2002.

inside the frame, or how the image relates to what is outside the frame?[16] In the context of Jeanneret and Klipstein's journey, if the notebooks constitute a kind of author—one can trace the lines and claim originality in the notebooks—then the photographs place this author into question.

What kind of travel, then, do the photographs constitute, or what does photography do to travel? Susan Sontag and Pierre Bourdieu attributed contrasting roles to photography in travel. Sontag associated photography with the rise of tourism: "As photographs give people an imaginary possession of a past that is unreal, they also help people to take possession of a space in which they are insecure."[17] Easing the anxiety of travel and of modernity, photographs make the traveller feel at home by capturing and so subduing an unfamiliar space, according to Sontag. If photography collapses the displacement of travel, the camera also can introduce distance. For instance, photography sustained Pierre Bourdieu's shift from philosophy to sociology in Algiers in 1956 by introducing a method of observation and "finding a way to approach a particular subject."[18] As he explained in an interview, instead of looking straight at the subject, he looked through his camera—a Rolliflex with a through-the-top view-finder—in an unobtrusive manner. By enabling detachment, the camera affected

"a conversion of [his] perspective that required a genuine change of [his] senses."[19] This duality of the collapse and expansion of distance may have been intrinsic to photographic discourse at least since Walter Benjamin, who effectively explained that mechanical reproducibility's destruction and reconstitution of aura ("the unique phenomenon of a distance however close [an object] may be") are at the center of the experience of modernity.[20]

Thus in Jeanneret and Klipstein's journey, photographs had begun to destabilize authorship. The camera expanded the field of documentation from landscapes and urban spaces to architectural corners, otherwise unseeable details and ethnographic encounters. Photography of the journey shifted the emphasis from the authors/voyagers to the temporal and spatial relation between the body holding the camera and the terrain.

17. *On Photography*, as quoted by Karen Burns in "Topographies of Tourism: 'Documentary' Photography and 'The Stones of Venice', *Assemblage* 32, 1997: 22-44, 25.

18. *Picturing Algeria: Pierre Bourdieu*, ed. Franz Schultheis and Christien Frisinghelli, New York: Columbia University Press, 2012, 12.

19. Ibid., 32.

20. "The Work of Art in the Age of Mechanical Reproduction" in *Illuminations*, New York: Schoken, 1968, 217-251, 222. See also, Samuel Weber, "Mass Mediauras, or: Art, Aura and Media in the Work of Walter Benjamin," in *Mass Mediauras: Form, Technics, Media*, Stanford: Stanford University Press, 1996.

TERRITORIES IN TRANSFORMATION

If photographs are part of an attachment that define what it means to travel at a certain moment, then we might shift our interest from the authors of the photographs to what they document. Rather than the self-discovery of Le Corbusier, the photographs portray a territory, which is disintegrating and reassembling. In *Origins of Totalitarianism,* Hannah Arendt wrote of the period before the First World War as a time when nation-states, which had appeared on the stage of history when peoples had acquired a consciousness of themselves as cultural entities and of their territories as home, had dissolved into either imperialism or tribal nationalism. She identified tribal nationalism as the nationalism of the peoples which had not achieved the sovereignty of a nation-state, the case for Austria-Hungary at the turn of the 20th century.[21] Amidst a history of changing boundaries and migrations, tribal nationalism became a "portable private matter," rather than a matter of public concern.

Voyage d'Orient and Le Corbusier's other books contain several references to the social transformations that he and Klipstein observed during their travels. As Francesco Passanti has shown, the journey was as much the discovery of vernacular for Le Corbusier as it was the discovery of the impacts of modernization.[22] In 1925, when writing *L'Art décoratif d'aujourd'hui,* Le Corbusier

ranted against the erosive impact of the railroad in the places he and Klipstein had encountered.[23] The train brought the outside, industrially produced kitsch that would replace local folklore, and Le Corbusier was convinced that cinema would complete the work of the railway by bringing outside images, impossible to ignore. At the same time, in *Voyage d'Orient,* there is a conversation with an architecture student from Prague about the aesthetics of iron bridges, in which Klipstein and Jeanneret defend the "beauties of modern engineering" and the importance of infrastructure that brings different places closer together.[24] (FIG. 6 IN THE PHOTO ESSAY) Thus physical and social transformation was one of the main topics of conversation for observant travellers and their interlocutors.

In *Voyage d'Orient,* Budapest becomes the example of a city of uncontrolled urban growth and transformation:

21. Hannah Arendt, *Imperialism, The Origins of Totalitarianism,* Vol 2, New York: Harvest, 1968, 107-123.
22. "Vernacular, Modernism, and Le Corbusier" in *Vernacular Modernism: Heimat, Globalization and the Built Environment,* ed. Maiken Umbach and Bernd-Ruediger Lueppauf, Stanford: Stanford University Press, 2005, 141-156.
23. Under the heading: "Le Paysan de Danube Opta" in *L'Art Decoratif d'Aujourd'hui,* 57.
24. Le Corbusier (Charles-Edouard Jeanneret), *Journey to the East,* trans. Ivan Zaknic, Cambridge: MIT Press, 2007, 42.

What should I speak of Budapest, since I neither understood nor liked her? She appeared to me like a leprous sore on the body of a goddess. One must climb to the citadel to see the irreparable condition of this aborted city. One is surrounded by a vibrant organism of palpitating mountains. A generous outpouring of nacreous fluid rises up slowly from the plain. The Danube encircles mountains, condensing them into a powerful body that faces the boundless expanses of the plain. But over this plain, there spreads a dull black smoke into which the network of streets disappears. Eight hundred thousand inhabitants have rushed here in the last fifty years."[25]

The passage demonstrates an aspect of spatial practice: the travellers climb to a higher point in order to obtain a sweeping view of the city. The aerial view would become a fascination for Le Corbusier, not only as an inspiration but also as a means of presenting an apocalyptic perspective of the world.[26] The passage contains an acknowledgement that they are not the only ones travelling and moving through this territory. An "arrival city" that grew by absorbing immigrants, Budapest displayed a unique rate of growth for Europe (twice the rate of Vienna and three times the rates of Paris and London) in the second half of the 19th century.[27] Yet what is striking is the lack of a photograph that shows the "swelling" of Budapest, the aerial view that is described above.

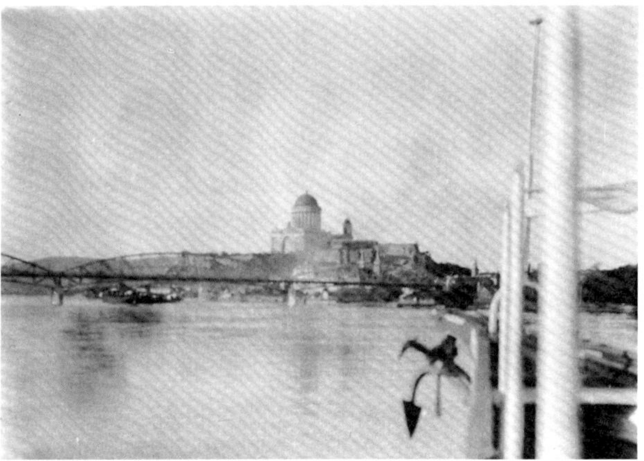

FIG. 3 HUNGARY. Esztergôm Cathedral. LC-108-57.

Instead of recording what could simply be an illustration, the travellers recorded their specific approach to the city from the Danube. (FIG. 3)

25. Ibid., 39-40.
26. "From the plane there is no pleasure but a concentrated mournful meditation" in *Aircraft*, as quoted by Kenneth Frampton in *Le Corbusier*, London: Thames & Hudson, 2001, 111.
27. See Douglas Saunders' study of migrations to the city in *Arrival City: How the largest Migration in History is Reshaping our World*, New York: Vintage Books, 2012. On Budapest's urban growth in the second half of the 19th century, see *Budapest and New York: Studies in Metropolitan Transformation, 1870-1930*, eds. Thomas Bender and Carl E. Schorske, New York: Russell Sage Foundation, 1994, 2-3. The book presents the unique culture of the city at that moment in history.

In contrast to the expansion of Budapest, the photographs of constitution celebrations in Istanbul portray a different aspect of modernity. Here, camera records a social transformation and its new public spaces. (FIG. 4 AND FIGS. 2 AND 3 IN THE PHOTO ESSAY) The horses are riding across what seems to be an open plain in a military parade, one of the festivities of the late Ottoman Empire attempting to modernize itself. The constitution of 1908 and the establishment of a parliament were part of the efforts to reform the state. Political and military gatherings like this began to occur more regularly along with the construction of monuments to commemorate important events.[28] These activities would comprise examples of modern, that is *national* public space in Istanbul in 1911 — very different than the mosques and cemeteries of before.

Could this open plain, the site of a military parade, a new ground in an old city, anticipate the designed public spaces of modernism? For instance, the inclined plane designed by Le Corbusier and Pierre Jeanneret (Le Corbusier's cousin and business partner) for the Palace of the Soviets competition in 1931 connected different spaces of gathering from the parking to the auditorium. A drawing submitted to the competition imagines a system of wide ramps and horizontal planes connecting the different

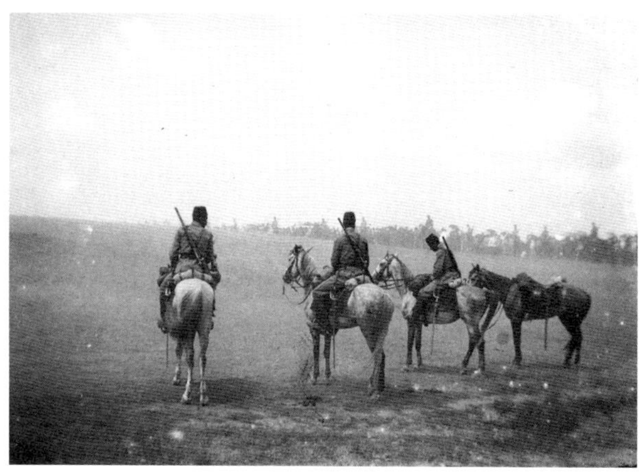

FIG. 4 ISTANBUL. Turkish army cavalry (possibly constitution celebrations). LC-108-358.

public spaces of the complex during May Day just as the parade enters the building.[29] It is the architectural response to modern mass movements like the military parade captured in the photographs.

28. Alev Erkmen, *Geç Osmanlı Dünyasında Mimarlik ve Hafıza: Arşiv, Jübile, Abide*, Istanbul: Akin Nalca Kitaplari, 2010. Based on Erkmen's account of the making of the Liberty Monument between 1909-1911, the site where the photographs were taken could be in Şişli looking across to Kağıthane. In 1911, this was a highly symbolic site where a military barrack had been established to control the 31 March Incident in 1909.
29. Kenneth Frampton, *Le Corbusier*, 99.

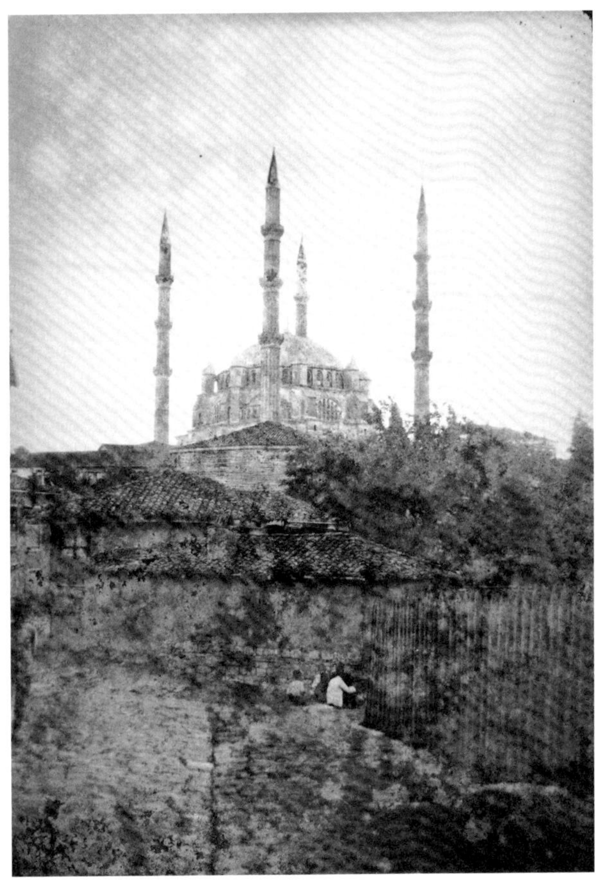
FIG. 5 EDIRNE. Street around Selimiye Mosque. LC-108-327.

PHOTOGRAPHIC URBANISM
Photographic urbanism may be one way
of recording and visualizing this territorial

transformation and its movements.[30] Jeanneret
and Klipstein's photographs probe buildings and
spaces. In a series of photographs of the Selimiye
Mosque in Edirne (former capital of the Ottoman
Empire, near Istanbul), the camera aproaches
the building from various angles and from
smaller streets as if to study the relation of the
building to the city and its topography. (FIGS. 5-6)
Photographs of the Hagia Sophia present view-
points where the space surrounding the building
gain as much significance as the architecture itself
(FIGS. 9-11 IN THE PHOTO ESSAY). From these photographs, it becomes apparent that it is not only the
building that dominates space, but there emerges
a possibility for other bodies to occupy it as well.

The fire in Istanbul literally highlights that
modernity is arriving in unexpected and disas-
trous ways. The city's skyline, backlit by flames,
becomes a case study for the urban silhouette.
(FIG. 1 IN THE PHOTO ESSAY) The camera moving

30. In writing about the role of the aerial view in urban planning,
Anthony Vidler has coined the term "photourbanism" and
described how it has been an aspect of French discourses on
the city. According to him, photourbanism is situated at two
poles. One is the aerial view which has dominated modern
urbanism and, has become a tool of city planners and social
scientists as well as of architects. The other is the street view,
the critical tool of surrealists, returning to the real to subvert
the hegemonic. See "Photourbanism: Planning the City from
Above and from Below."

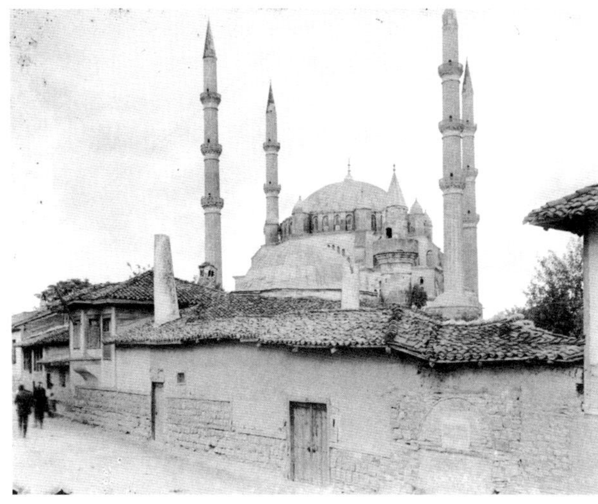

FIG. 6 EDIRNE. Street around Selimiye Mosque. LC-108-197.

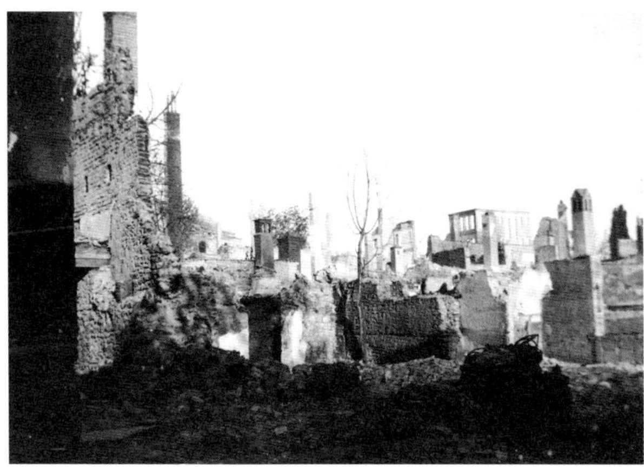

FIG. 7 ISTANBUL. Destroyed areas by a fire. LC-108-373.

across urban terrain after the event of the fire further dissects the spaces of the city taken apart by the disaster. Later, Le Corbusier used one of these photographs in a book and wrote that in the aftermath of the fire, the houses of regular people had become palaces.[31] Both the photographs and the "monumentality" they capture resembles the spaces in Werner Herzog's *Lessons of Darkness*, portraying Kuwait's landscape after the first Gulf War (1992). In both Herzog's movie and Jeanneret and Klipstein's photographs, the camera records a terrain filled with what they perceive to be monuments. (FIG. 7 AND FIG. 56 IN THE PHOTO ESSAY)

These photographs show the embodied practice of the two travellers moving through cities and landscape, observing and recording territories in transformation. (FIG. 8) What the camera seems to have enabled is a way of distancing oneself in urban space, detaching the photographer from the viewed subject and exploring the space around buildings. This "space between" is perhaps a precursor to Le Corbusier the architect's urban spaces, a space of distant views, but also a space that presupposes a body.

Here we can speak of a photographic urbanism, which instead of focusing on surveys

31. *Une Maison, Un Palais: À la Recherche d'une Unité Architecturale*, Paris: Éditions Crès, 1928.

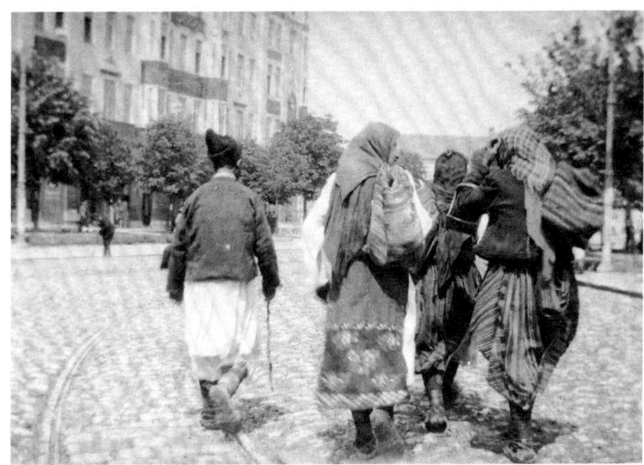
FIG. 8 Group of women and farmer on a street (possibly in Bucharest). LC-108-561.

and surveillance, is based on a moving body with its trajectories and different speeds. Such an urbanism captures temporality to a degree. A concept that Le Corbusier later coined as an "architectural promenade" also involves photographic urbanism. As he described it, the architectural promenade corresponds to architecture unfolding as a body moves through it.[32] While the architectural promenade is by necessity related to surveillance and surveying, to power and discipline, it is also more than this. It is an attempt to capture the experience of the street without the specificity of the street corner.[33] Yve-Alain Bois has analyzed this experience in terms of the discourses surrounding the picturesque.[34] Architectural promenade, if it were to be considered as a spatial practice, is both a discursive activity as Bois has shown (intellectually mapped onto previous understandings of the picturesque) and an embodied one, requiring lived experience.

Thus, the photographs taken during Jeanneret and Klipstein's *Voyage d'Orient* allow us to dissociate these ideas, like architectural promenade, from a single author and situate them in travelling bodies — not only the bodies of the travellers but also those of other passers-by, migrants, newcomers to cities (like those in Budapest). The photographs remind us that the ground on which travellers are moving is not necessarily static, but is constantly changing as well. In shifting the focus to that ground, they remind us how transient the urban, how provisional a monument, and how fragile a city may be. Then and now, from one image to another, photographic urbanism unfolds the spaces of a city.

32.   *Œuvre Complète*, 7 vols., Zurich: Editions d'Architecture, 1965, Vol. 2, 24.
33.   On the characteristics of this movement, see, Stan Allen, "Le Corbusier and Modernist Movement: the Carpenter Center for Visual Arts, Cambridge, MA" in *Practice: Architecture, Technique and Representation*, Amsterdam: G+B Arts, 2000.
34.   "A Picturesque Stroll around Clara Clara" in *October 29* (1984): 32-62.

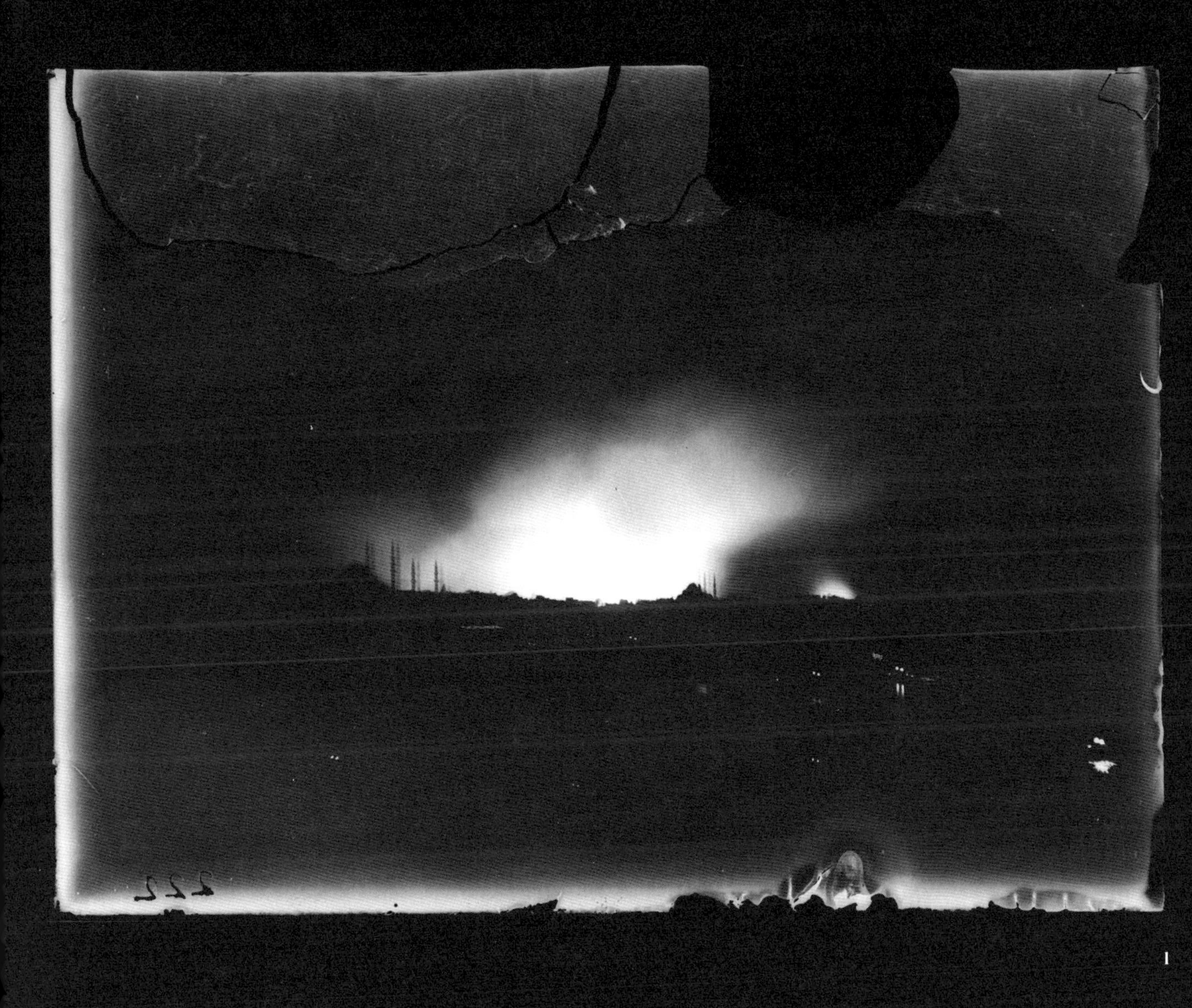

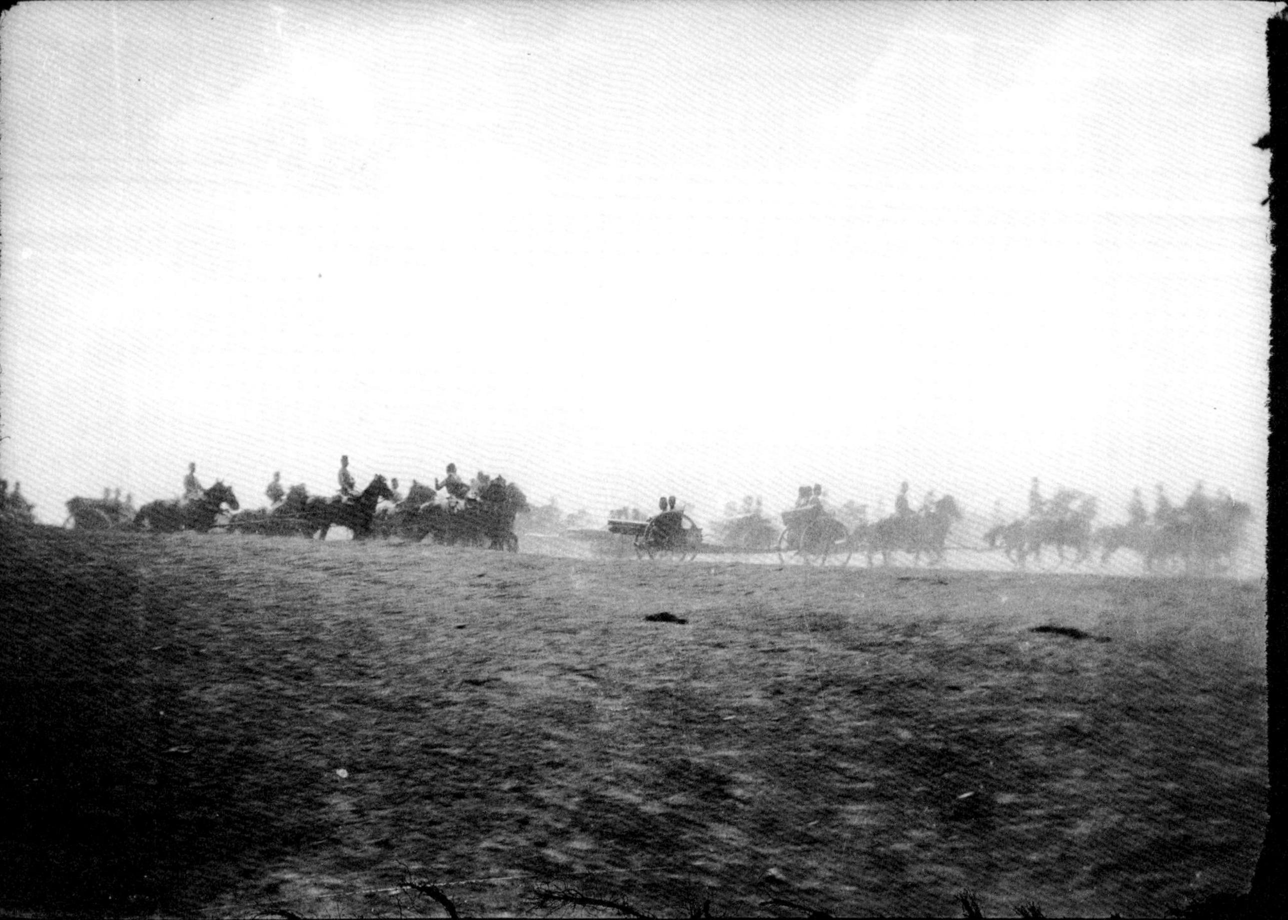

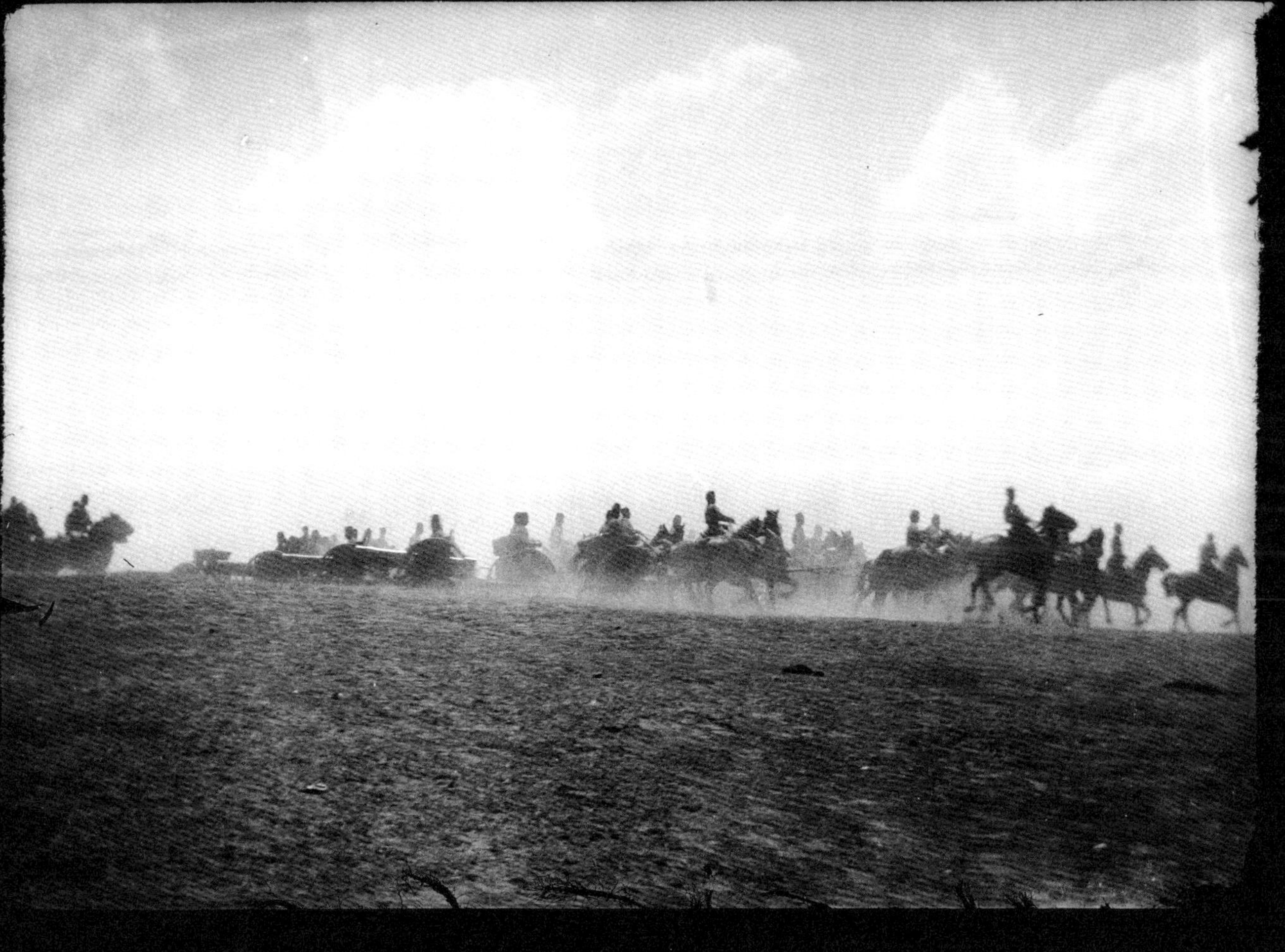

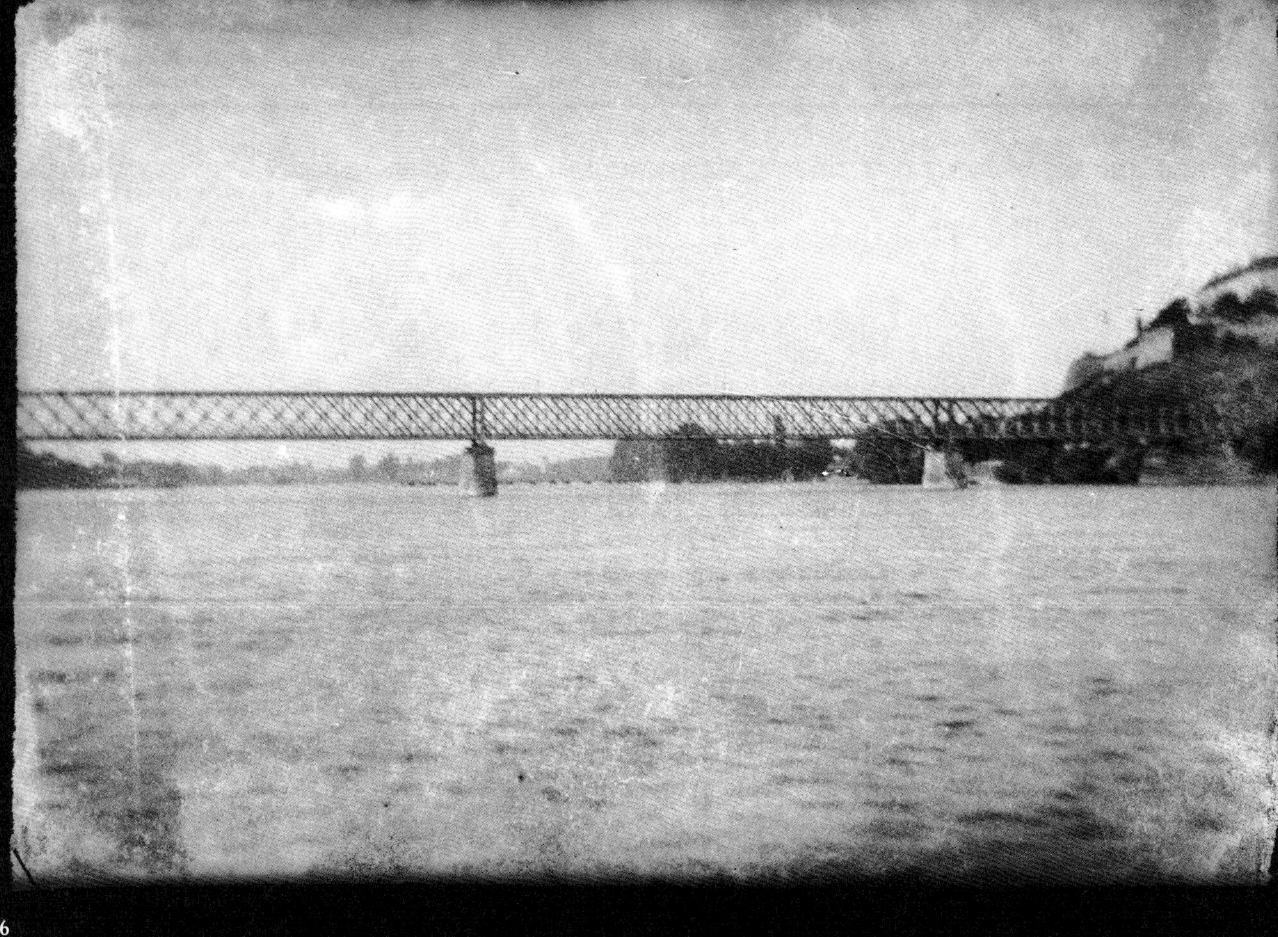

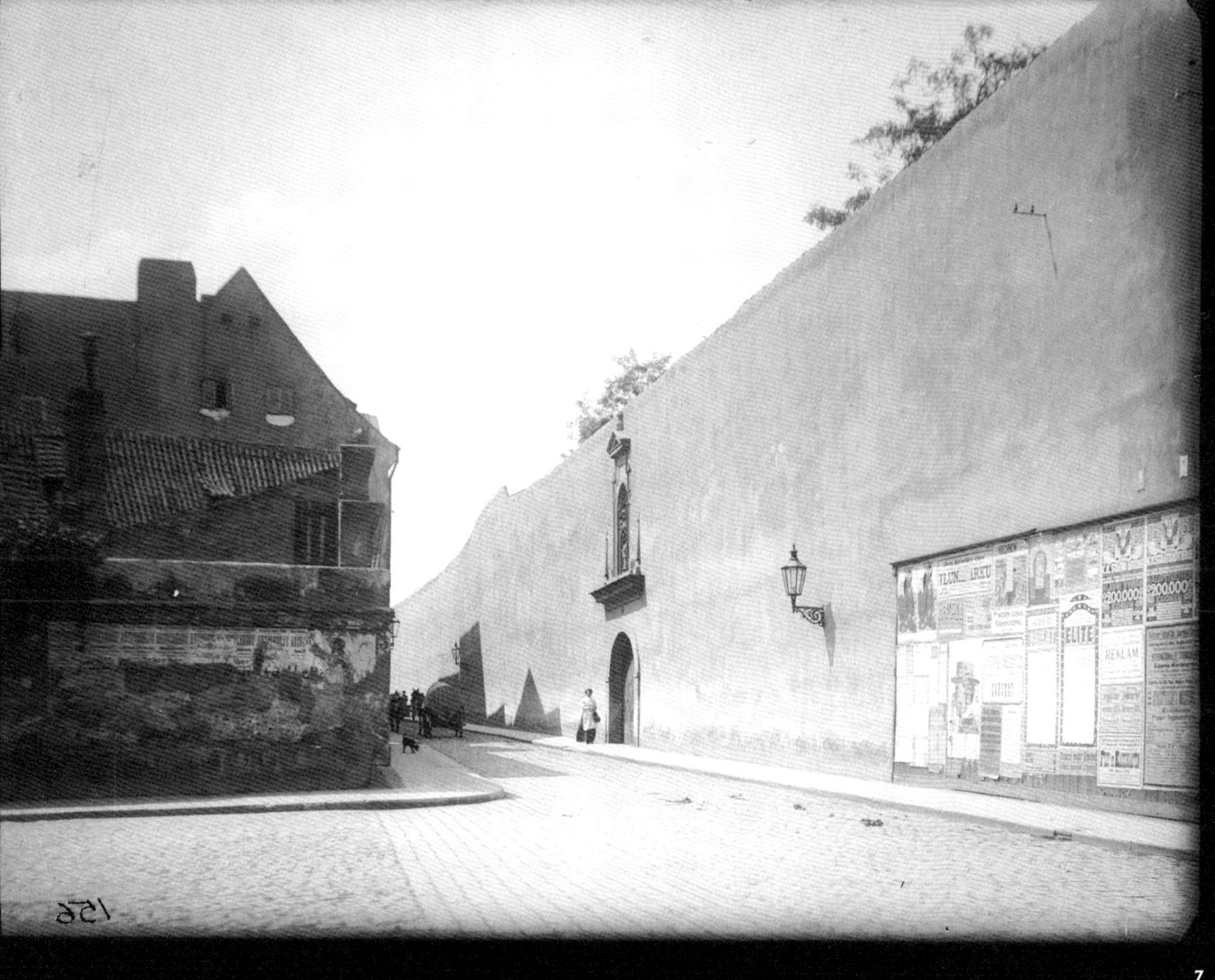
156
REKLAM
ELITE
200.000
7

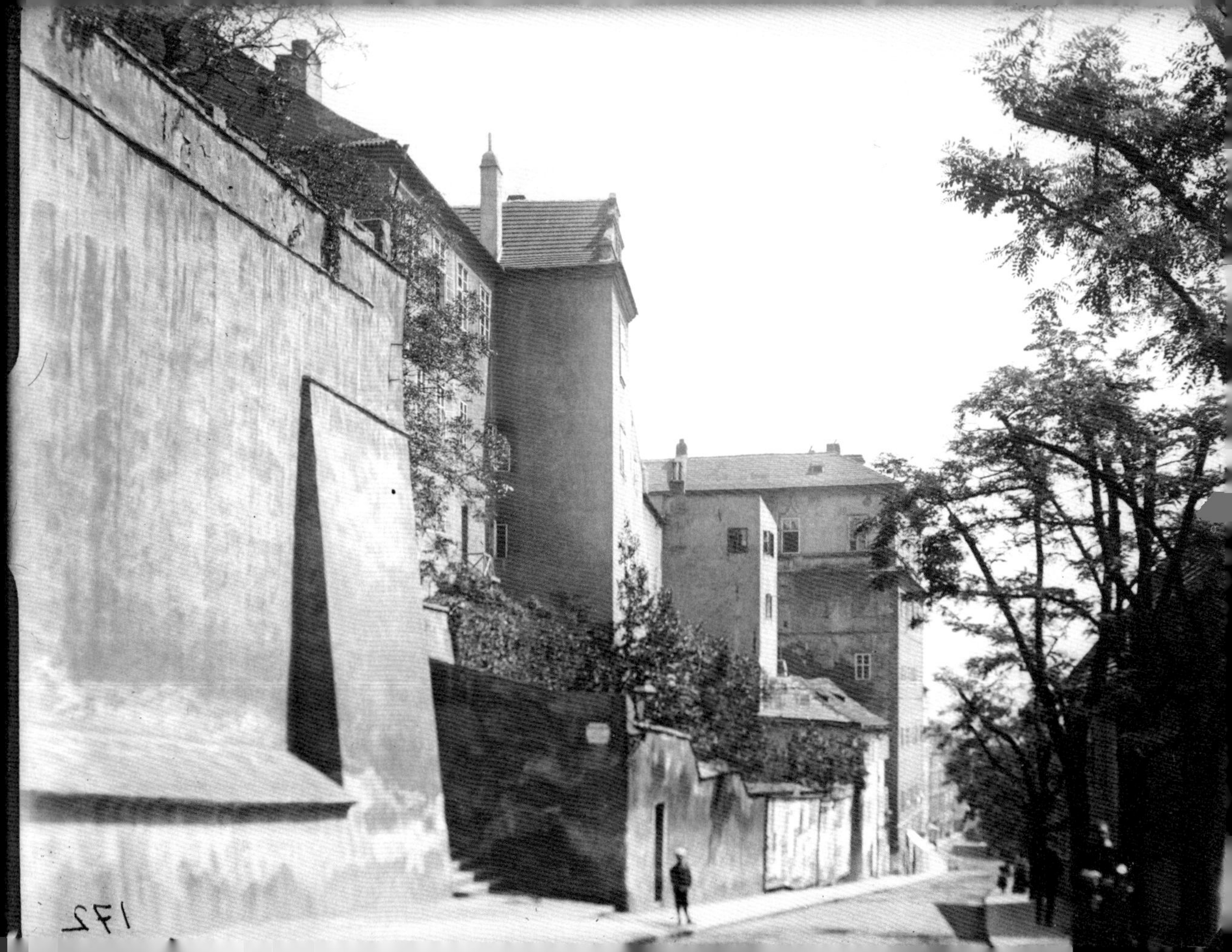

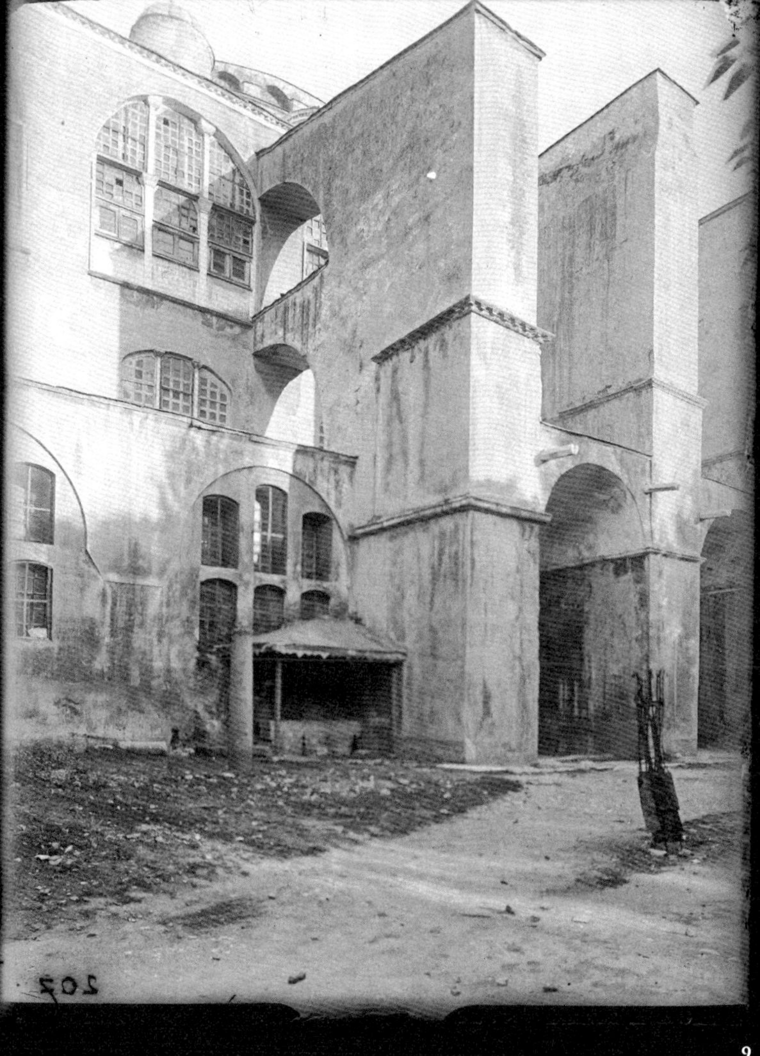

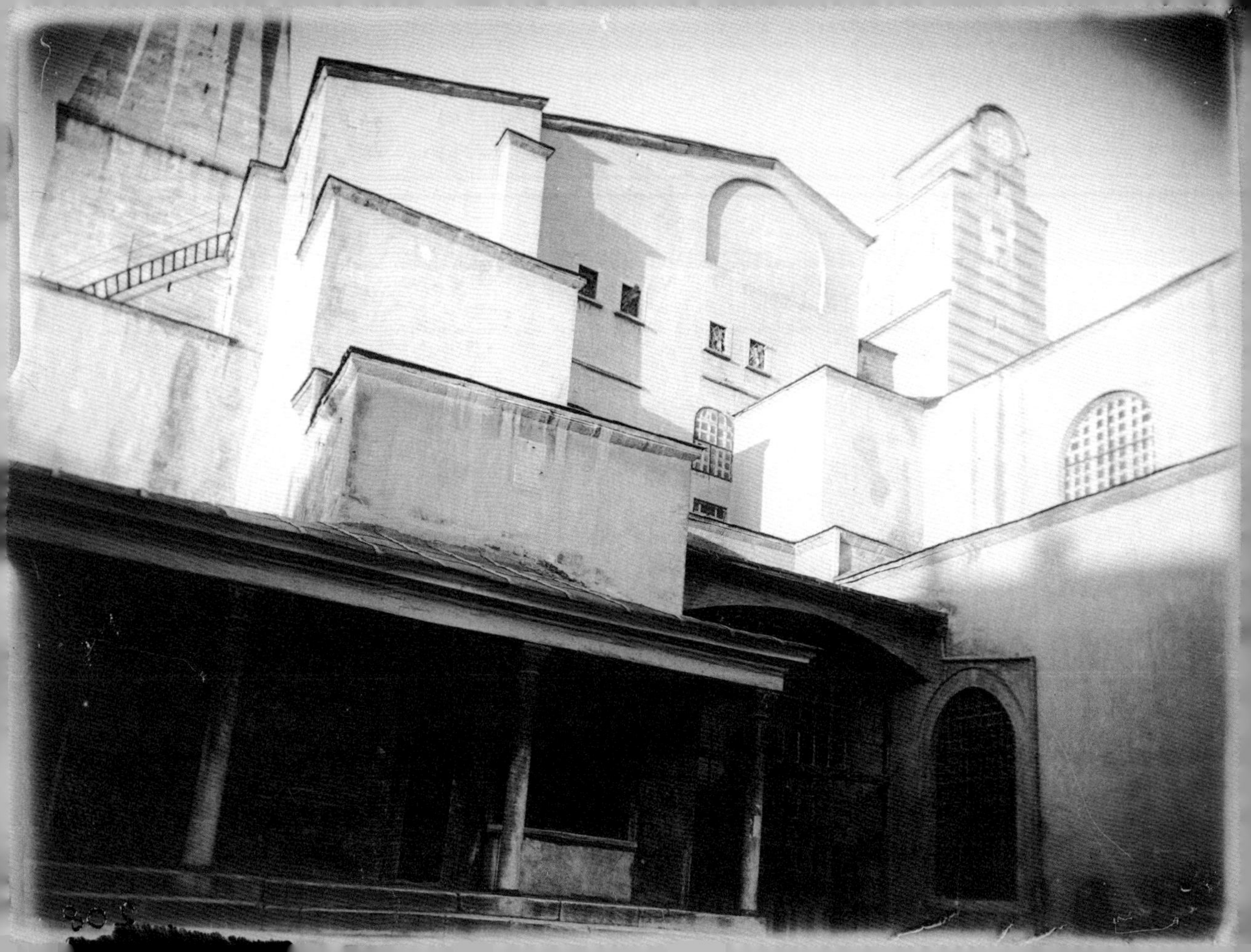

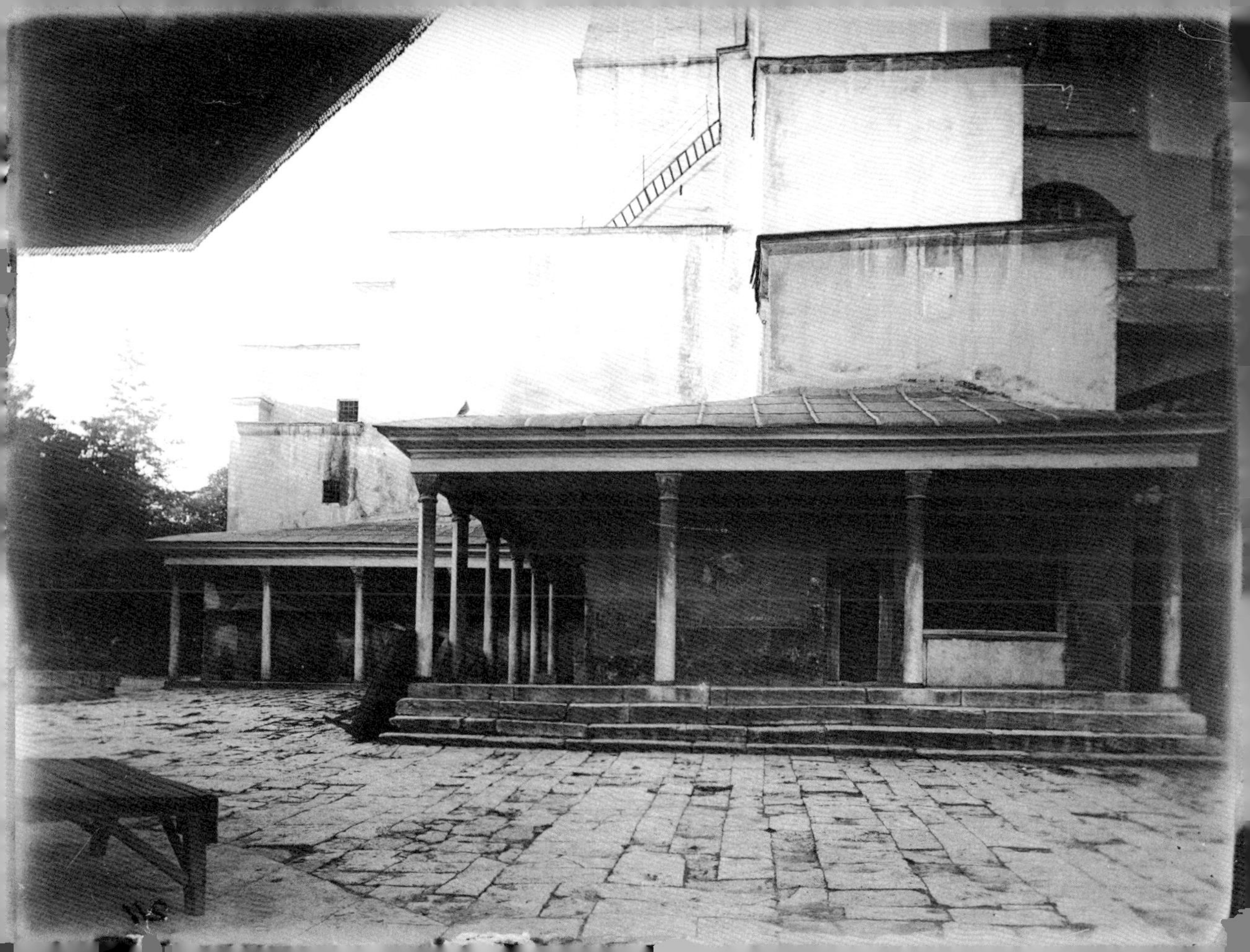

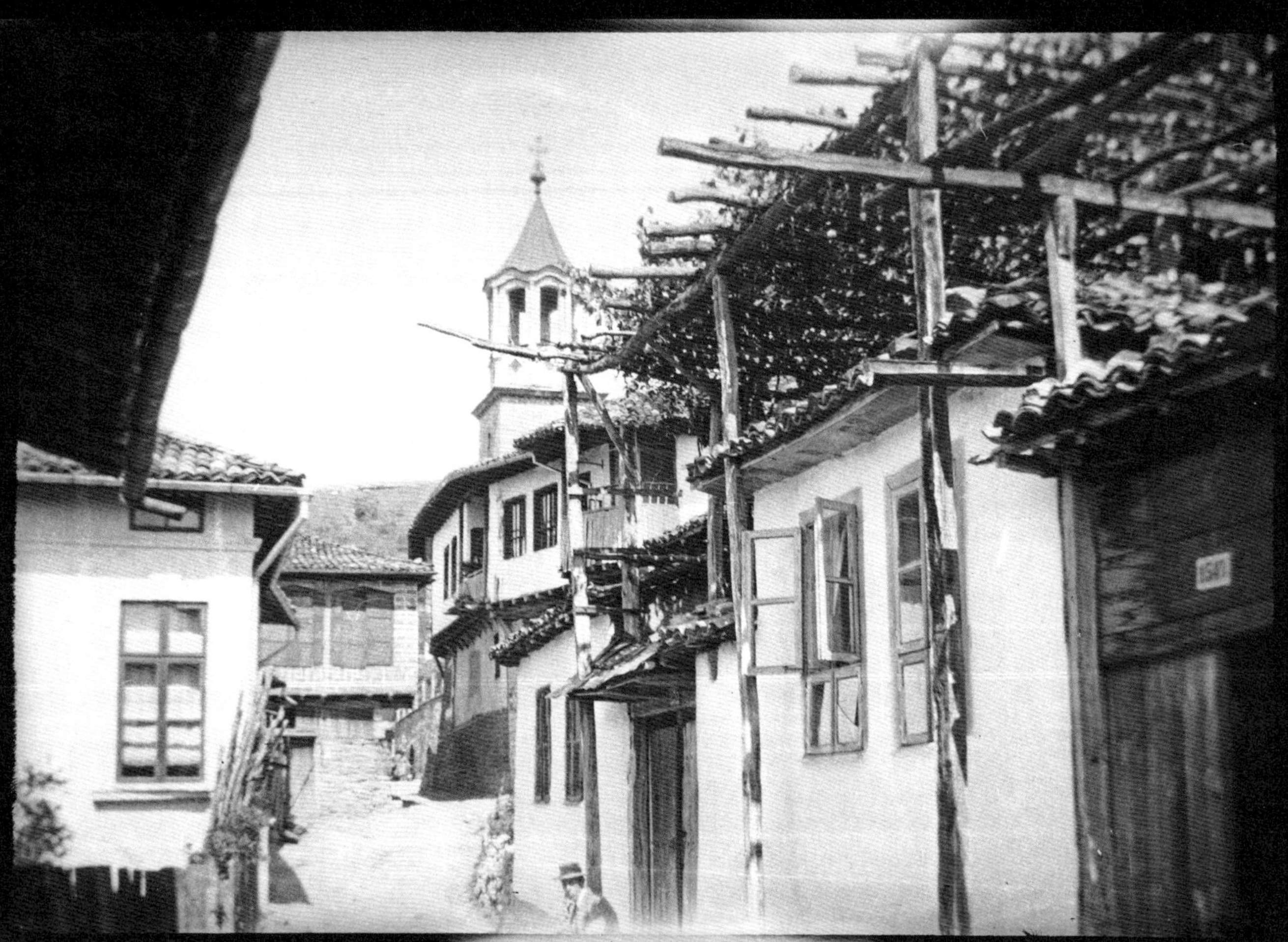

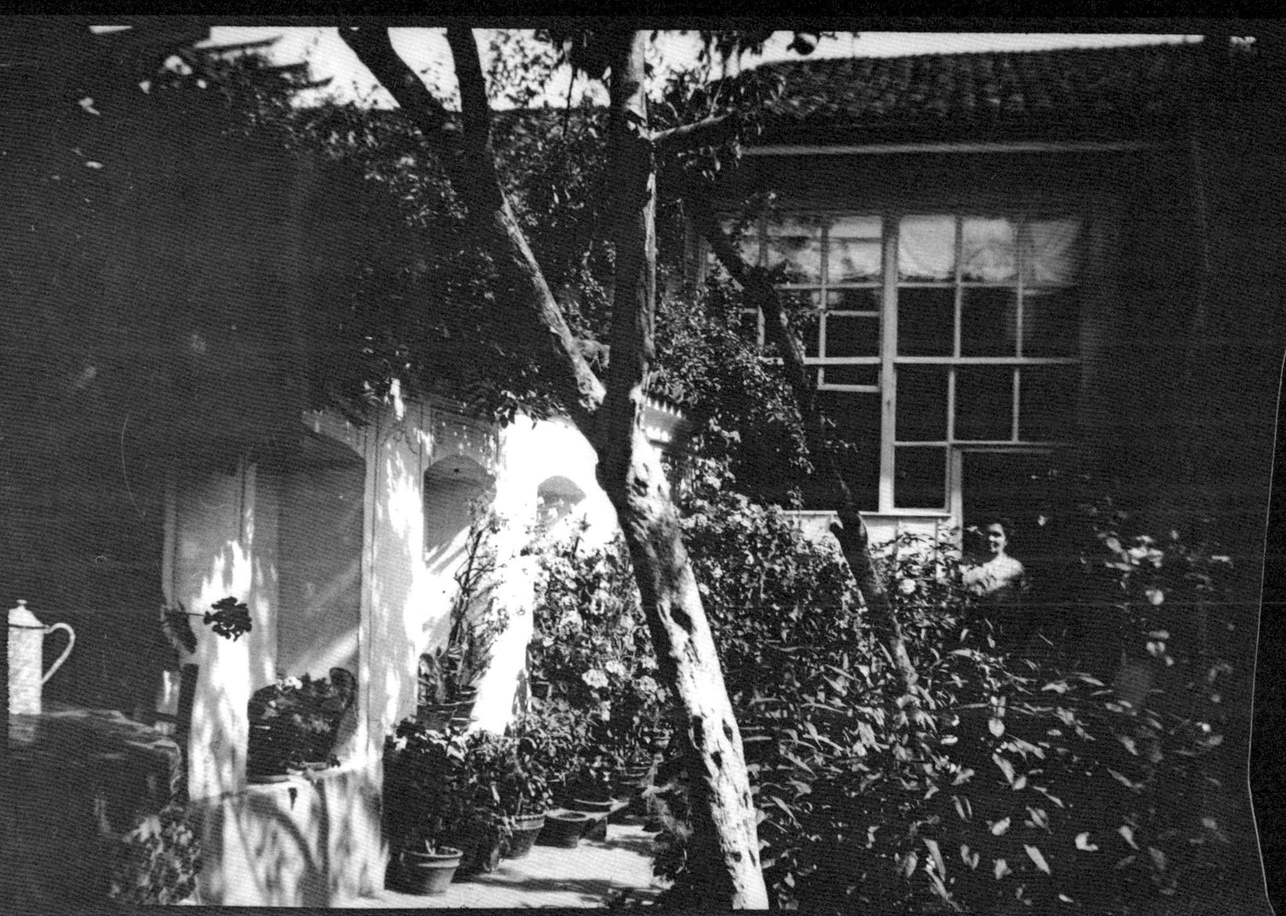

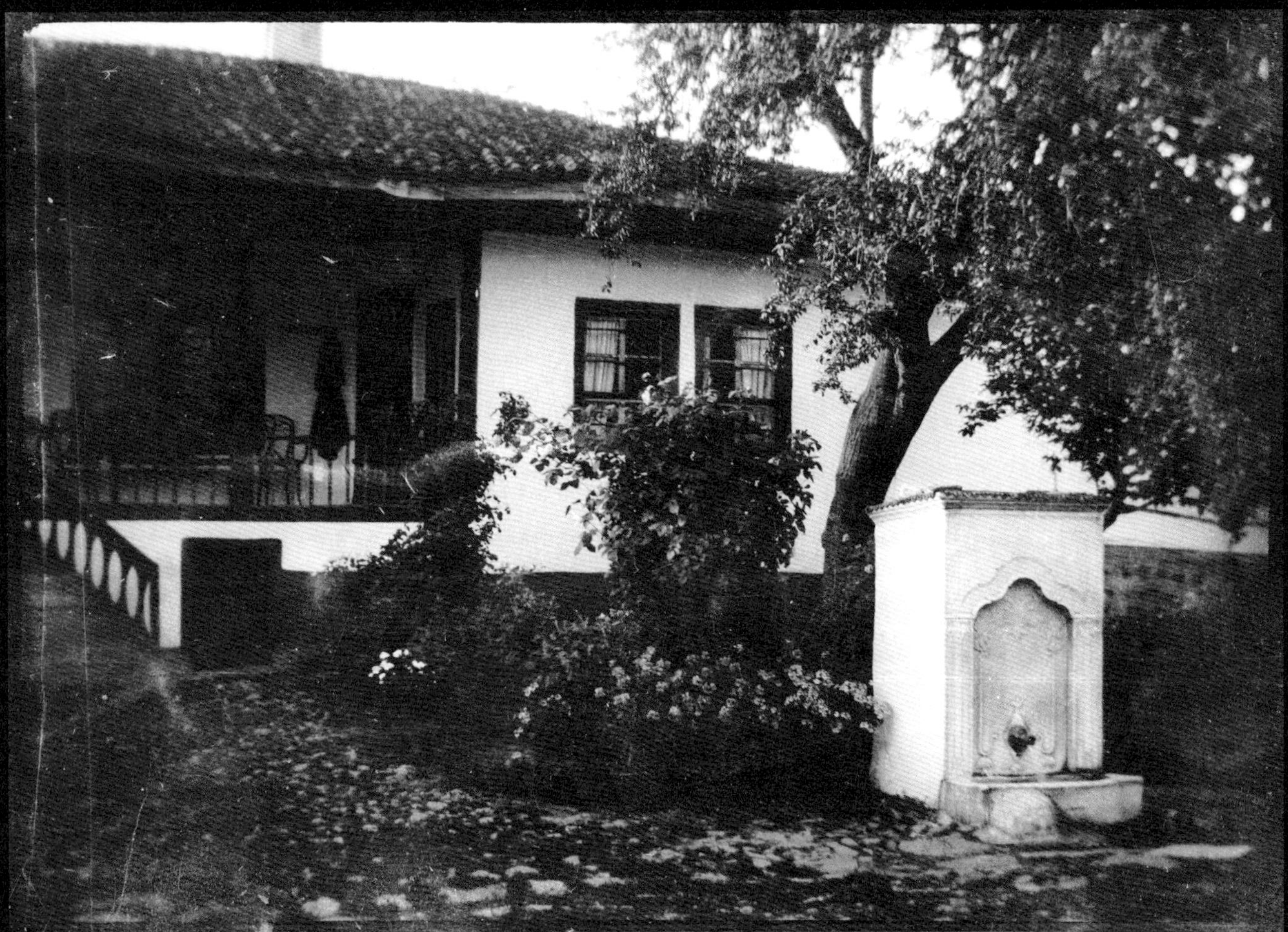

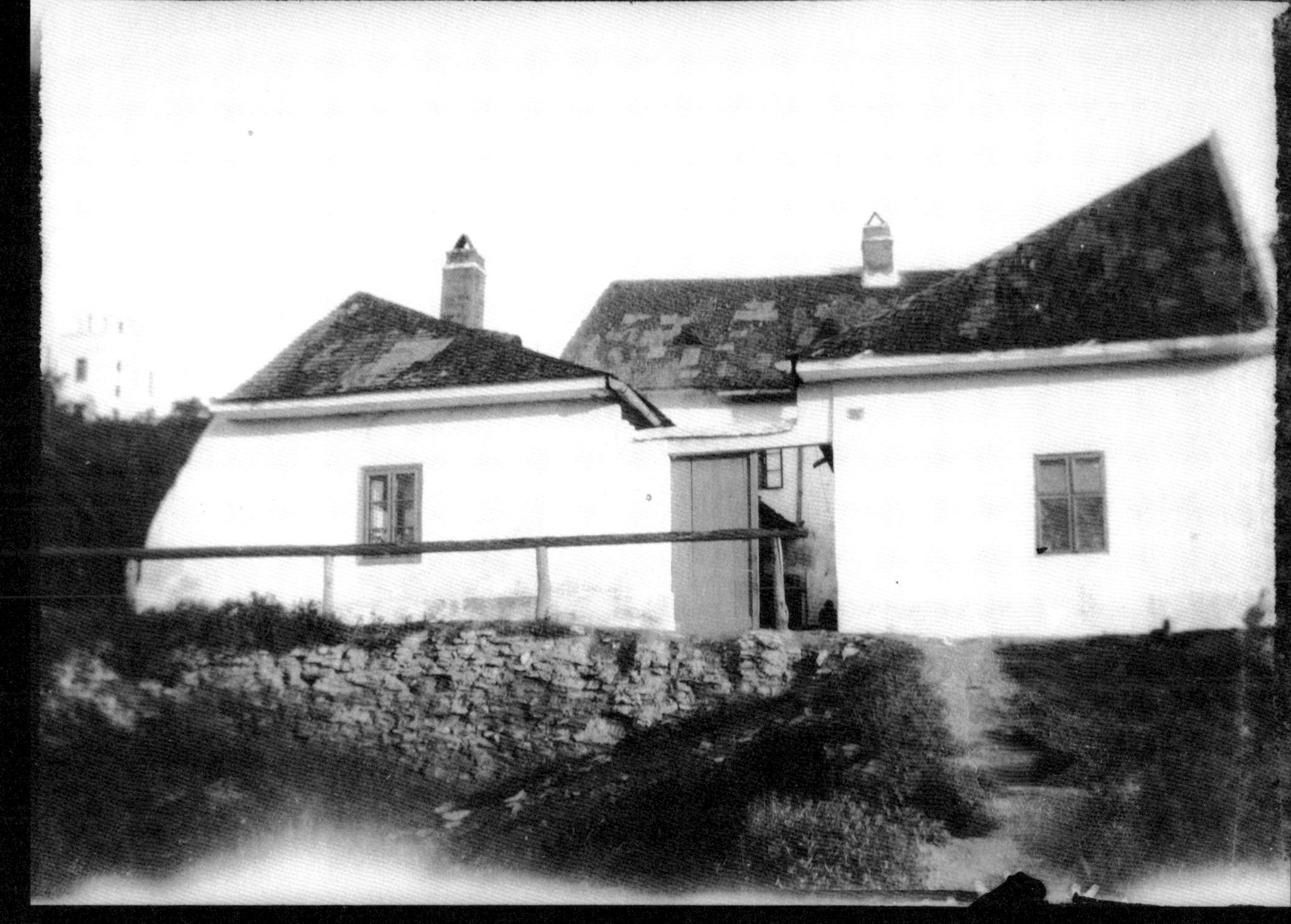

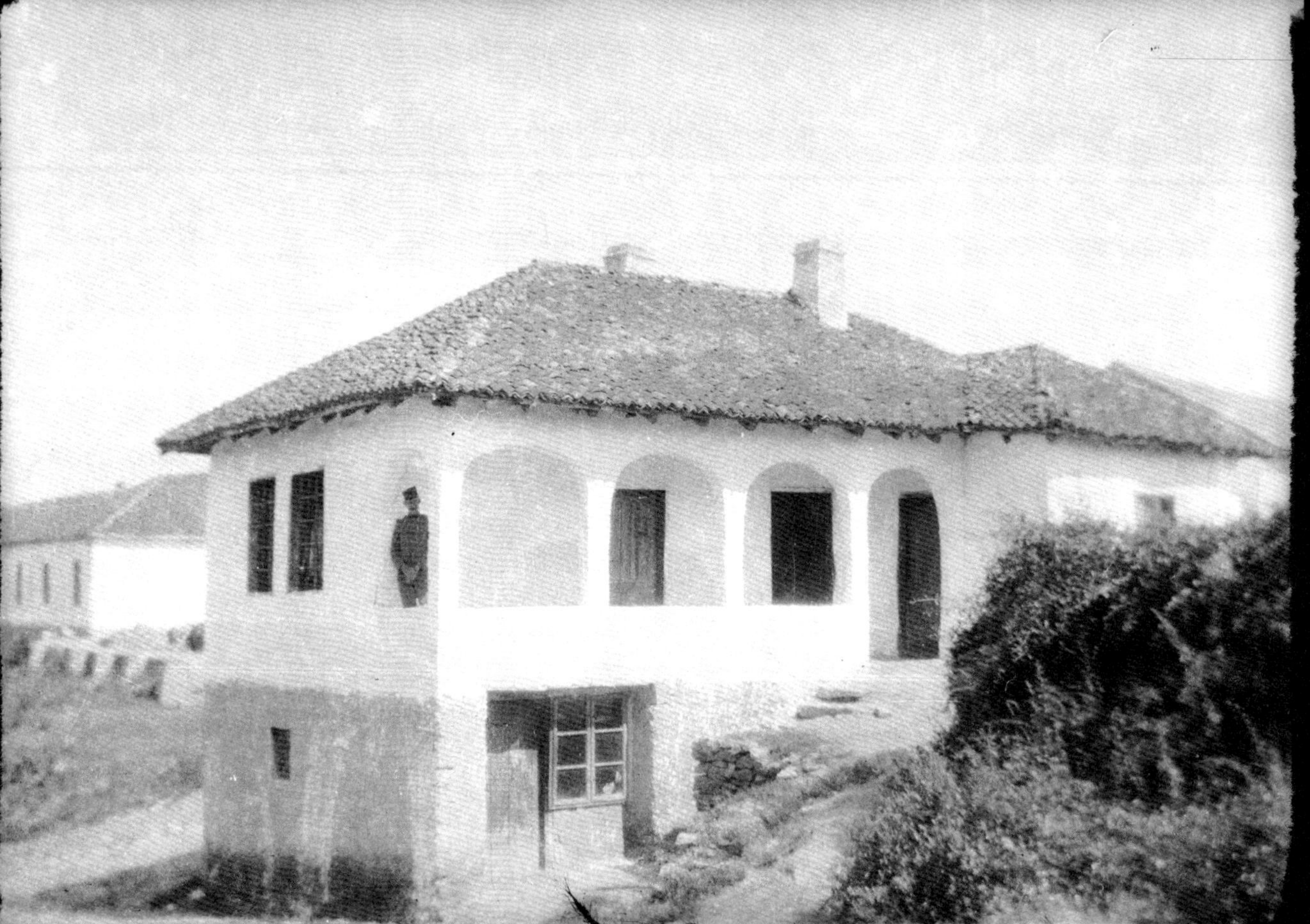

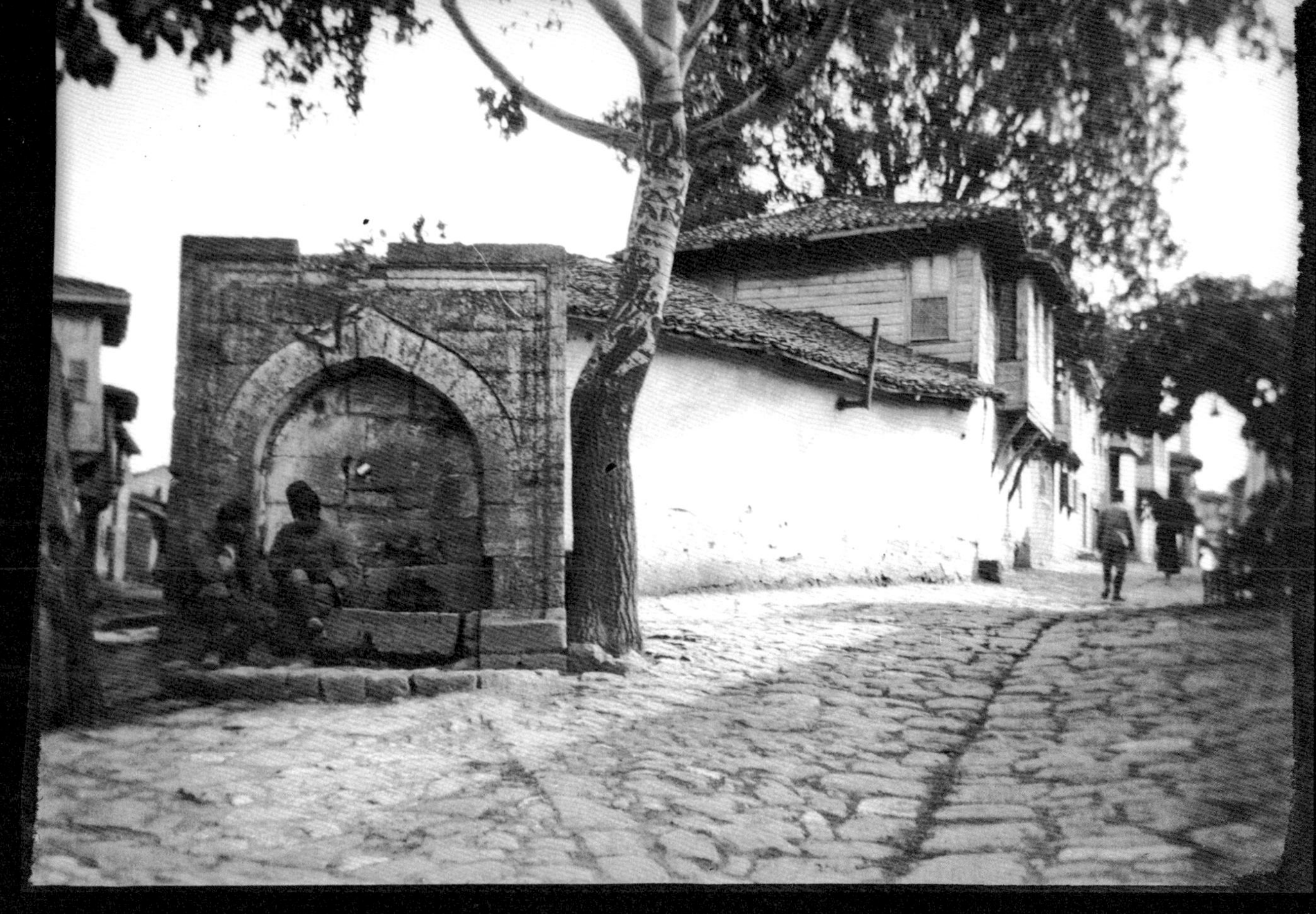

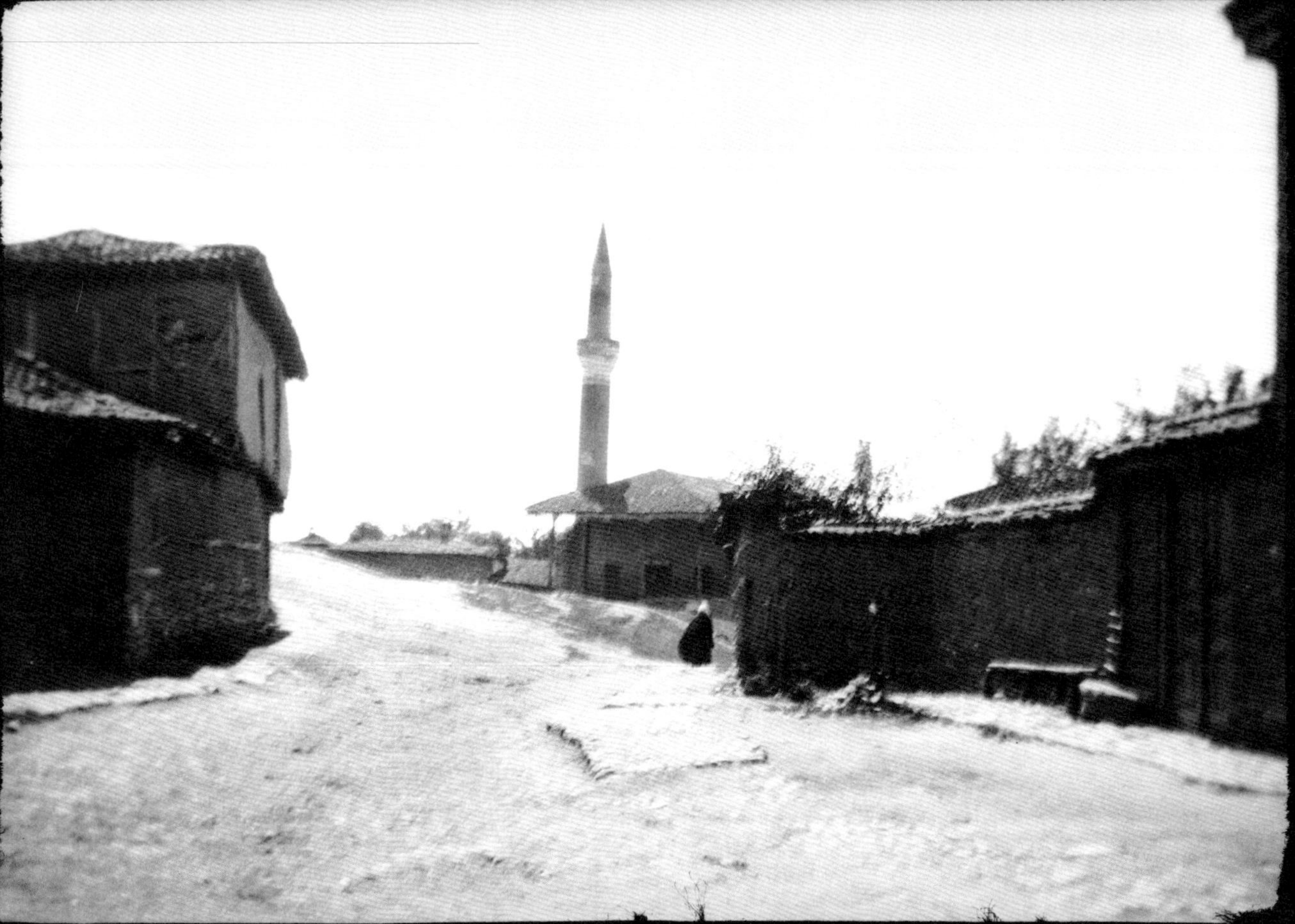

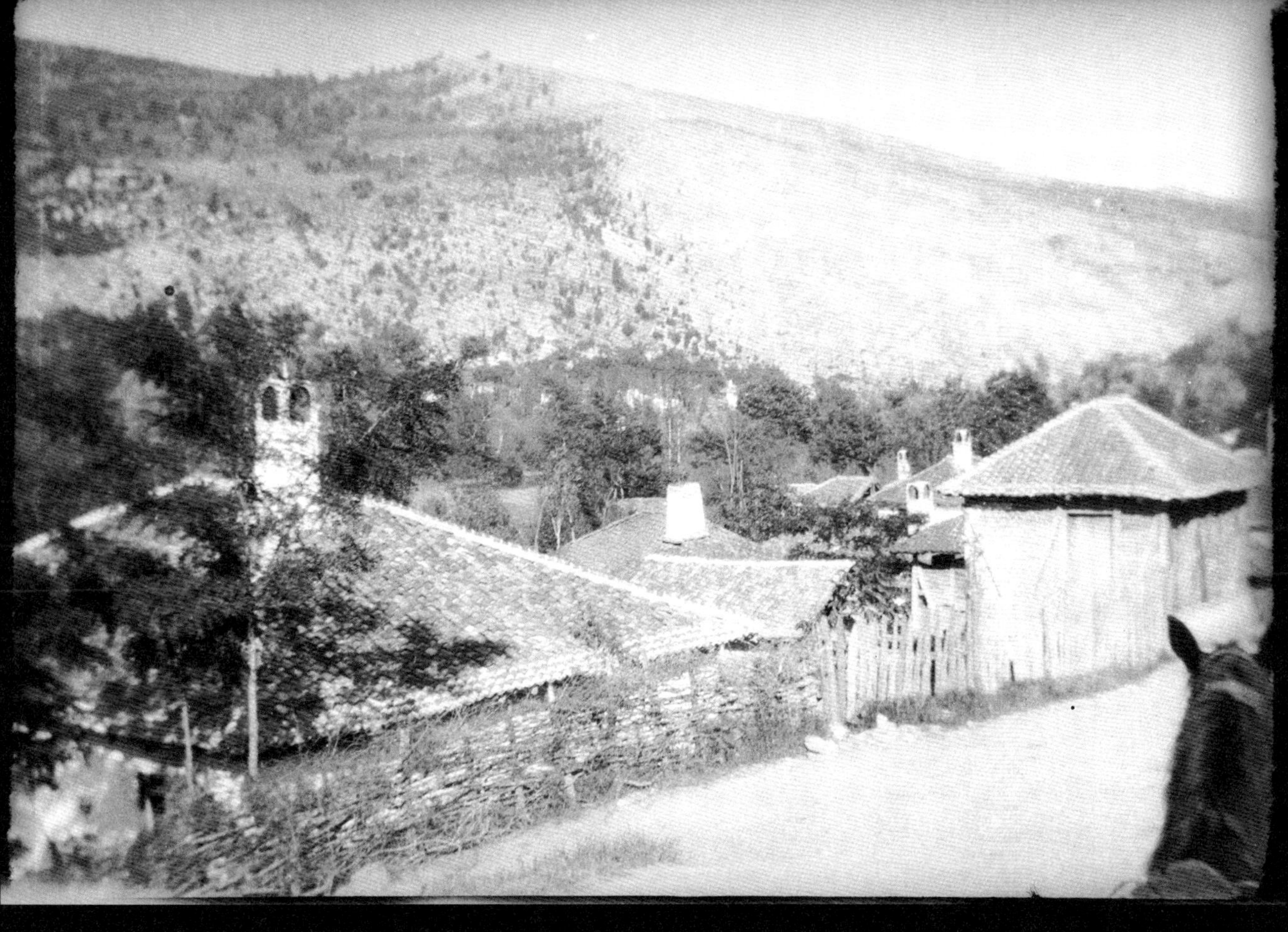

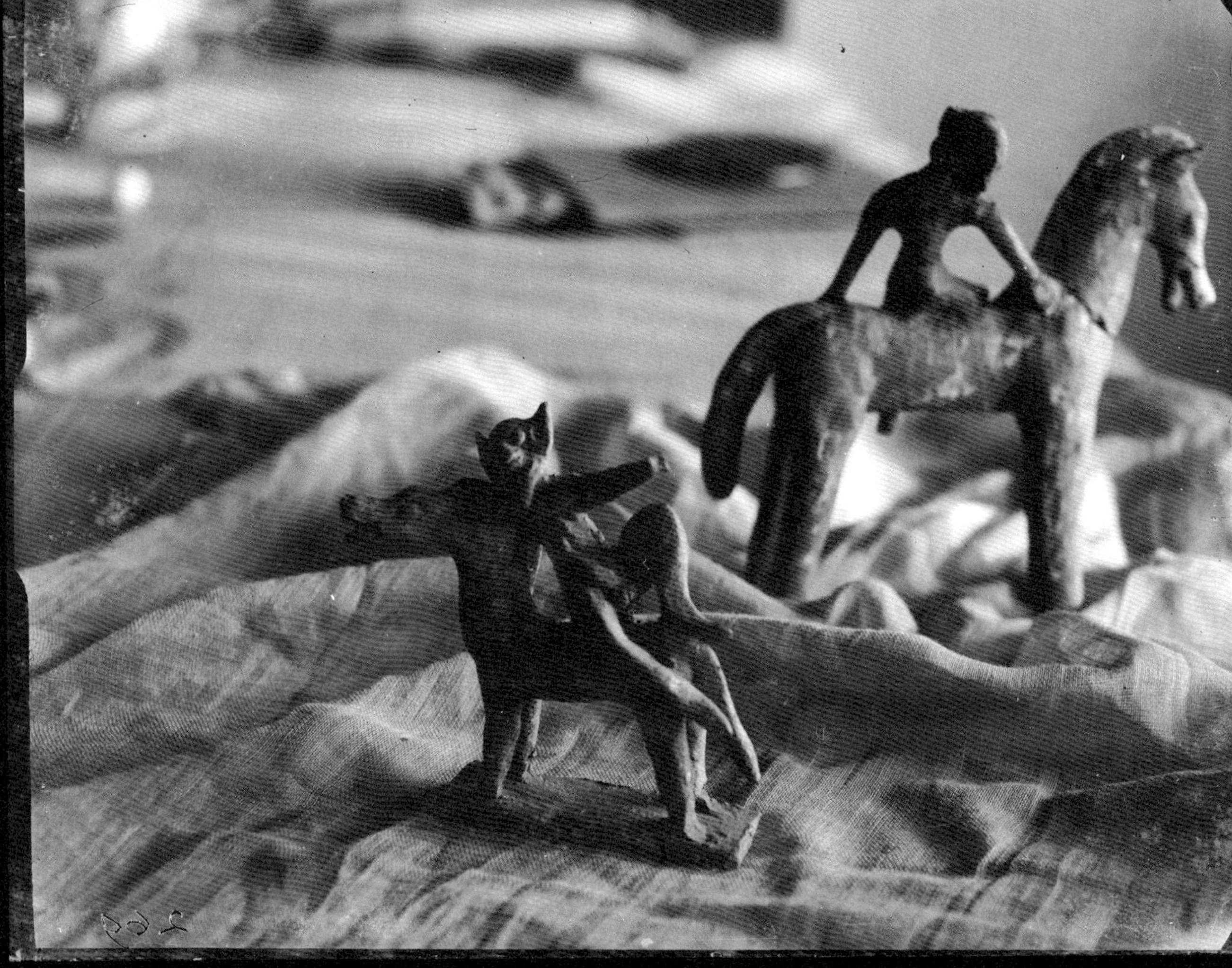

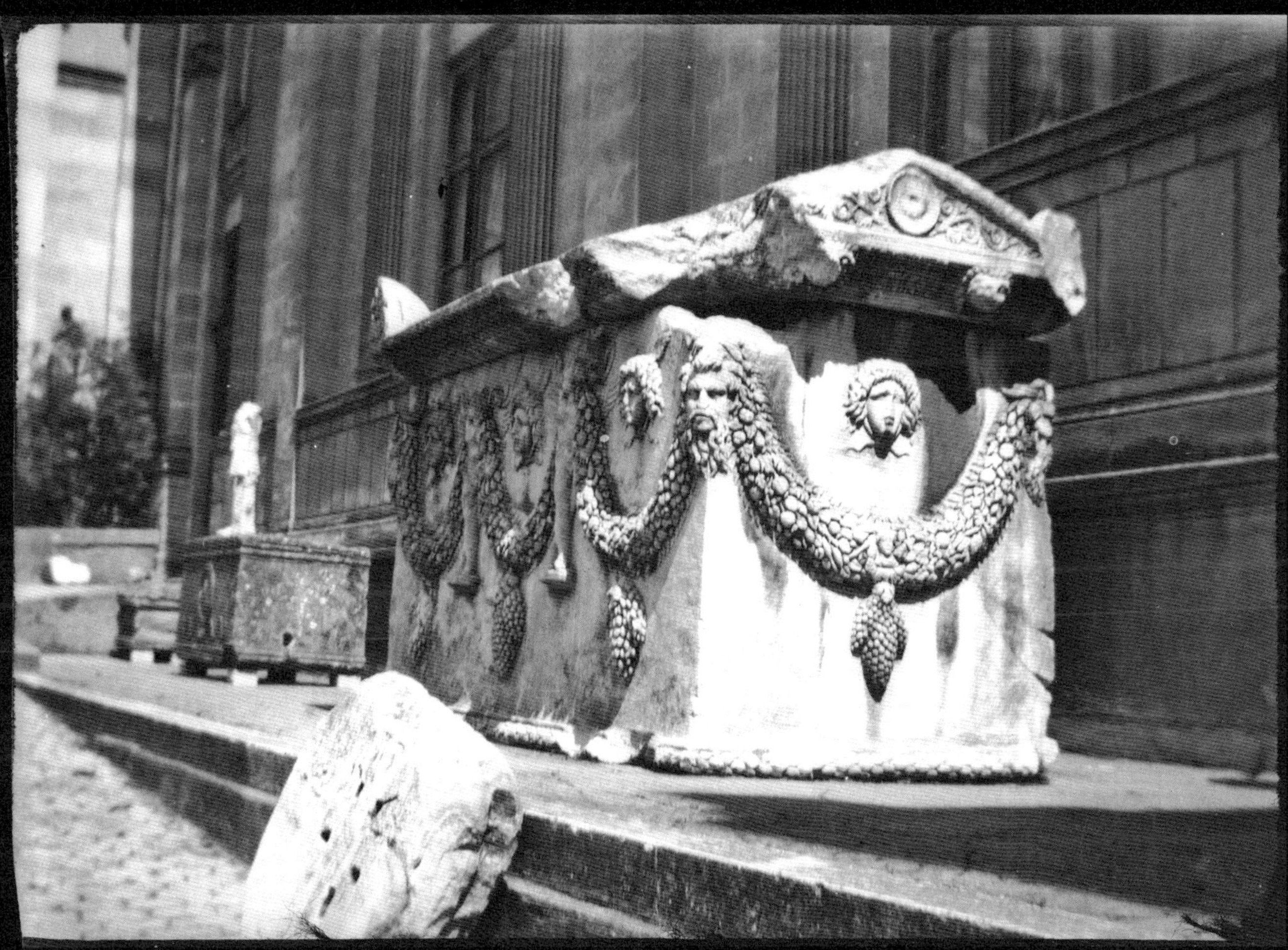

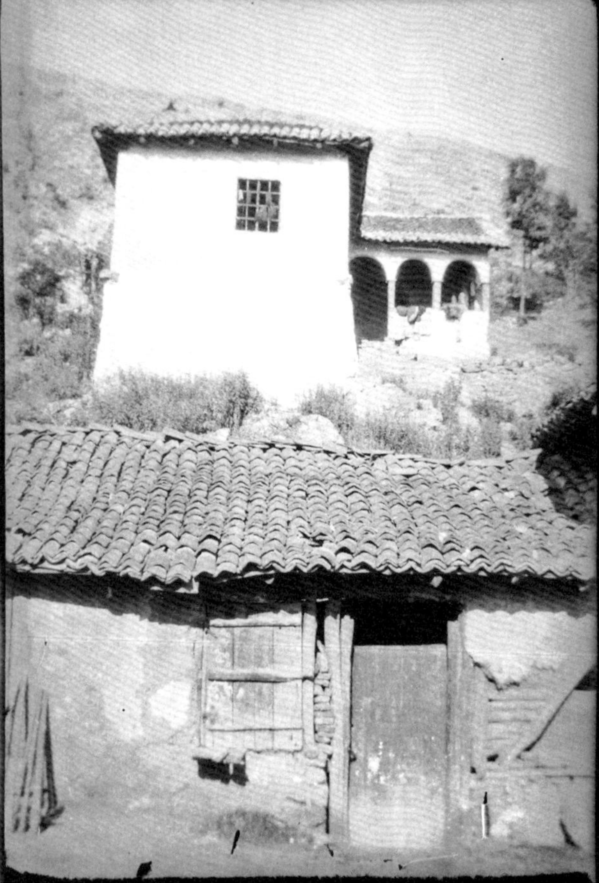

22

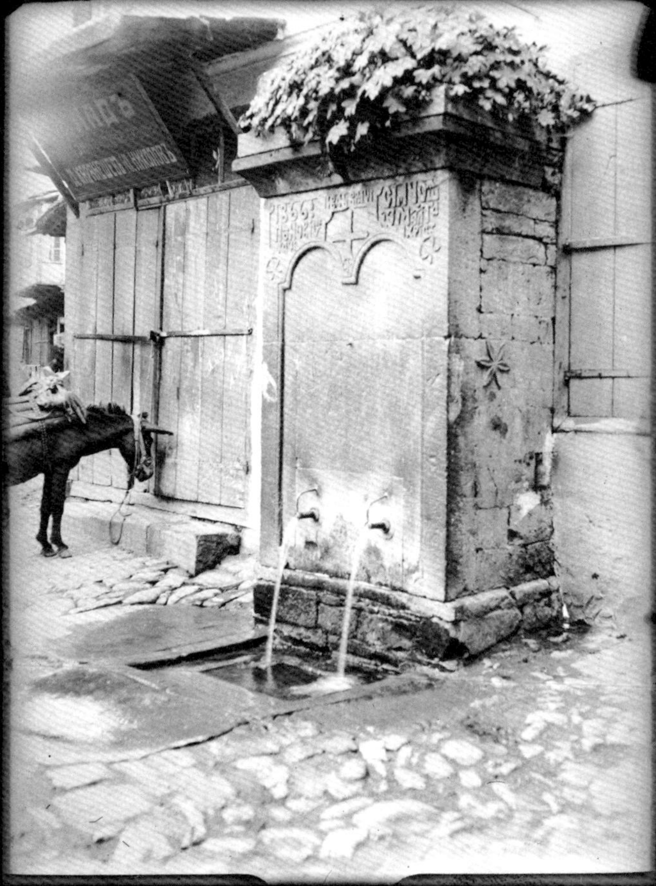

23

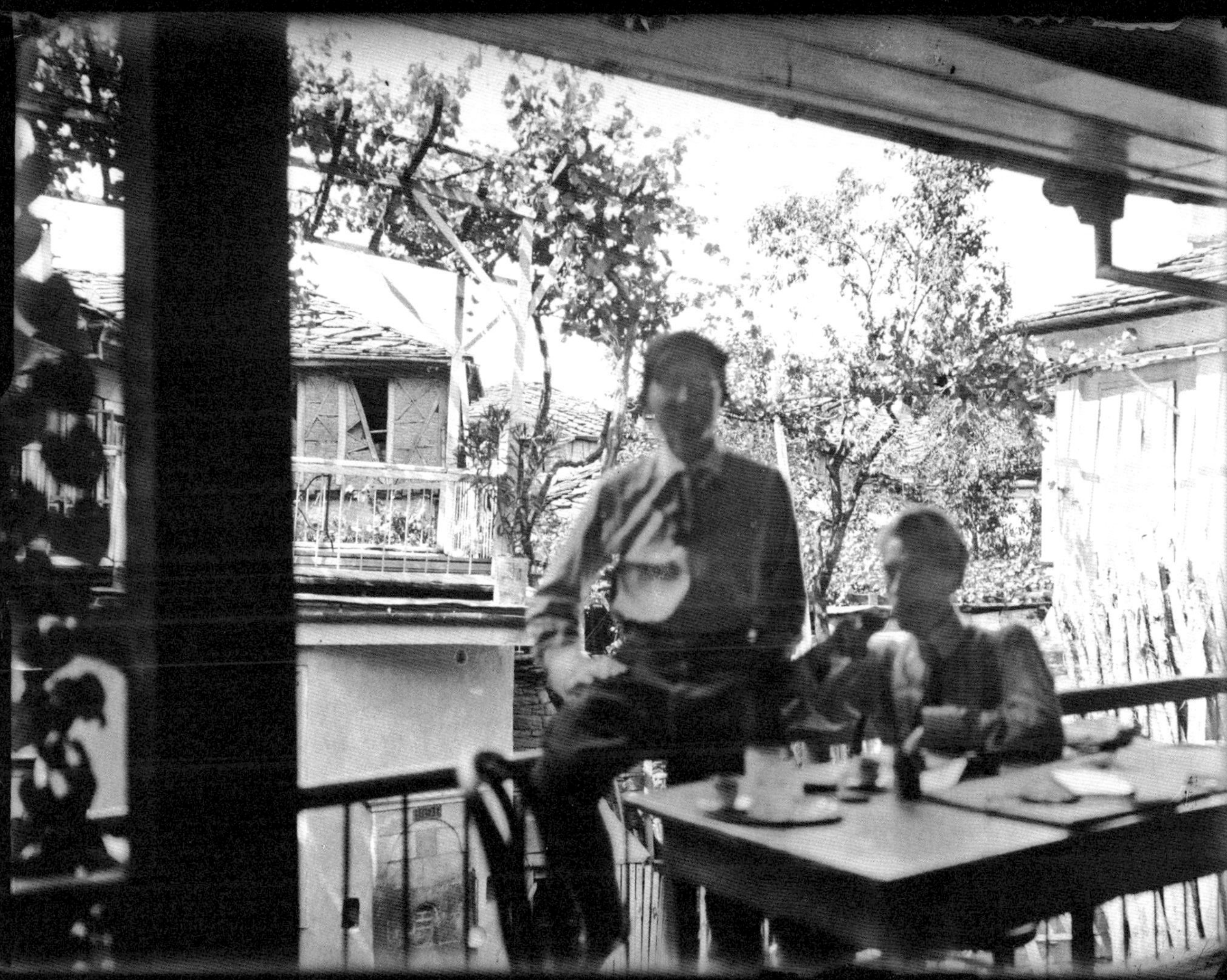

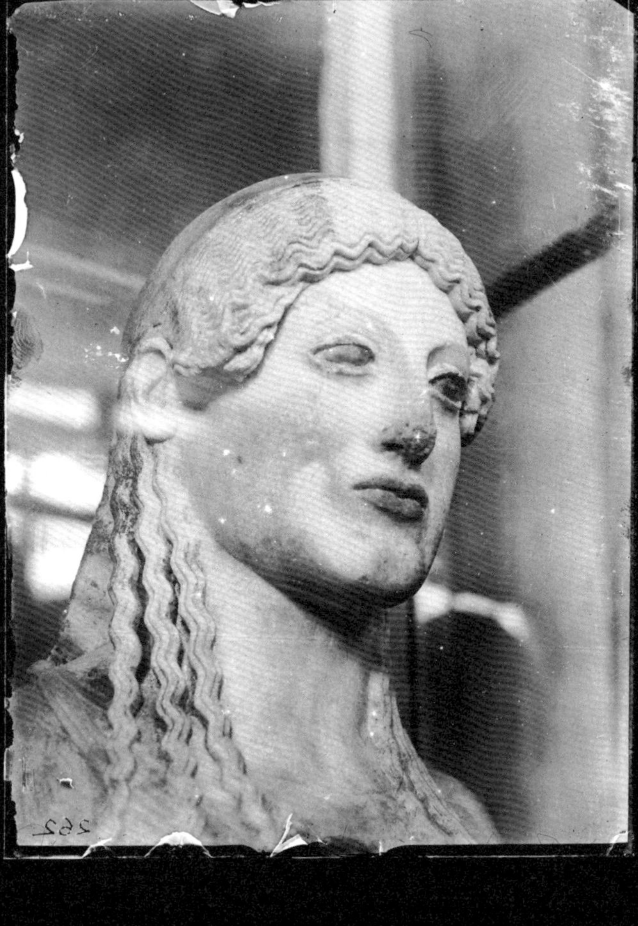

25
26

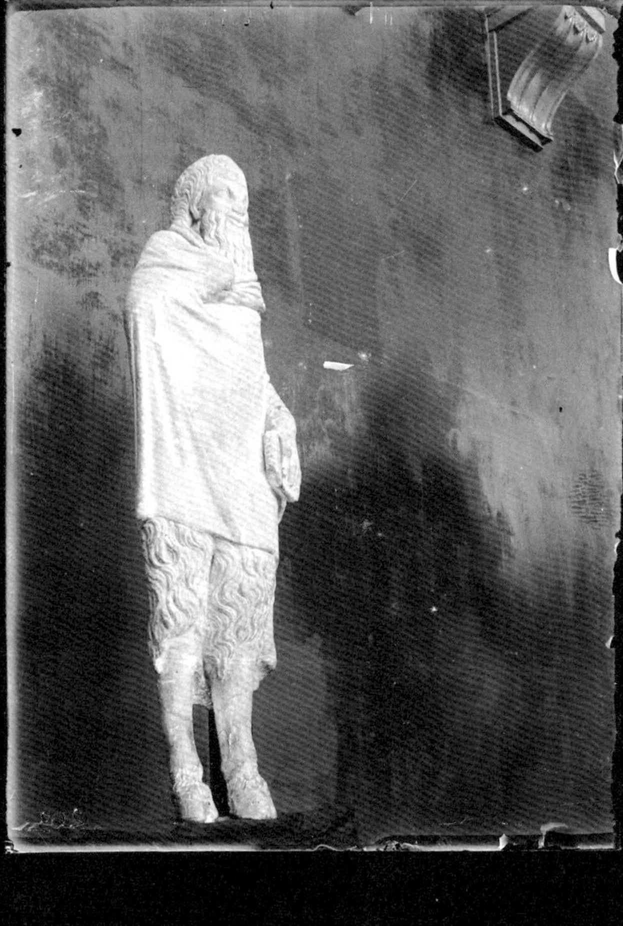

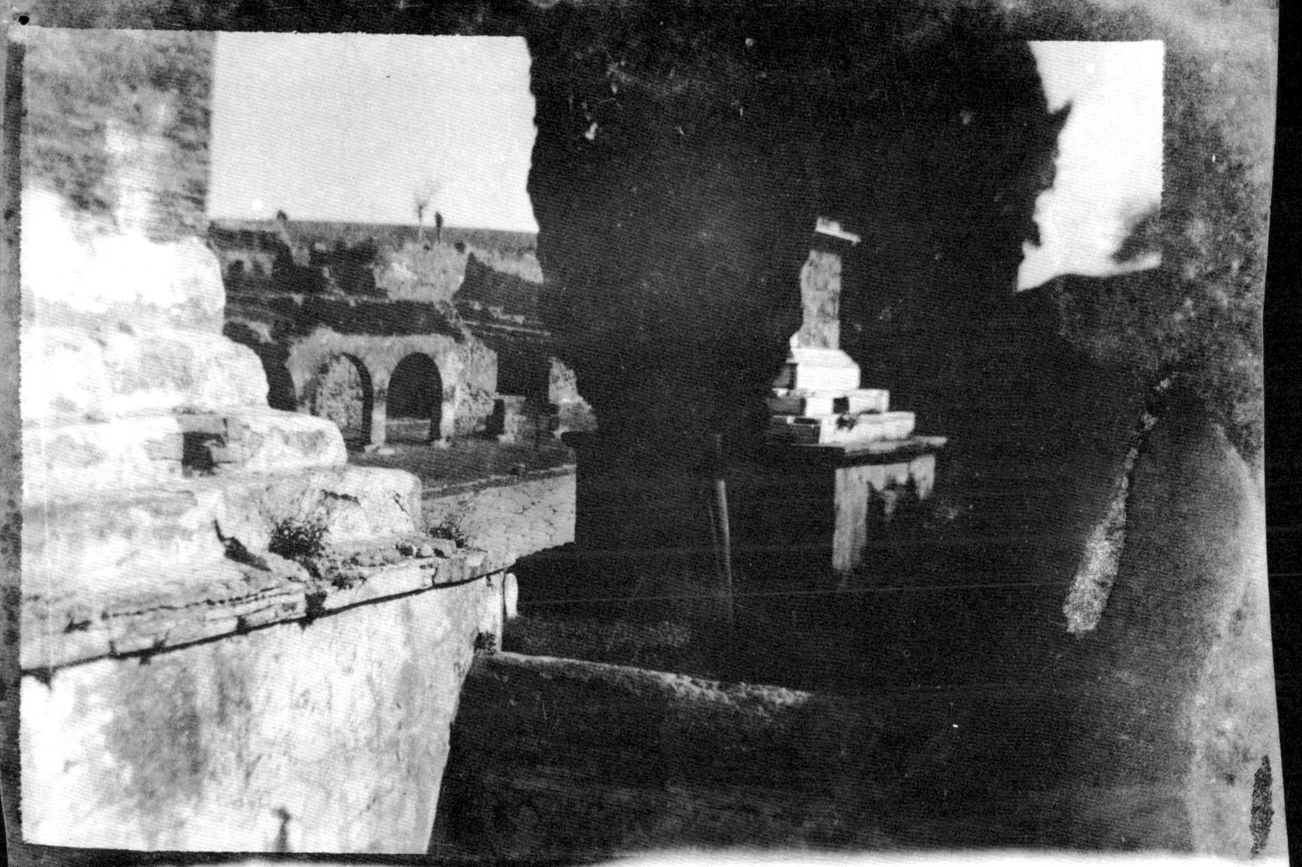

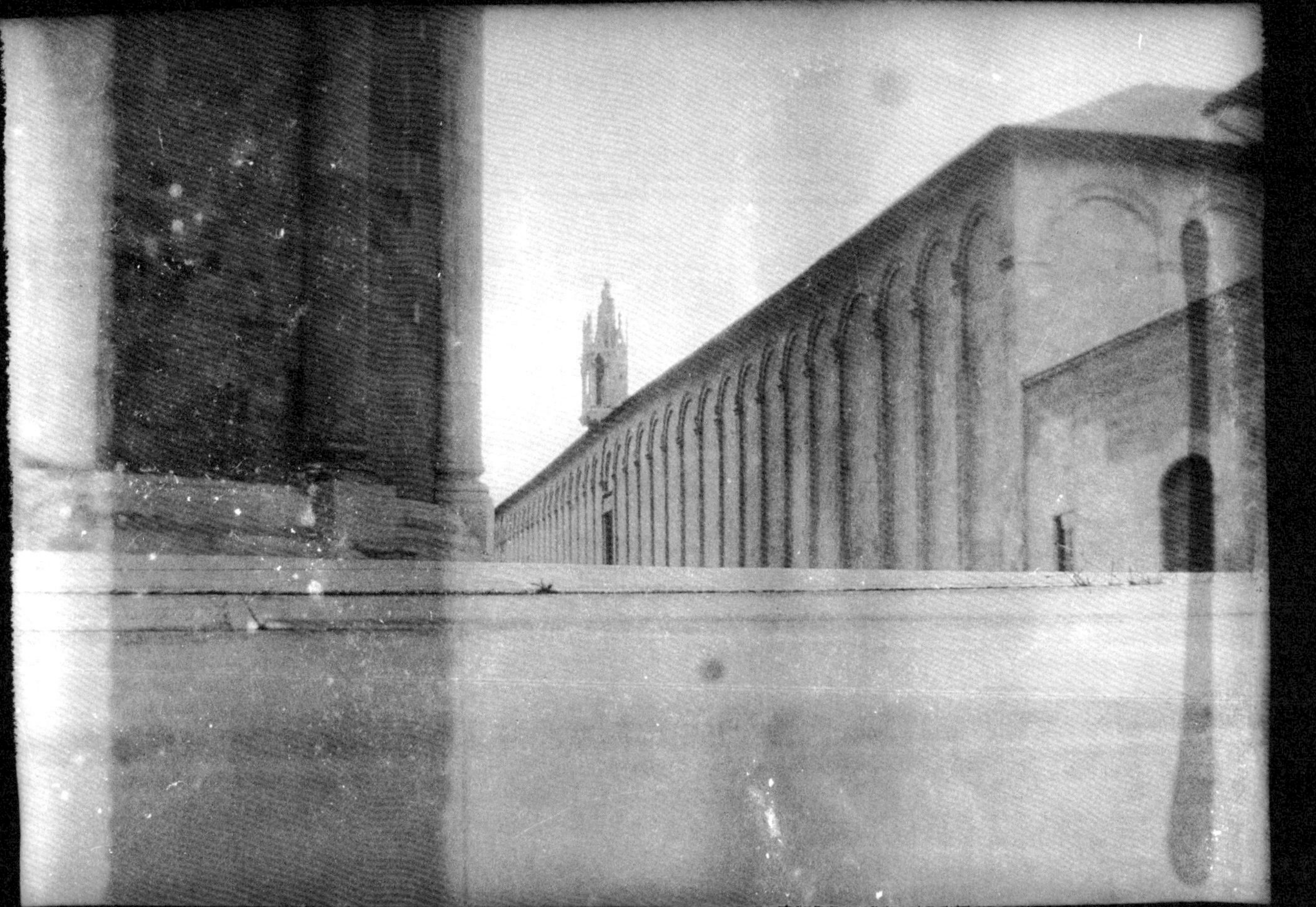

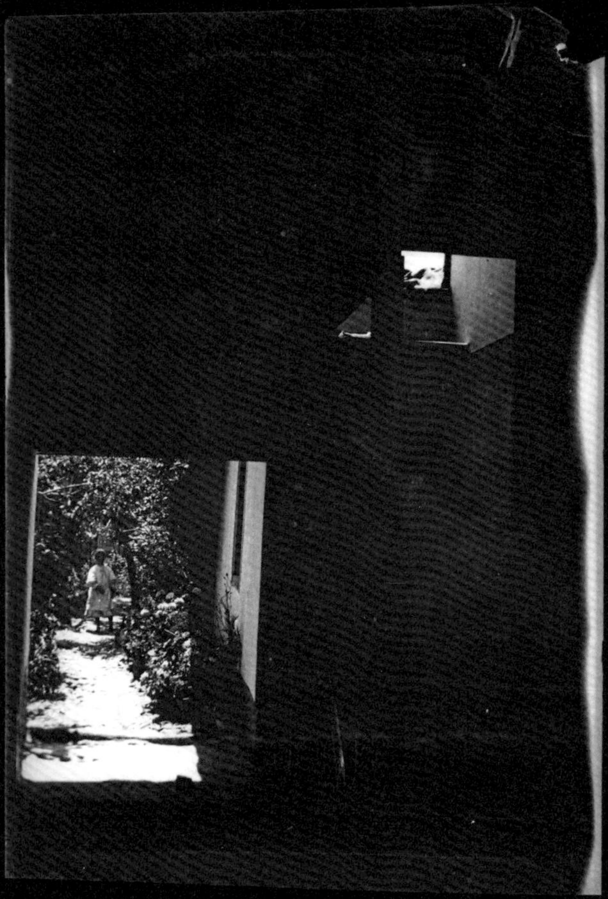

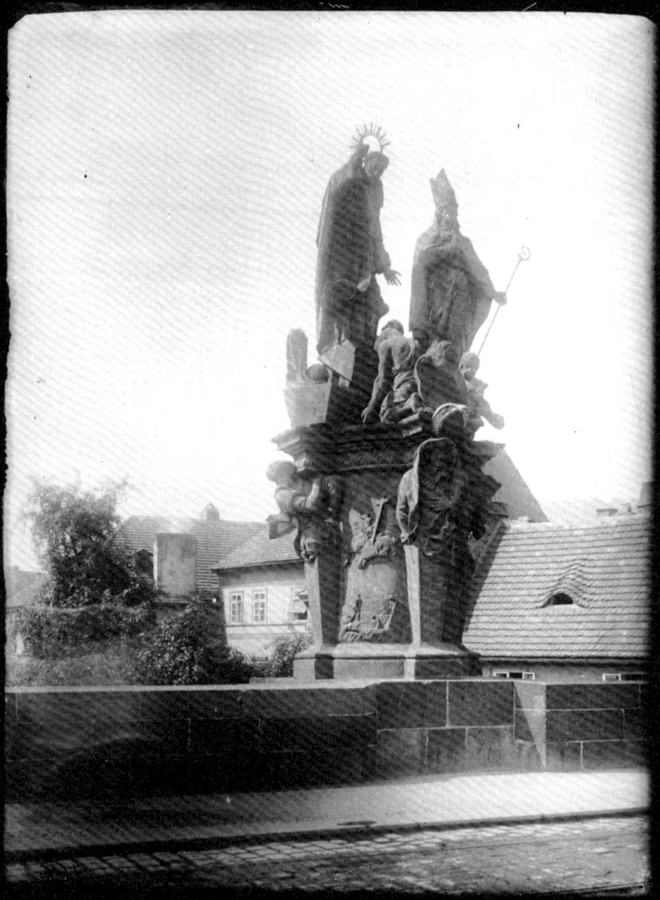

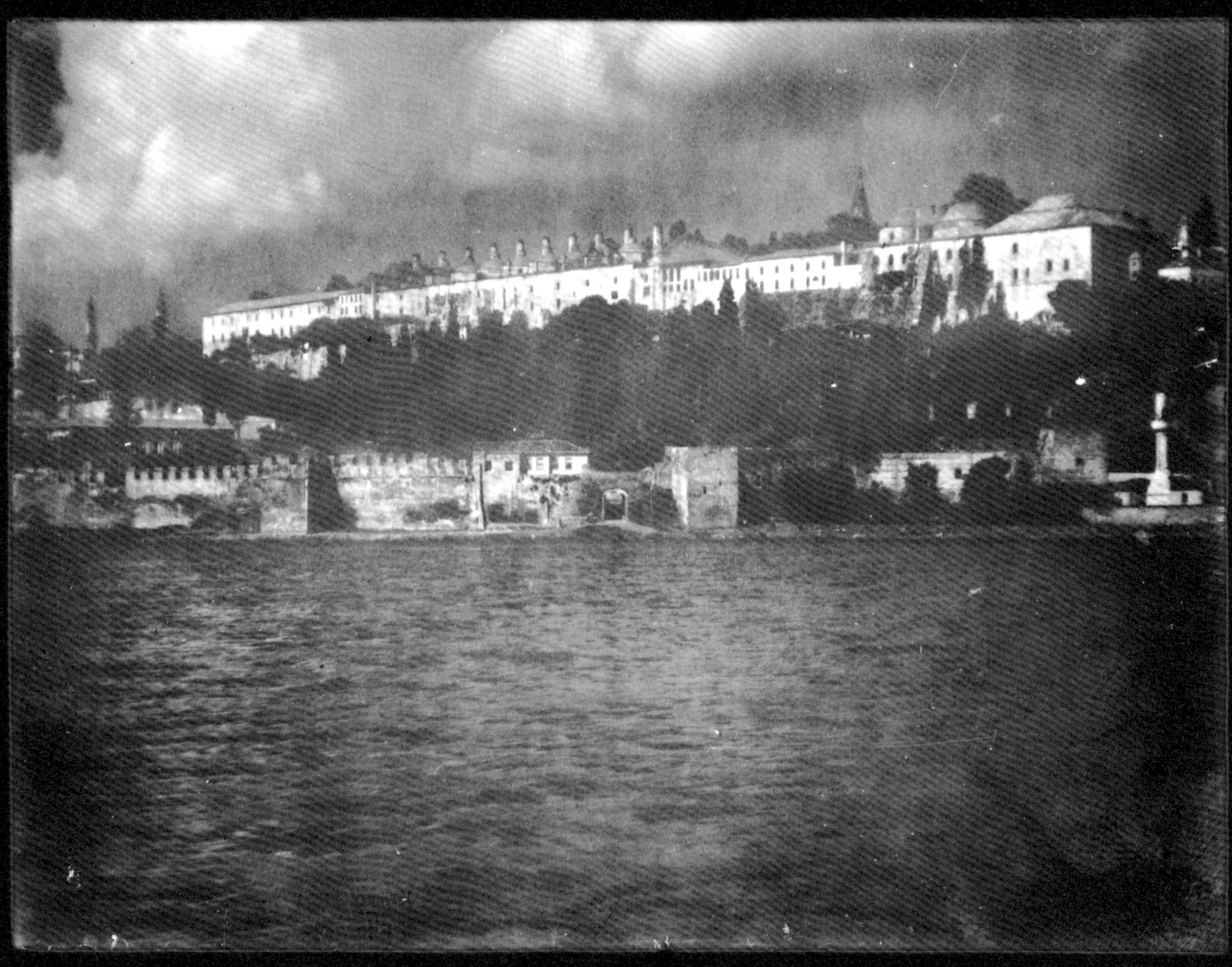

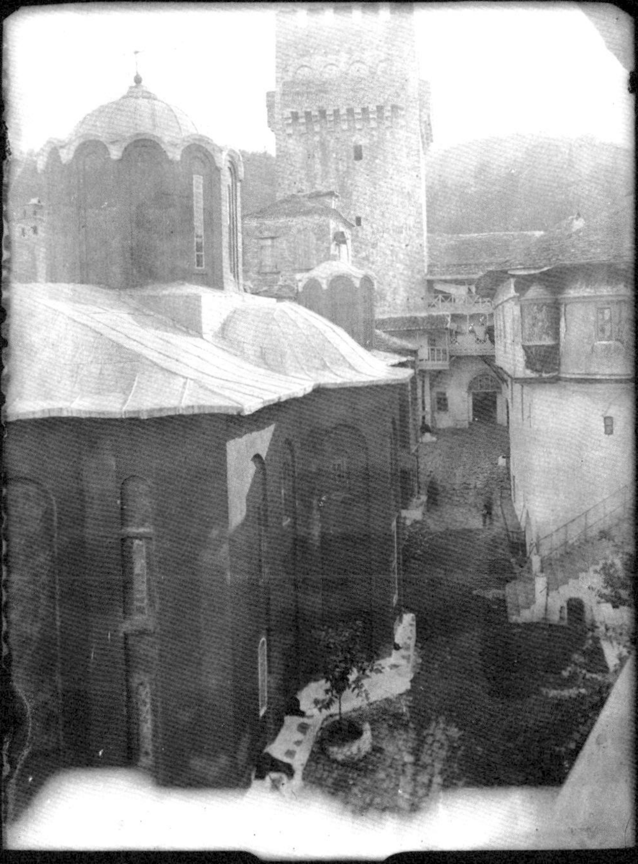

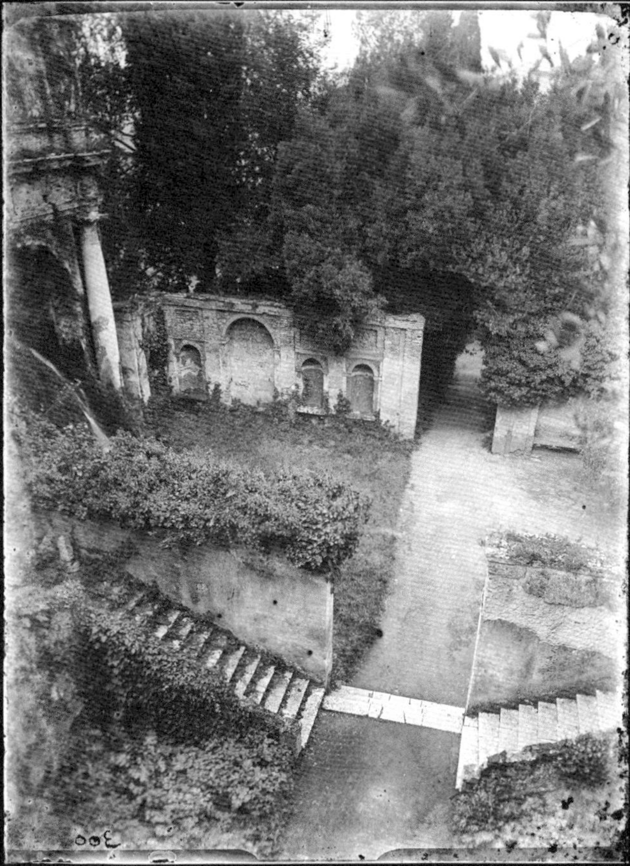

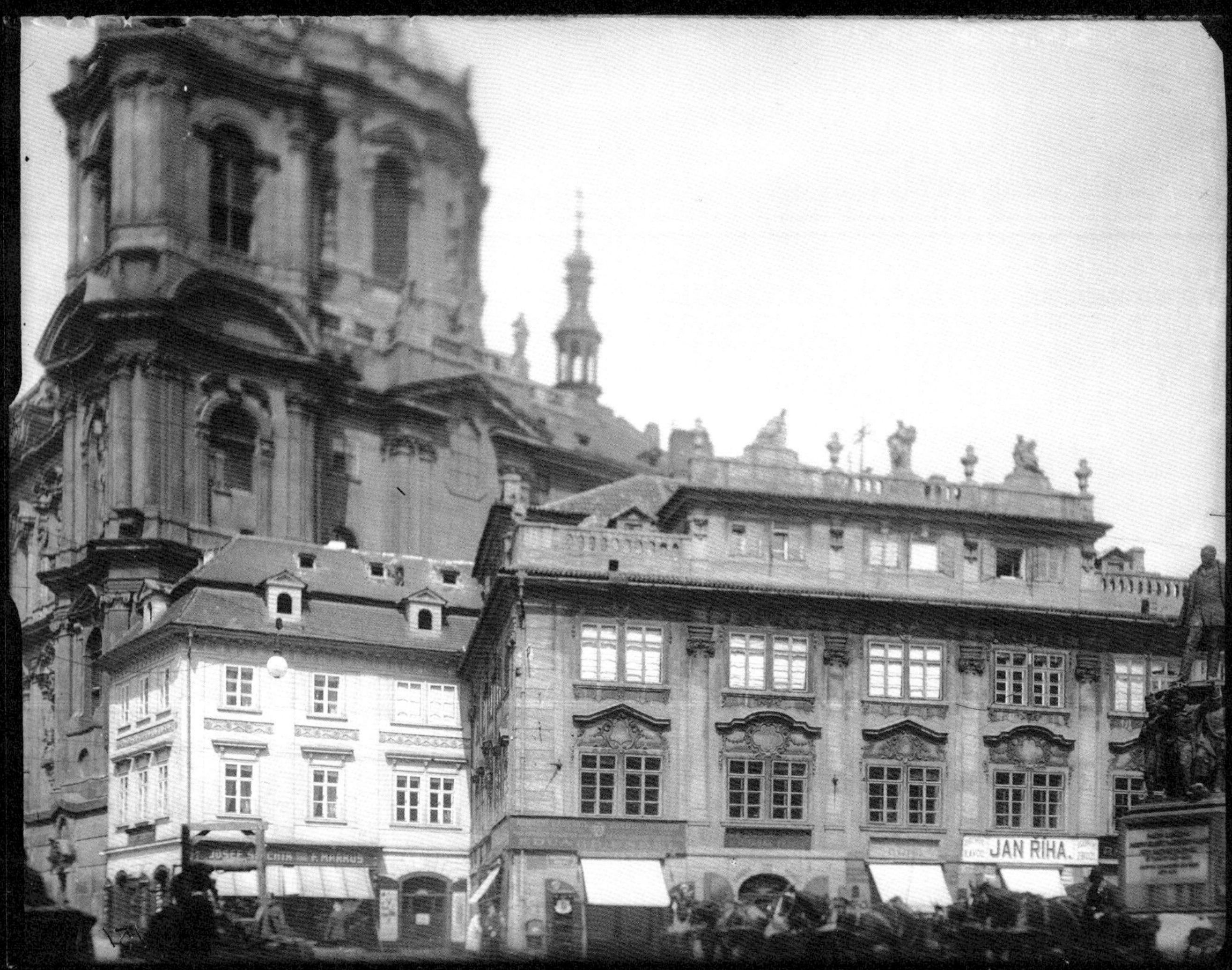

36

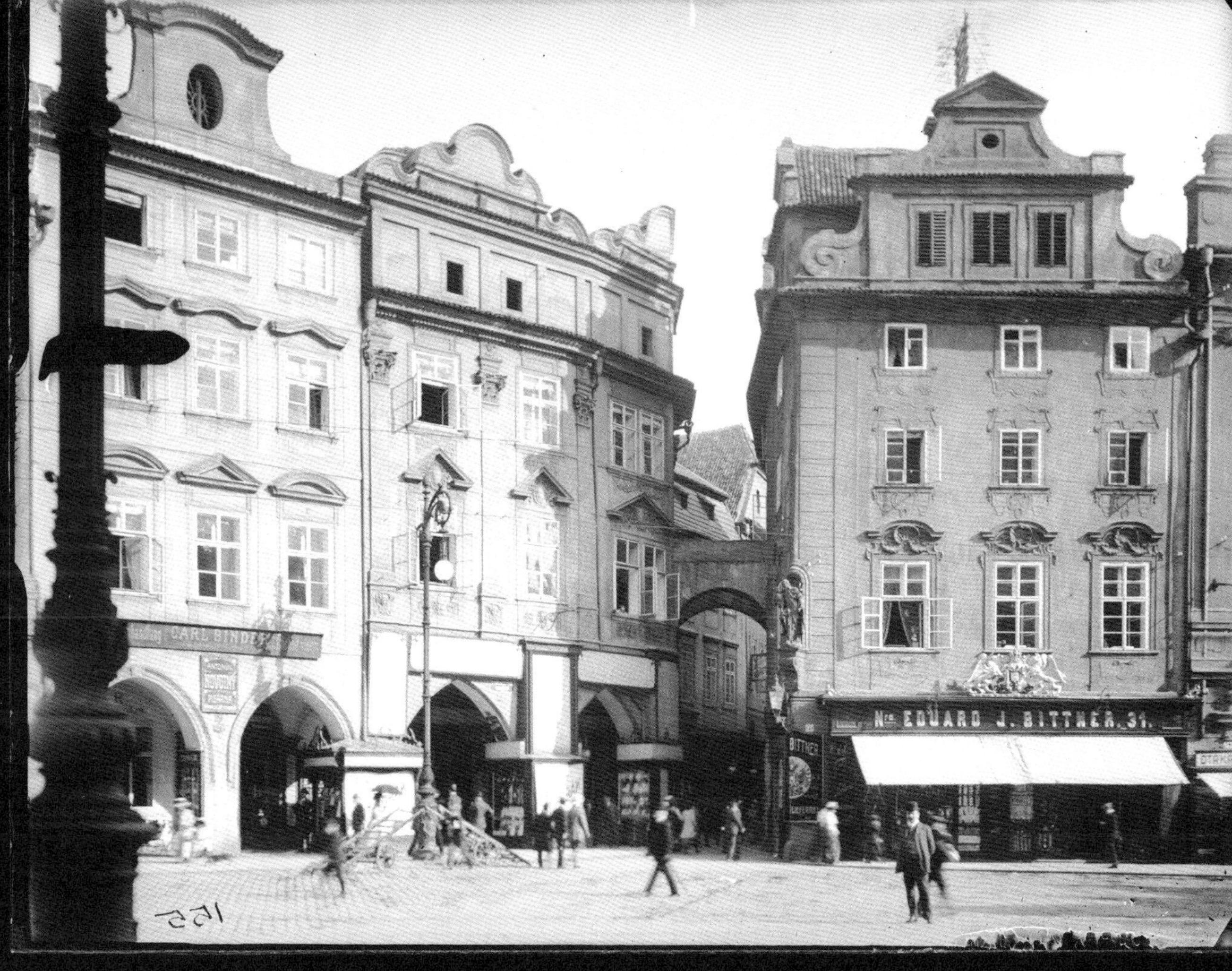

CARL BINDER
Nᵒ EDUARD J. BITTNER 31.

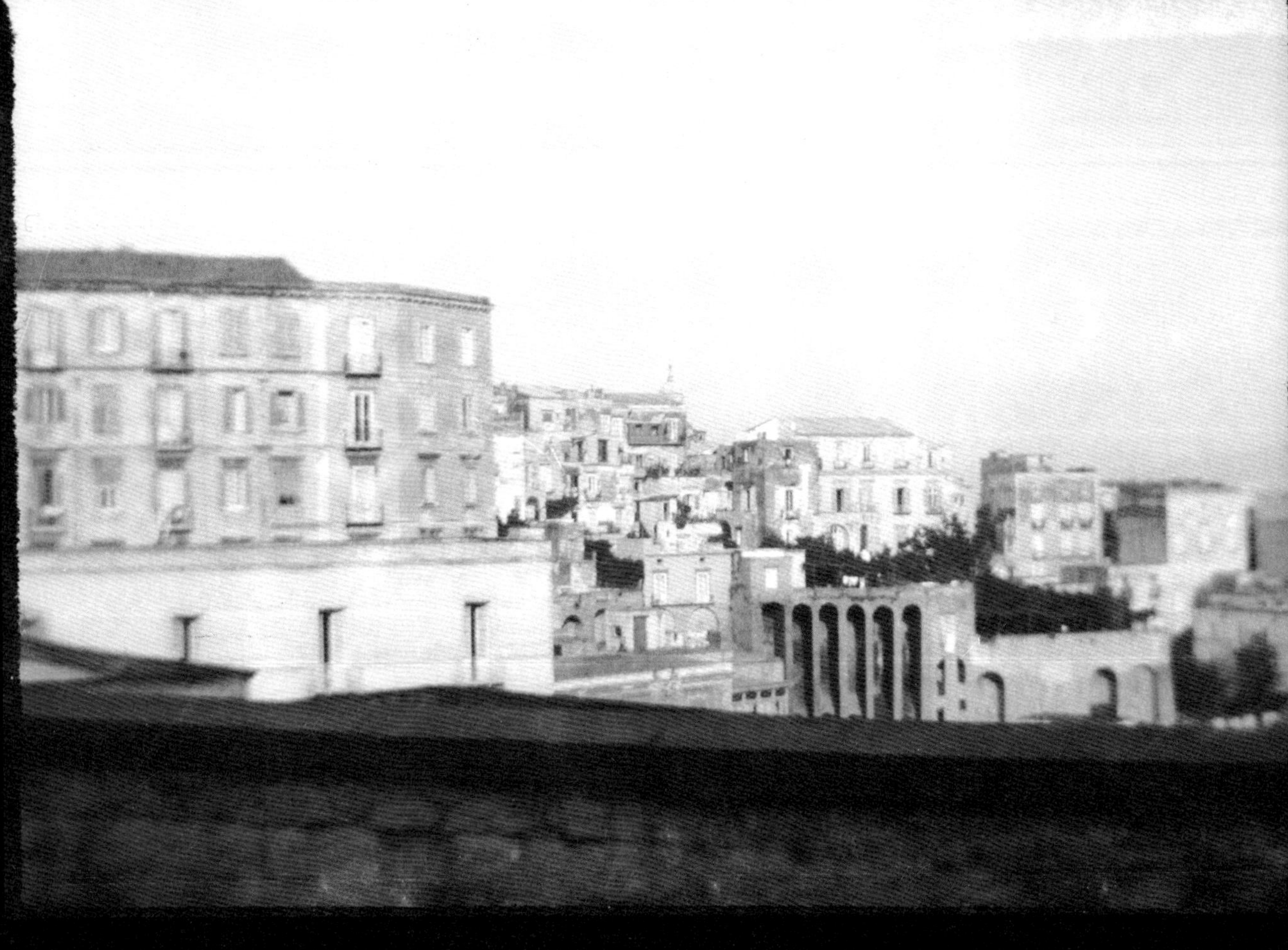

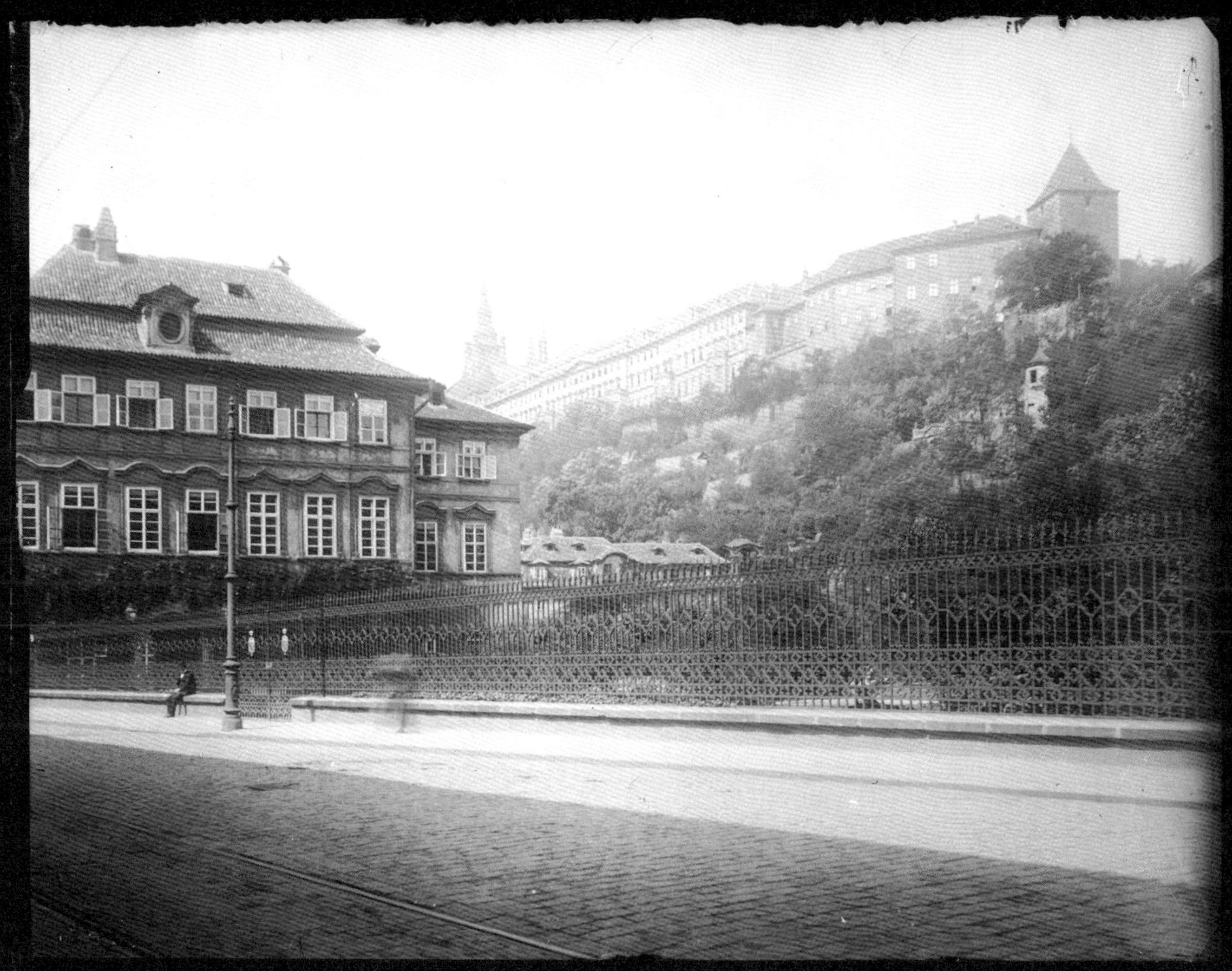

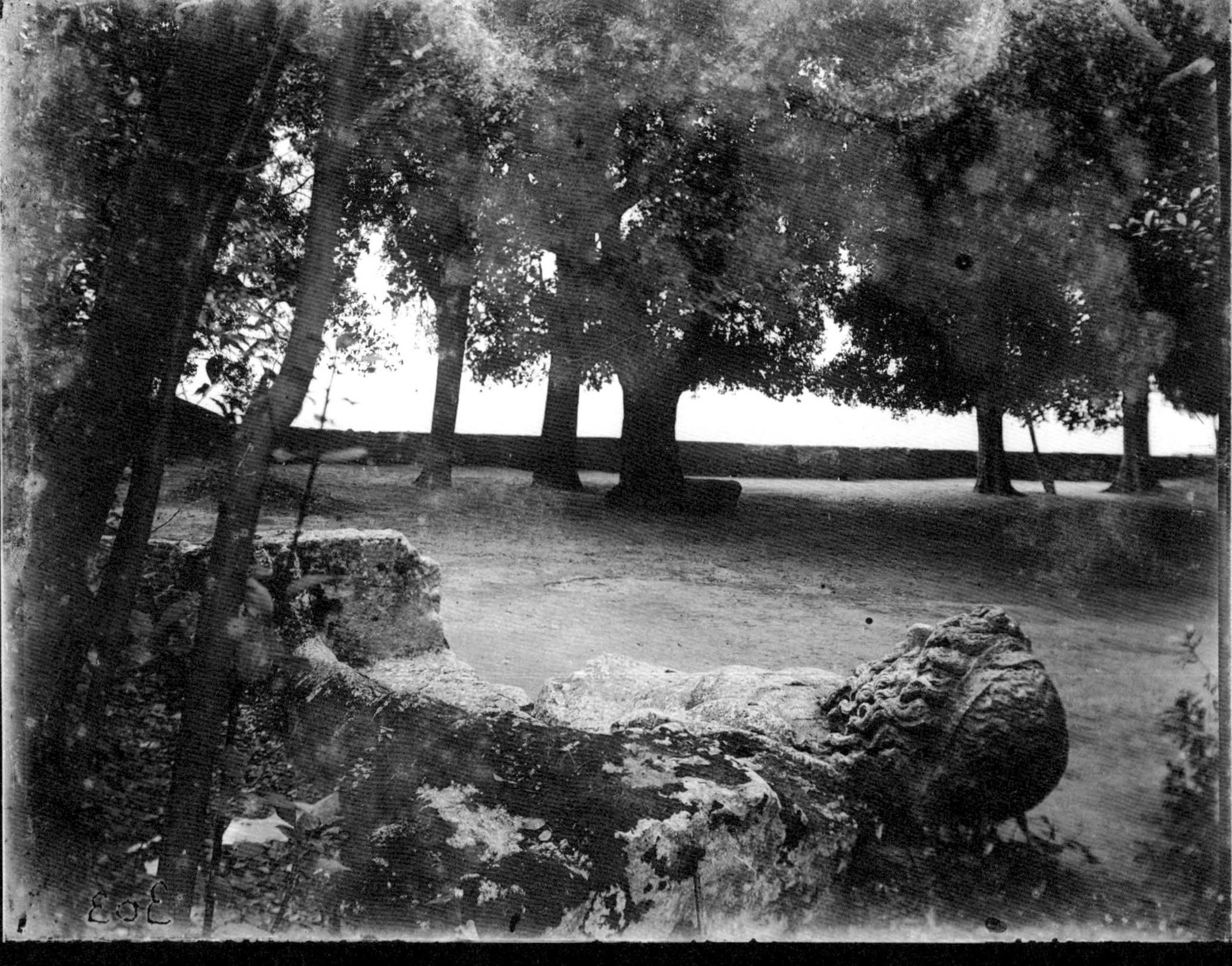

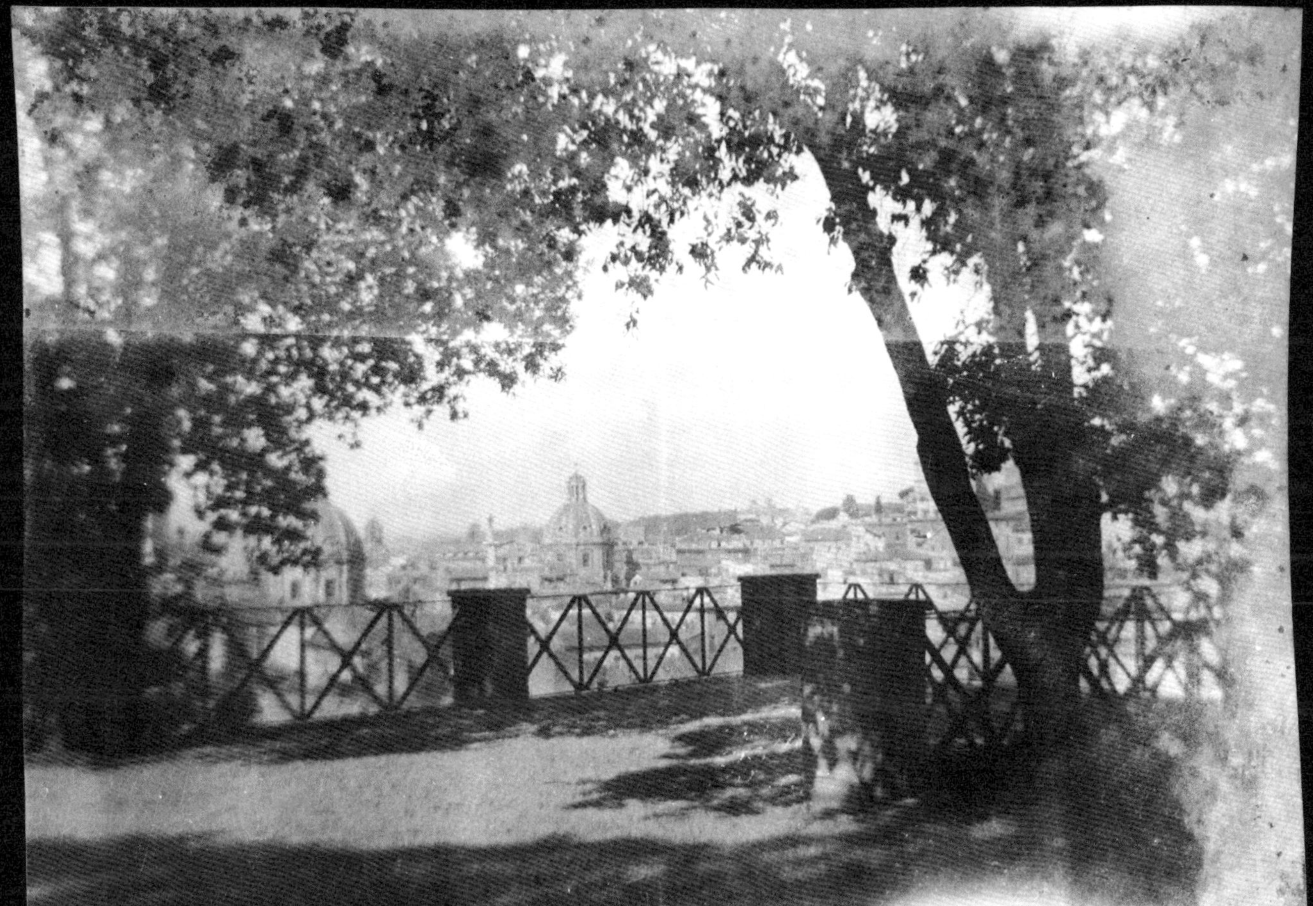

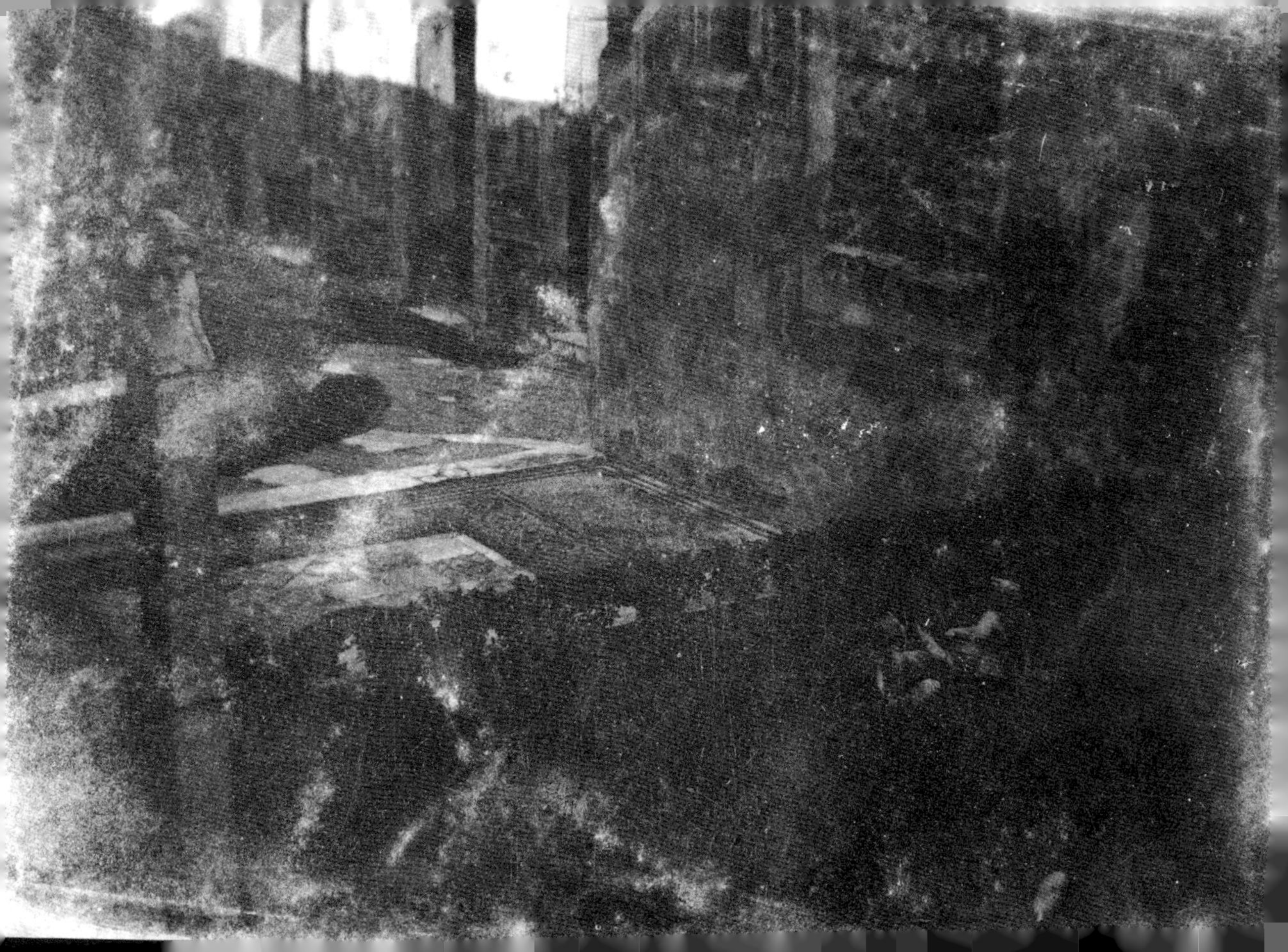

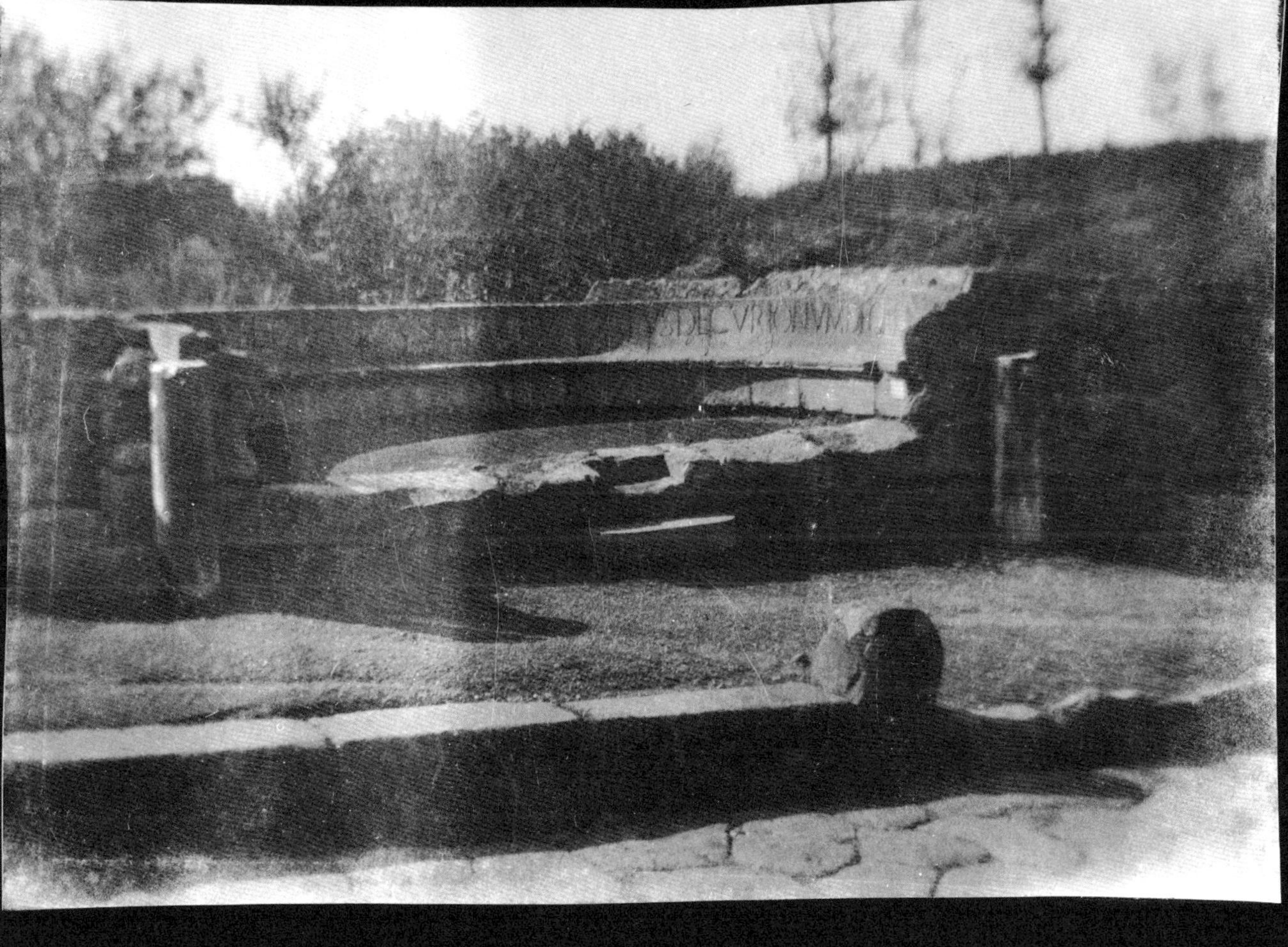

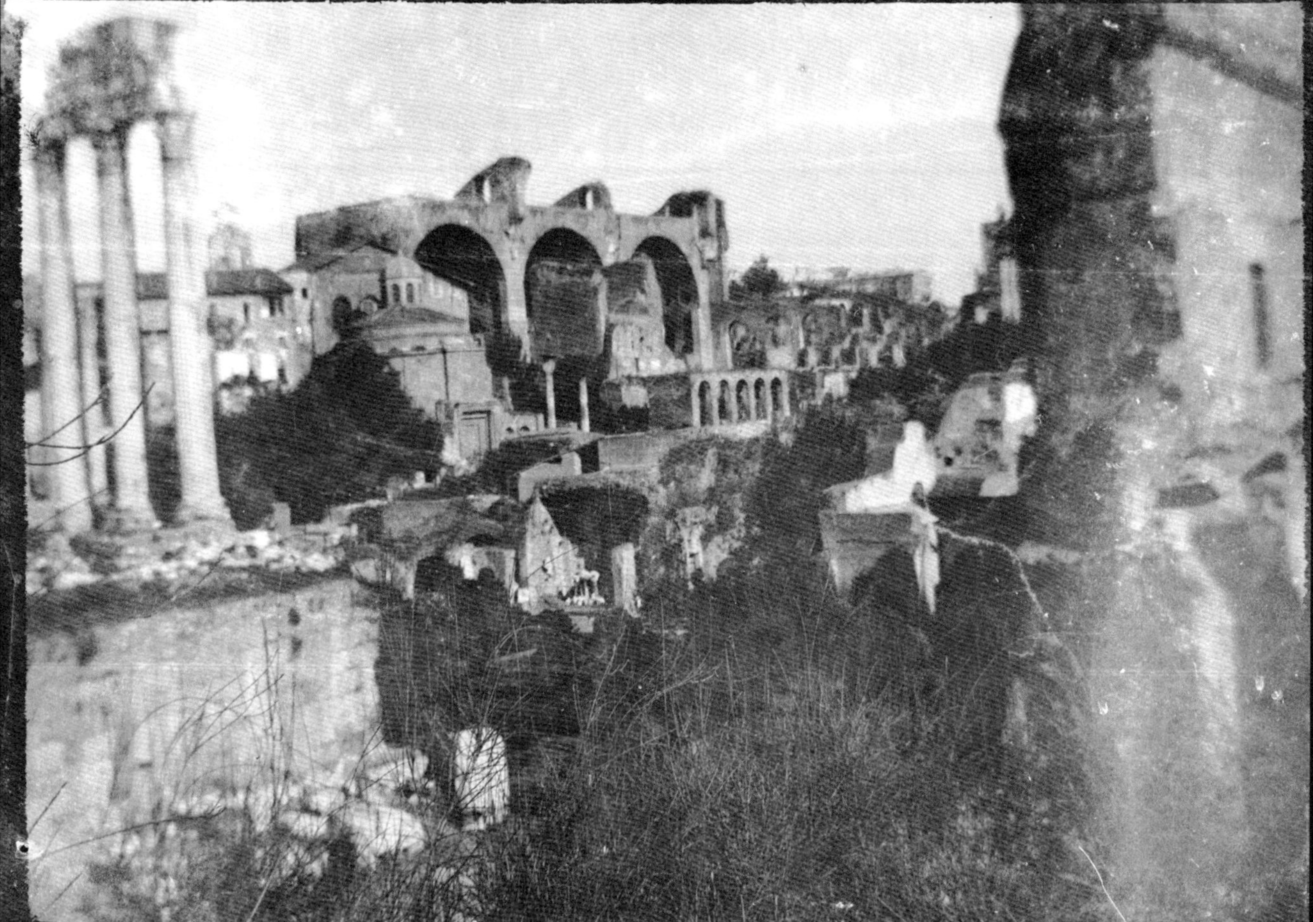

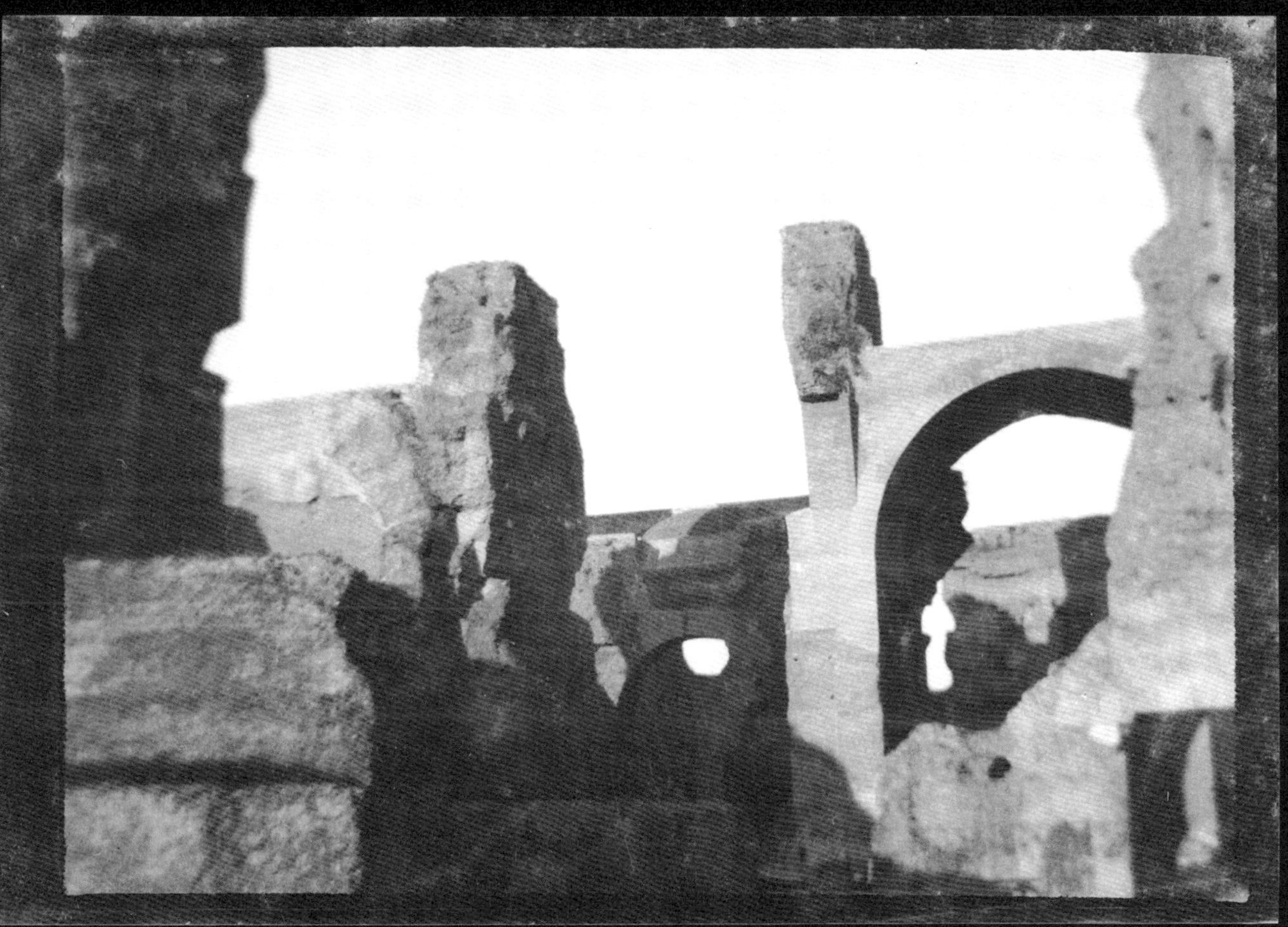

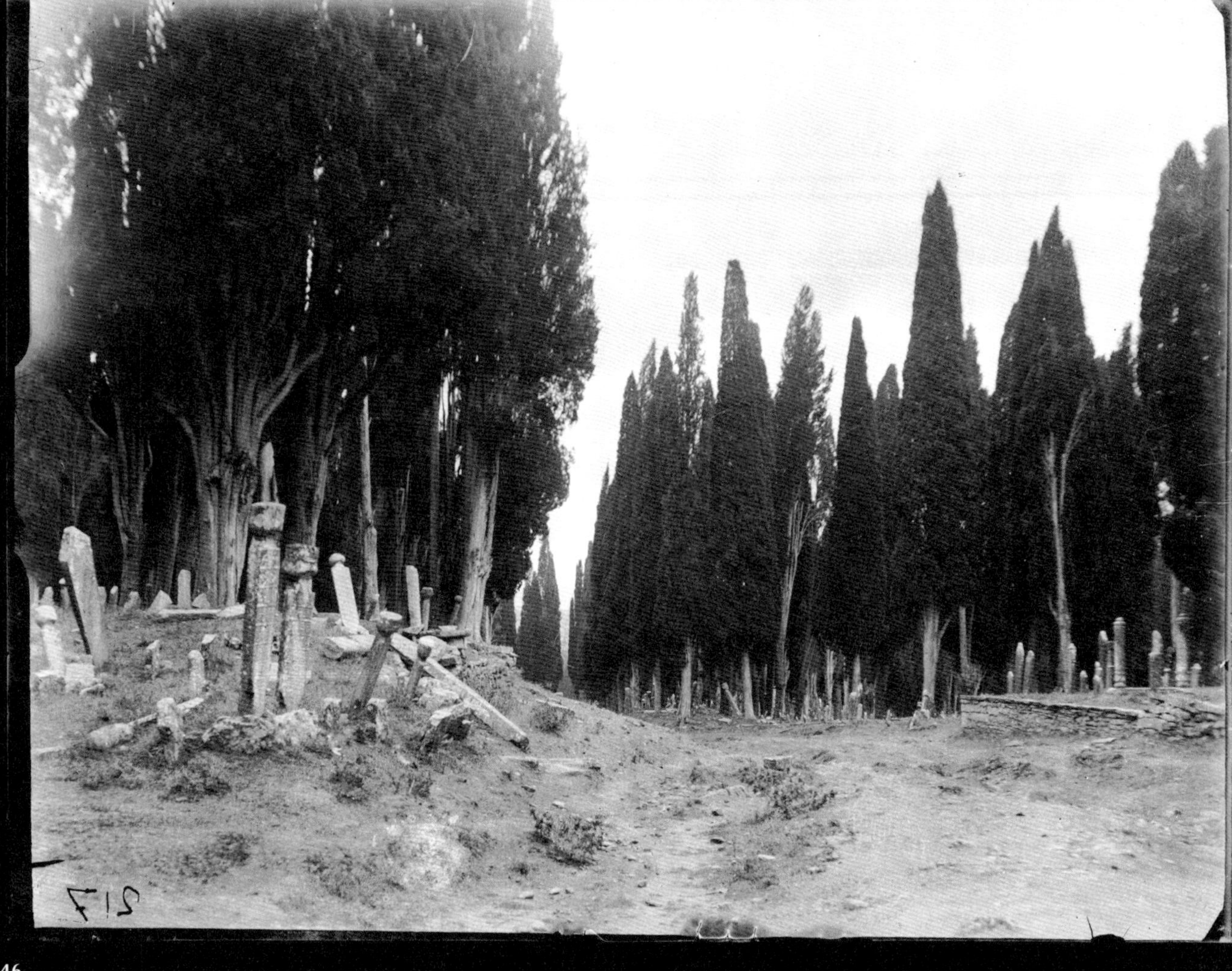

217

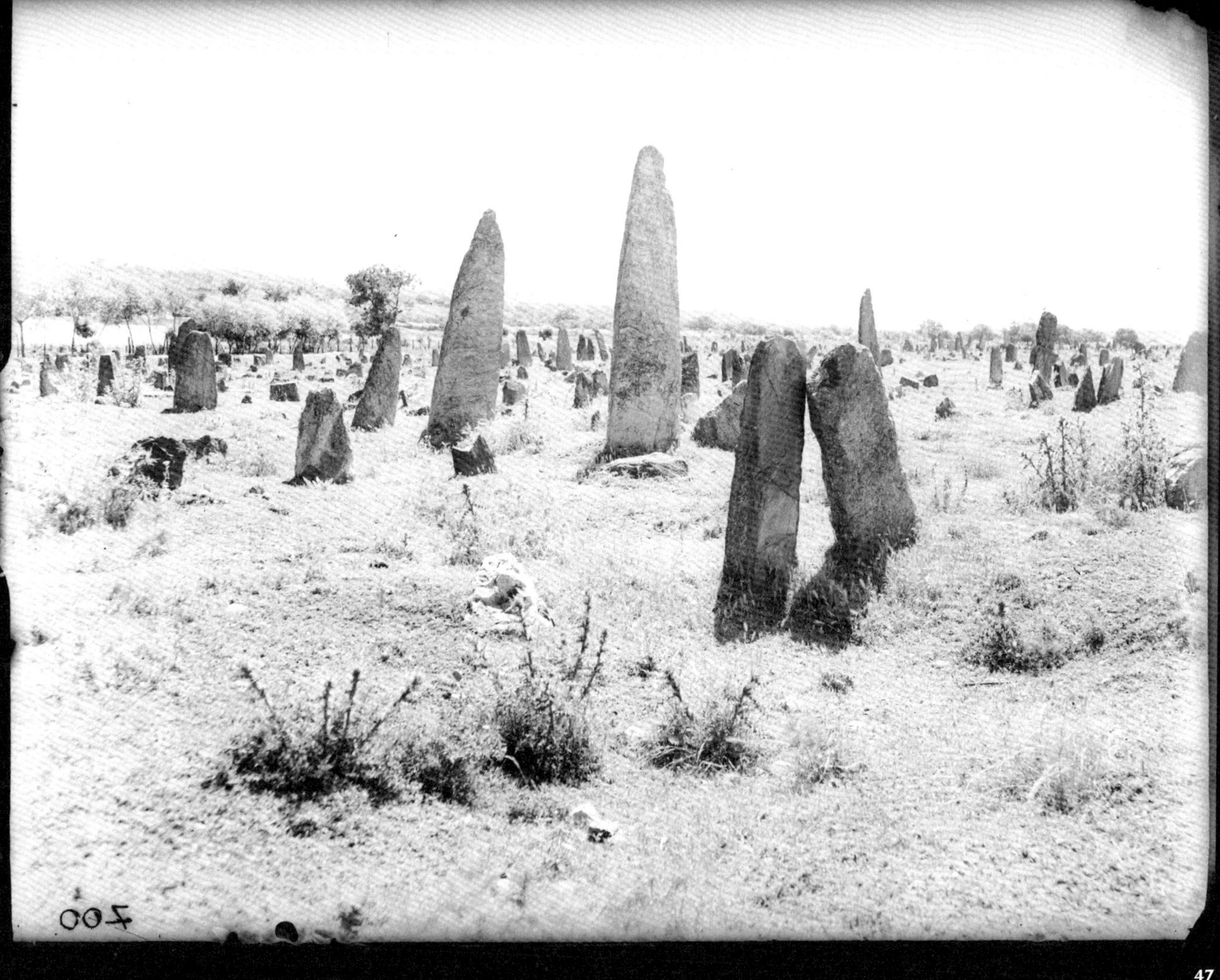
005

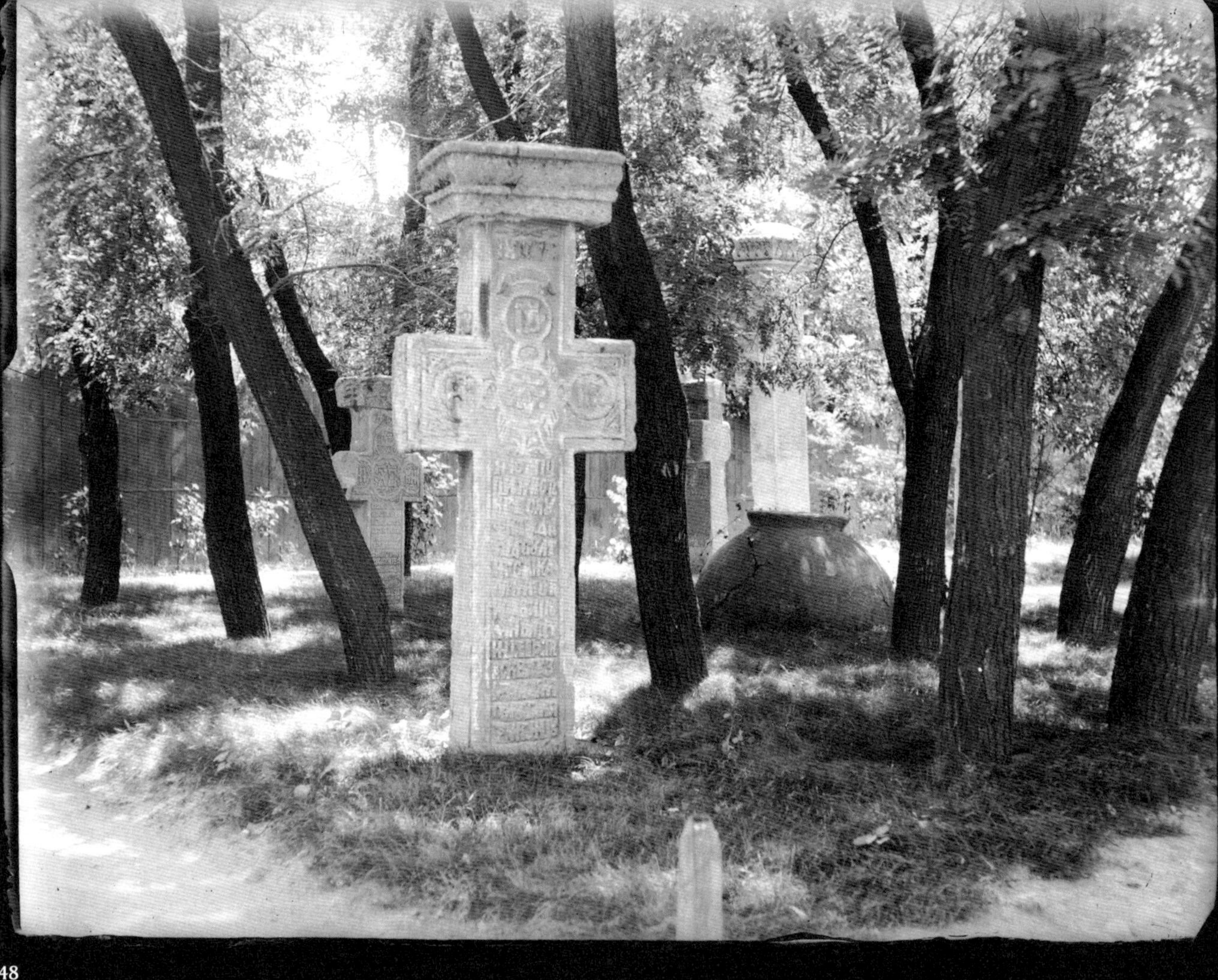

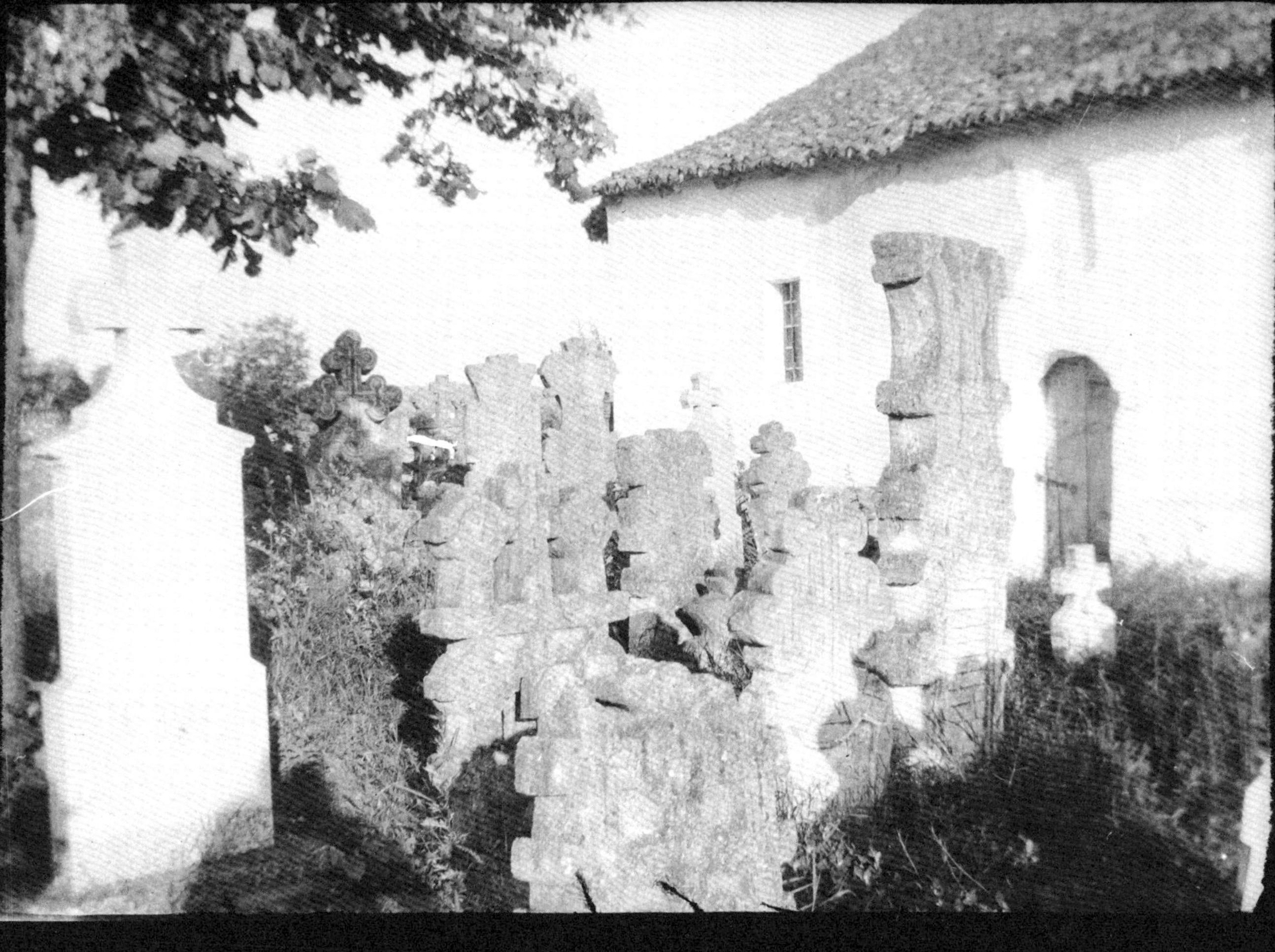

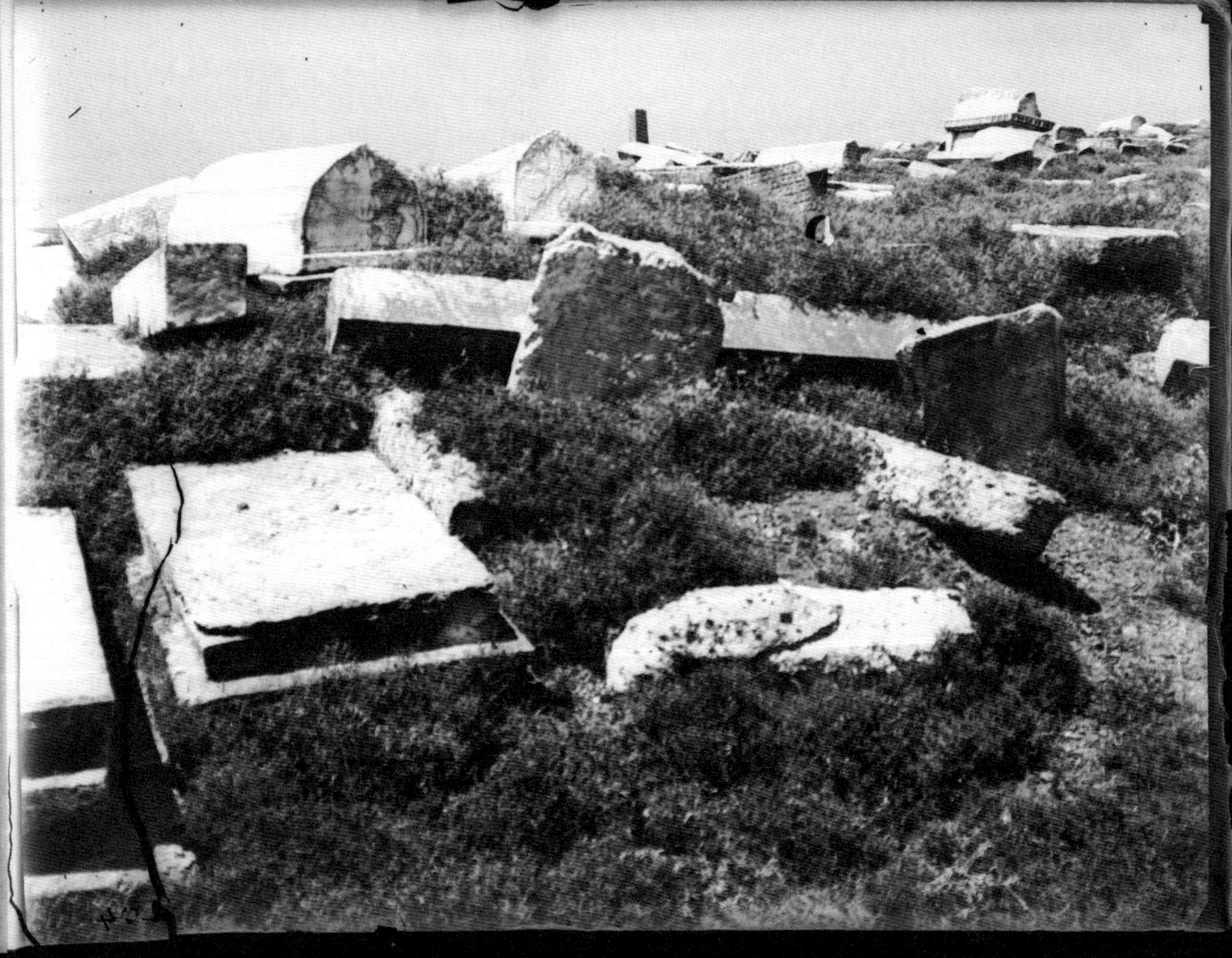

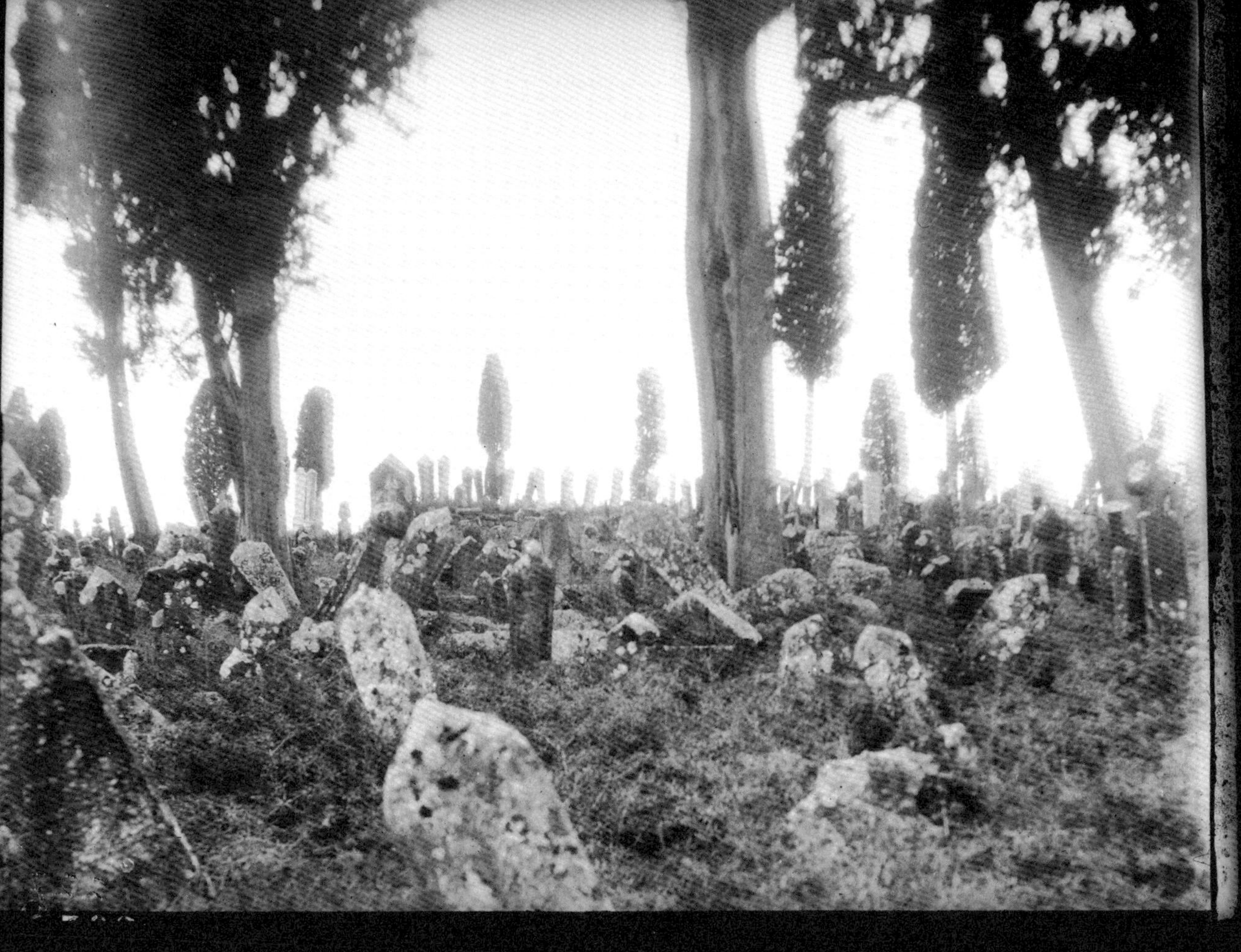

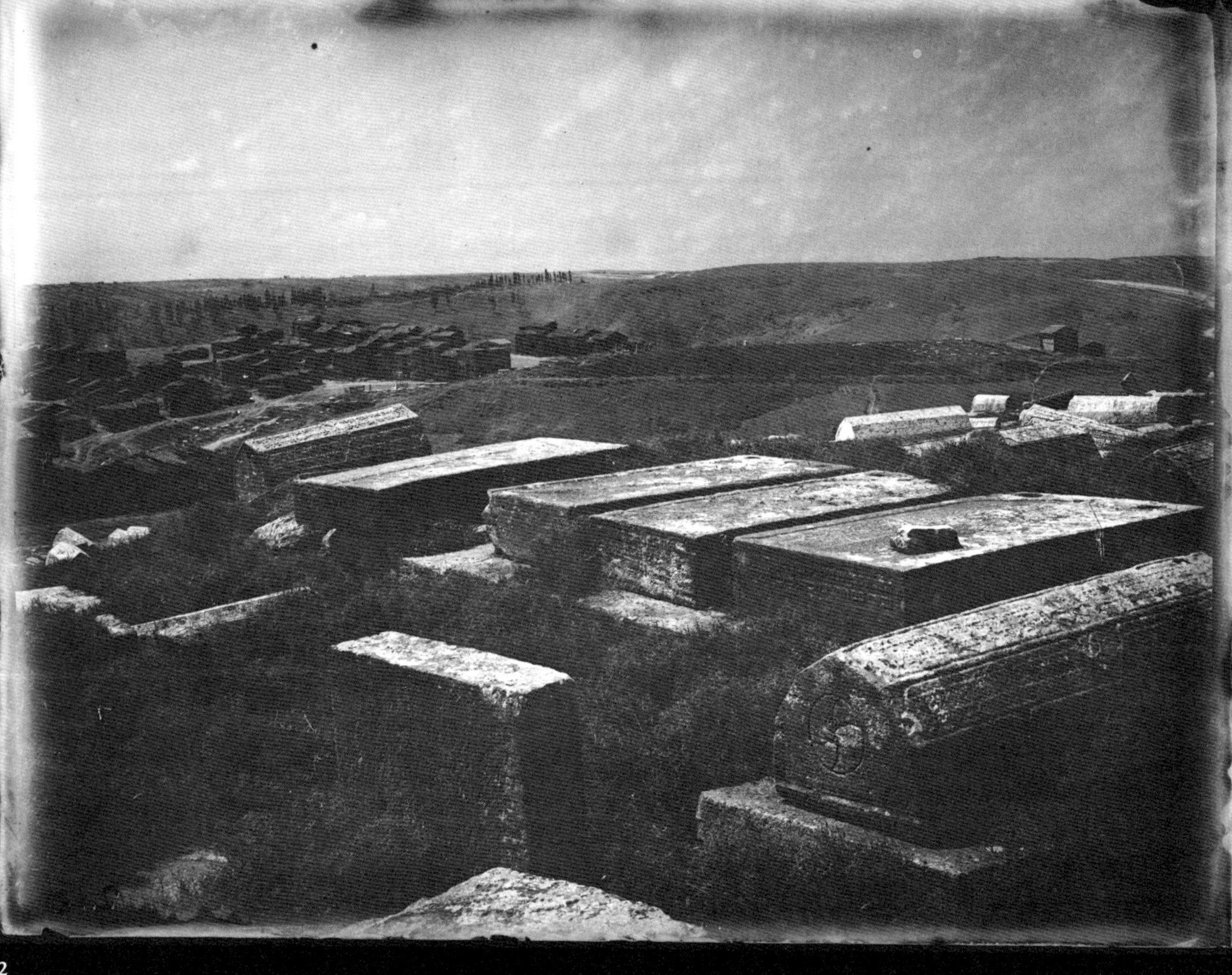

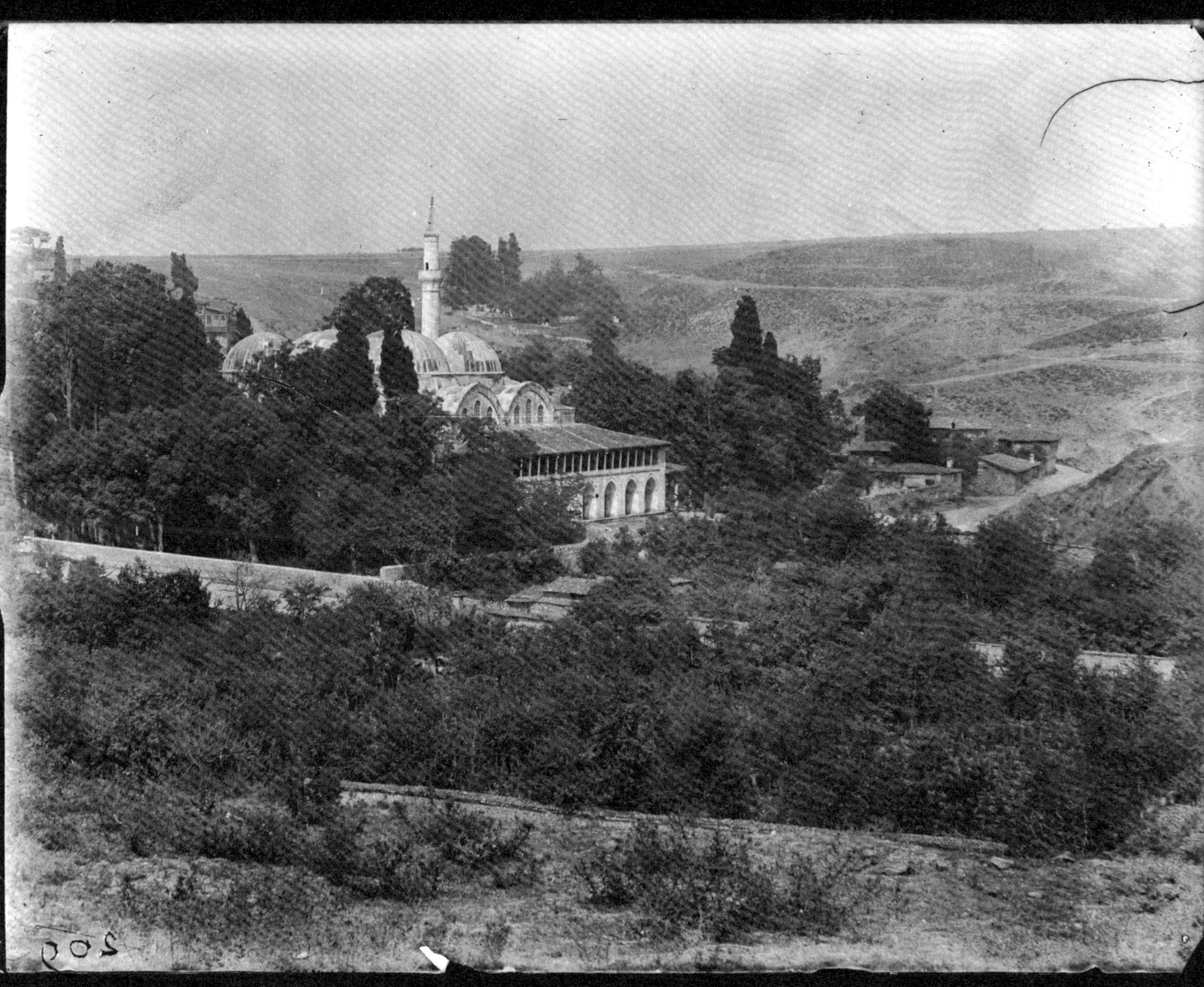

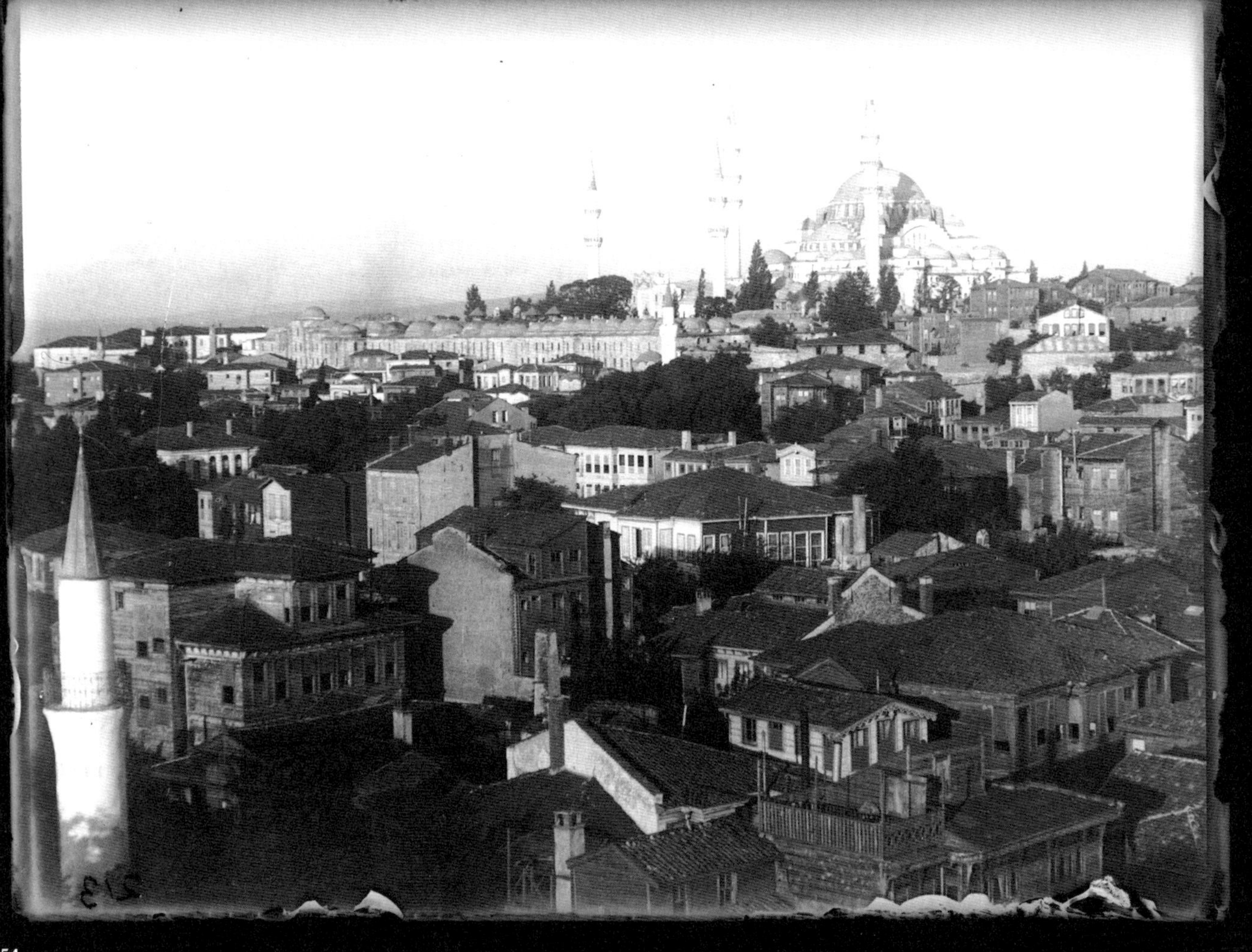

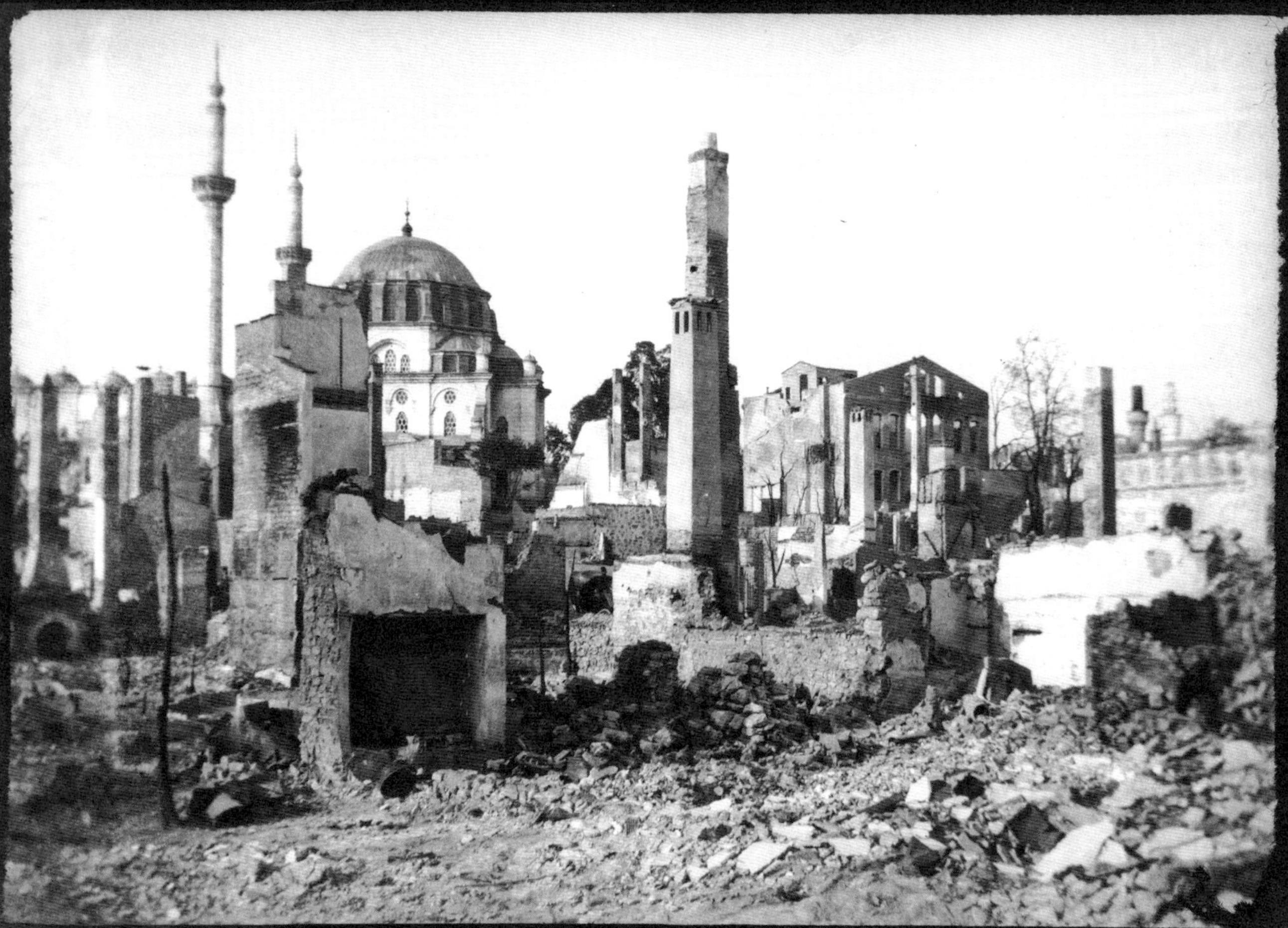